P9-CDI-254

ALSO BY WILLIAM C. REMPEL

*Delusions of a Dictator: The Mind of Marcos
as Revealed in His Secret Diaries*

AT THE DEVIL'S TABLE

The Untold Story of the Insider
Who Brought Down the Cali Cartel

AT THE
DEVIL'S
TABLE

363.45

Rempel

WILLIAM C. REMPEL

RANDOM HOUSE / NEW YORK

Published in the United States by Random House, an imprint of The Random
House Publishing Group, a division of Random House, Inc., New York.

RANDOM HOUSE and colophon are registered trademarks
of Random House, Inc.

Library of Congress Cataloging-in-Publication Data
Rempel, William C.
At the devil's table : the untold story of the insider who brought
down the Cali Cartel / William C. Rempel.
p.   cm.
Includes bibliographical references and index.
ISBN 978-1-4000-6837-1
eBook ISBN 978-0-679-60487-7
1. Cali Cartel. 2. Drug traffic—Investigation—Colombia—Cali. 3. Cocaine
industry—Colombia—Cali. 4. Organized crime—Colombia—Cali.
5. Drug traffic—Investigation—Colombia—Cali. I. Title.
HV5840.C723515   2011
363.4509861'52—dc22
2010045786

Printed in the United States of America on acid-free paper

www.atrandom.com

123456789

First Edition

Book design by Susan Turner

For Bill and Dorothy

| *Contents* |

| *Prologue* |

WRONG NUMBER

Washington, D.C.
Monday, June 12, 1995

A LATE SPRING STORM HAD TURNED THE U.S. CAPITAL WET AND dreary. Under heavy overcast, the streets were so dark at midday that drivers turned on their headlights. But on C Street the sun was shining in one corner of the State Department, the office of the assistant secretary of state for international narcotics and law enforcement affairs—fondly referred to by its occupants as the office of the "secretary for drugs and thugs." The staff of Ambassador Robert S. Gelbard was celebrating news that U.S. and Colombian drug agents had just captured one of the biggest names in the Cali cocaine cartel. After months of Gelbard's incessant cajoling, urging, and browbeating, the Bogotá government had finally brought down a prominent trafficking target. It was hardly a crippling blow to the world's richest criminal enterprise. The boss of bosses, the head of the cartel, remained at large and under the protection, it seemed, of the most powerful political forces in Colombia. Still, Gelbard and his staff dared to hope that the Cali syndicate could be dismantled.

Across the Potomac in Langley, Virginia, a telephone operator picked up an incoming call at about one thirty. "Central Intelligence Agency," she said pleasantly.

"Yes, hello. Please pardon my English," responded a Latin-accented voice in perfect English. "I'm calling from Colombia. I have some important information about the Cali drug cartel—the head of the cartel, I know his location."

"Yes, sir. And how may I direct your call?"

"Well, your agency has people here. They are trying to find this man. I am offering my assistance."

"Thank you, sir. How may I direct your call?"

After a long pause, the man said that he knew no one at the CIA by name but would gladly talk to anyone interested in capturing Miguel Rodríguez Orejuela, godfather of the Colombian cocaine syndicate. The operator seemed neither skeptical nor impressed. She simply remained pleasant and asked to be provided a specific office, officer, or telephone extension.

The caller pressed her: "Do you have a fax number?"

"I'm sorry."

"Do you have a number for tips or anonymous sources?"

"No, I'm sorry. Perhaps you can call back later."

ABOUT TWENTY-FIVE HUNDRED MILES SOUTH, the man who had just called the CIA returned a black telephone receiver to its cradle. He was tall and dark haired, with a neatly trimmed beard. His dressy-casual attire, typical of the tropics, gave little hint of his background. To strangers in the busy downtown Telecom building, he might have passed for a middle-aged university professor, an off-duty judge, or a bank vice president.

He lingered for a few moments in the soundproof privacy of the phone booth. His hands were still trembling. He had risked his life to place that call. He took a slow, deep breath and replayed the conversation in his mind. It seemed absurd—until he realized that the operator wasn't inept . . . she was screening calls. He was just another nuisance caller, a nutcase. And maybe he was, in fact, crazy.

If Miguel and the other Cali cartel bosses ever suspected that he had dialed the CIA, he was dead. No trial, no defense—just a few bullets to the brain . . . if he was lucky. There were worse ways to die. He had come close to some of them. But on that afternoon in mid-June, he knew what he was doing. He was desperate—but he was no nutcase.

He was forty-seven and a family man—and for the previous six and a half years he had been a top aide to one of the most ruthless and powerful crime bosses in the world. Now he wanted out of the cartel . . . out of an organization that discouraged retirement or resignations.

As he stepped from the phone booth, he kept an eye out for anyone familiar, ready with an excuse to explain his presence in the Telecom building. After all, convenient cartel phones were nearby. But they wouldn't do. Cartel wiretaps were everywhere. He knew better than most that there wasn't a private telephone anywhere in Cali that was genuinely private.

He emerged into the humid eighty-six-degree heat of a Cali afternoon. Across the street was the redbrick Iglesia de San Francisco, an eighteenth-century church and civic attraction, with its distinctive Mudejar-style bell tower. He slipped into its cool, dim sanctuary and approached the altar. He had to think about his next move. He had confided to no one his desperate plan to bring down the cartel boss, not even to his wife, although he was putting her and their children in grave danger. He told himself that she wouldn't want to know, she would be terrified—and worse, she might be unable to hide her fear. He had to withhold the truth for her own protection—to protect all of their lives. He had never felt so alone.

Beyond the Father, Son, and Holy Mother to whom he prayed, the man falling to his knees near the altar of Iglesia de San Francisco that afternoon trusted no one but the CIA . . . and he couldn't even get past the Langley switchboard operator.

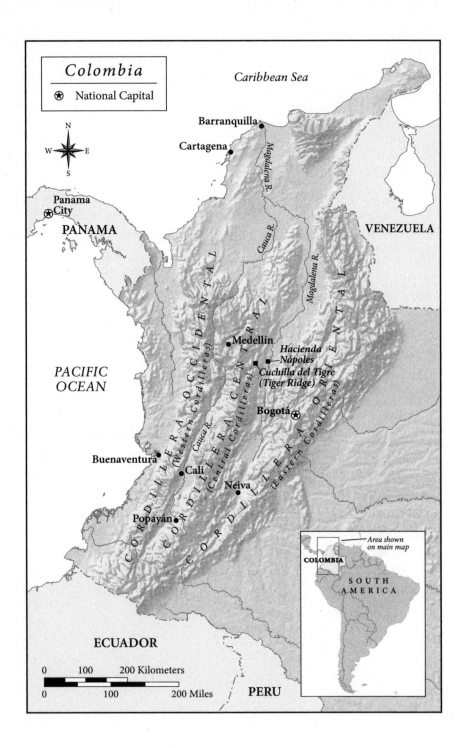

Caribbean Sea

N
W   E
S

Barranquilla

Cartagena

PANAMA

Panama
City

PACIFIC
OCEAN

Magdalena R.

Cauca R.

Magdalena R.

VENEZUELA

CORDILLERA OCCIDENTAL
(Western Cordilleras)

Cauca R.

CORDILLERA CENTRAL
(Central Cordilleras)

Medellín

Hacienda
Nápoles
Cuchilla del Tigre
(Tiger Ridge)

Bogotá ⊛

CORDILLERA ORIENTAL
(Eastern Cordilleras)

Buenaventura

Cali

Neiva

Popayán

ECUADOR

Area shown
on main map

COLOMBIA

SOUTH
AMERICA

0   100   200 Kilometers

0   100   200 Miles

PERU

PART ONE

The Cartel War Years
1989–1993

SIX AND A HALF
YEARS EARLIER

Bogotá, Colombia
Mid-January 1989

JORGE SALCEDO STOWED HIS CARRY-ON BAG IN AN OVERHEAD COM-
partment and dropped into a window seat of the aging Boeing 727.
It was an early morning flight out of Bogotá to Cali, Colombia, and he
was a reluctant traveler. Besides the inconvenient hour, the forty-one-
year-old businessman really could not afford to take time away from his
latest venture, a small refinery he was developing to reprocess used
motor oil. The project was behind schedule, and here he was flying off
on a mystery trip. He had no idea why he was going to Cali. In fact,
until arriving at Bogotá's El Dorado International Airport an hour earlier, he didn't even know his destination.

"Jorge, you need to come with me. Some people want to meet
you," his friend Mario had said on the phone. He was emphatic. He
told Jorge to pack an overnight bag—then hung up. Now they were on
the plane together.

"What's the deal, Mario?" Jorge couldn't hide a tone of impatience as he turned to his friend settling into the aisle seat. "What are we doing here?"

Like Jorge, Mario was in his early forties—fit, trim, and exuding confidence. Even in casual civilian clothes, he looked military, like someone out of Central Casting. But the recently retired major Mario del Basto was the real thing, a highly decorated soldier.

"After takeoff," he assured Jorge, "we'll talk." He gave a nod toward strangers still standing in the aisle.

Jorge had always trusted Mario. The two had been good friends since soon after Jorge joined the Colombian army reserves in 1984. Mario, an officer in the regular army, became commanding officer of Jorge's Cali-based reserve unit. The major relied on Jorge as an intelligence officer with valuable skills in weaponry, electronic surveillance, radio technologies, and photography.

The army reserve was an unpaid, volunteer position, but it gave Jorge the taste of a military career like that of his father, General Jorge Salcedo. The senior Salcedo had been a contender for chief of Colombia's armed forces, and he remained a prominent public figure nearly twenty-five years after his retirement in the mid-1960s.

Jorge saw reflections of his father in Major del Basto. Both were career army officers. Both wore uniforms with chests full of medals for valor. Both had extensive experience fighting antigovernment guerrillas.

Growing up the son of a general provided Jorge with many advantages, from financial security and social respect to opportunities for travel—including an extended stay in the United States while his father was on assignment in Kansas. It also influenced his views on groups like FARC (Fuerzas Armadas Revolucionarias de Colombia, or Revolutionary Armed Forces of Colombia), against whom his father waged war. At home and in the reserves, Jorge saw the guerrillas as irredeemable terrorists, and he came to share frustrations widely held in the military that government-sanctioned peace talks simply allowed guerrillas to regroup and resupply.

"We're trying to talk them to death," Mario complained to Jorge.

Even for a military hero like Major del Basto, such criticism of the civilian leadership was dangerous. He shared his opinions only with close friends until his rage could be contained no longer. At the close of 1988, del Basto rejected a promotion to colonel and quit the army. He blasted President Virgilio Barco for coddling FARC. Then he disappeared. Jorge hadn't heard from Mario for days—not until the mysterious phone call that led him aboard this Avianca airlines flight.

"WE'RE GOING TO SEE some Cali guys," Mario began moments after they were airborne. He was leaning across the empty middle seat between them. Engine noise protected their privacy.

"Do I know them?"

"It's possible. They're important local businessmen."

Jorge had lived in Cali as a boy, when his father was the army brigade commander there. Again in the early 1980s, he resided there while working as a partner and engineer at a battery-manufacturing plant just outside Colombia's third-largest city.

"What I can tell you," Mario went on, "is that these people have a serious problem with Pablo Escobar. He's bombing their businesses, threatening their families—it's a terrible situation."

Jorge's expression abruptly hardened to a glare. "Don't tell me—we're going to see the Cali *cartel* guys?"

By January 1989, everyone in Colombia knew about the raging feud between Escobar's Medellín cartel and his rivals in Cali. For nearly a year, headlines carried gruesome accounts of bombings, dismemberments, and shootings. The number of innocent-bystander deaths mounted. Like most of his friends and cohorts, Jorge feared and loathed Pablo Escobar. The drug boss had declared war on the Colombian government in a campaign to overturn Bogotá's extradition treaty with Washington. His paid assassins targeted national officials, local police, criminal investigators, and judges. A Medellín hit team struck especially close to home when it gunned down one of Jorge's boyhood friends, a popular minister of justice named Rodrigo Lara Bonilla.

Jorge didn't know much about Escobar's rivals in Cali, except by reputation. They were regarded as less violent—at least they did not kill public figures. In fact, the southern bosses were widely known as "the Gentlemen of Cali." Nonetheless, Jorge never considered taking sides. The war between the cartels was none of his business.

"You should have told me," Jorge said. "Maybe I don't want to meet them."

Mario shrugged. "But they want to meet you."

Jorge shook his head in wonder. A big organized crime outfit wanted to see him. *Why?* Mario looked around to see that no one was listening and continued.

Soon after leaving the army, Mario said, he had been called to Cali and offered a position managing security for the Rodríguez Orejuela family. Jorge recognized the name. They were owners of a national chain of discount pharmacies and a professional soccer team, among many other legitimate interests. But it was common knowledge that they were also big-time traffickers. Like Escobar, they denied any drug ties. Unlike Escobar, they kept a low profile.

"These guys are afraid for their lives and for their families," Mario said. "Pablo is trying to kill them—men, women, children, everyone." He said it was especially unfair to the Rodríguez Orejuela clan because "they are not violent people." Mario described his new job as keeping innocent women and children safe from Escobar's hired killers.

"And they think you can help, too."

"So, it's not the cartel drug business," Jorge said with obvious relief.

"No, of course not." Mario dropped his voice so that even Jorge could barely hear him: "But don't talk about cartels. They hate the word. There is no Cali cartel, you understand? They're businessmen."

"I see. All right, but—why me?"

Jorge considered himself a businessman who recycled motor oil and an engineer who designed manufacturing systems or tinkered with cameras and radios. In the army reserves he specialized in surveillance and intelligence, a relatively new area of personal interest. Still, he saw no obvious reasons for a summons to Cali.

He asked again: "Why?"

Mario smiled, sat back, and said nothing.

* * *

JORGE WASN'T LOOKING for a job that morning in January. He already had business deals brewing on several fronts—including potentially lucrative negotiations with the Colombian military. Jorge had recently begun representing some European companies interested in landing defense contracts in Colombia and other Latin American countries, clients he picked up during the previous year while attending an international exhibition of military suppliers in London. He returned with samples of night-vision gear, encrypted radios, and surveillance devices he hoped to sell to army procurement officials in Bogotá.

But what most intrigued one of the Bogotá generals was the business card of David Tomkins, a colorful arms dealer based near London. Tomkins and a group of retired British special forces soldiers offered to instruct the Colombian army in guerrilla-fighting techniques. Jorge relayed their proposal.

"These trainers, they are also mercenaries?" asked the general. He had once served as an aide to Jorge's father. He knew he could trust the old general's son. "Would your contacts consider a clandestine mission against the FARC?"

Within a few days, Jorge was flying back to England. There, he presented Tomkins with a proposed assignment: attack and destroy FARC's showcase mountain headquarters known as Casa Verde. The Colombian military would secretly support the raid—providing arms, explosives, and transportation—but it had to be done in such a way that the army could deny involvement.

The British mercenaries had flexible ideologies that could accommodate a wide array of customers, but they tended to be staunchly anticommunist. To clinch the deal, Jorge pointed out FARC's longstanding support from Fidel Castro. The Brits eagerly signed on. Their field leader was a Scotsman named Peter McAleese, a tough former Special Air Service (SAS) sergeant and paratrooper who once survived a jump with a failed parachute.

FARC had many enemies. Guerrilla bands had attacked remote villages, seized farmers, miners, and ranchers for ransom, and even dared to kidnap drug traffickers. When the British commandos arrived in Colombia, they were welcomed by an unlikely alliance of rich cattlemen, miners, and leaders of the Medellín cocaine cartel. Primary funding for the mission came from José Rodríguez-Gacha, a major landowner and a trafficking partner of Pablo Escobar's. With dissident military officials providing arms and munitions, the Brits were backed by a Faustian ensemble—what Colombians called *la mesa del Diablo* . . . "the Devil's table." And Jorge served as maître d'.

Through the summer of 1988, Jorge—code-named Richard—was the secret liaison between the commandos and their Colombian supporters. If the mission were exposed, the army would disavow any knowledge. Jorge was responsible for keeping the Brits fed, housed, supplied, and out of public view. One of the few with whom he shared details of the operation was Mario del Basto. Jorge took him to jungle training sites and introduced the major to Tomkins and McAleese.

Preparations for the attack dragged on for months. The Brits were ready, but the dissident military officers hesitated. They were fearful of a political backlash and ultimately unwilling to risk their military careers. In the end, the same cabal of military officials who had launched the secret plan called it off.

Nonetheless, the commandos left happy and well paid, thanks to the wealthy Medellín ranchers and traffickers who reimbursed the Brits for training ragtag elements of their private armies. One drug boss had even sent his son for jungle combat training. In November 1988, Tomkins and McAleese were the last to fly home. In a farewell meeting with Jorge, they embraced and said they were eager for future assignments. "Until next time," McAleese said.

Jorge immediately returned to his neglected business interests, but now—eight weeks later—he was flying to Cali and wondering why.

A CAR FROM THE InterContinental hotel was waiting for them at Cali's Alfonso Bonilla Aragón International Airport. Luxury hotel suites were also waiting, stocked with fresh fruits and flowers—compliments of the Rodríguez Orejuela family. A message said that their afternoon appointment with "the gentlemen" was delayed. A car would pick them up around ten o'clock that night.

The timing was not coincidental. In light nighttime traffic, anyone trying to follow the car would be more easily detected. Jorge knew Cali well and realized immediately that they were doubling back, circling, and watching to be sure that no one was tailing them. Jorge felt his first twinge of anxiety. Since childhood, he had been prone to mild attacks of claustrophobia. In the backseat of the Cali cartel car, his throat tightened. He took a deep breath and wiped a sweaty palm on his slacks. He didn't want Mario to notice. But he also couldn't help feeling that his friend had put him in a difficult spot.

The winding drive finally ended at a high-walled compound. Their car entered through a large gate that shut behind them. Jorge glanced around as he stepped out. He saw security lapses everywhere. Dozens of bodyguards milled about, bristling with firearms, but they seemed most intent on swatting mosquitoes. No one inspected the car. Curiously to Jorge, all sentries were inside the walls. He saw no one posted outside.

Even in the dark, Jorge could see that the auto court was full of cars—mostly Mazda sedans and midsized SUVs—parked at haphazard angles. A handful of smaller cars effectively blocked all the others. In an emergency, all but a few would be trapped.

A cartel security man greeted them just outside the door to the main house. José Estrada was about forty, a retired army sergeant. He escorted Jorge and Mario through a seemingly empty house. The floors were polished white marble. The white walls and ceilings were freshly painted. The furniture was luxurious white leather. Jorge saw no books, no toys, no children, none of the clutter of family life. It looked like a showcase for interior designers or a furniture showroom. The style gave Jorge his first clue to the manners and tastes of the drug lords: practical, efficient, and businesslike.

The visitors were ushered into a spacious office where four men were waiting. So, these were the Cali cartel godfathers, Jorge thought—men who could play God with human lives, dictate government policies, and influence the national economy. They were not particularly imposing physically. At nearly six feet two, Jorge was taller than anyone in the room. As Mario made the introductions, Jorge greeted each boss with a smile and a handshake. They seemed pleased to meet him—and completely harmless, almost benign.

Pacho Herrera, thirty-seven, was the youngest of the four. This was one of his houses—his white palette, his sterile rooms. He looked as if he had just stepped off the pages of a gentleman's fashion magazine. Pacho was the only unmarried godfather. He was homosexual. Jorge thought that Pacho had the empathetic, easygoing manner of a young priest. What he didn't know was that the gay gangster ran the most brutal wing of enforcers in the cartel.

Chepe Santacruz, forty-five, was in denim and cotton and looked the part of a farmer or rancher who had just come in from the stables. He seemed jovial and self-deprecating, even a bit mischievous. But he sometimes took his penchant for teasing too far. His rough edges showed in the coarseness of his conversation. Chepe was proudly unsophisticated. He also was a street fighter. And in brawls, as in practical jokes, overkill was his trademark.

Gilberto Rodríguez Orejuela, almost fifty, was the talker, an often charming raconteur who had the look of a well-fed professor. He immediately put Jorge at ease and seemed to be the official host, the presiding officer of the meeting. Throughout the evening, Jorge recognized Gilberto's unspoken authority as others in the room deferred to him.

Gilberto's younger brother Miguel, forty-five, was a stern-faced man who seemed endlessly weary. He said little, but missed nothing. In deference to his place in the cartel, he was known as Don Miguel or simply El Señor. Chepe liked to call him Limón, or "Lemon," for his pinched expression and sour disposition. No one else dared use the nickname to the don's face. Miguel ran daily operations of the cartel, making him the boss of bosses. But he and Gilberto were close partners, and all important cartel matters came before the four-member brain trust that greeted Jorge and Mario.

The two visitors took seats in white leather chairs. A white-uniformed maid offered cold fruit juices. The Gentlemen of Cali moved right into the night's agenda. First, they wanted help with personal security.

Pablo is "a bandit . . . a criminal . . . a crazy guy," Chepe declared. He told Jorge that Escobar was threatening to kill everyone with ties to the Cali bosses—wives, children, friends. "No one is safe," Chepe said.

"Yes, I understand," responded Jorge, thinking of his former classmate, the assassinated justice minister. "Escobar killed my friend Rodrigo Lara Bonilla, a very good man."

Jorge felt a surge of emotion. He had rarely talked about his friend's murder, but here in the company of Escobar's enemies he had rediscovered his deep-seated anger. He felt no need to suppress it. It was clear they all shared a powerful sentiment—hatred.

Gilberto seemed both surprised and delighted to hear of Jorge's personal loss at Escobar's hand. "It was a terrible tragedy," he sympathized. "It was also stupid. Sometimes, Pablo ignores his own best interests. He goes to war and expects to win friends. He's a fool. A dangerous fool."

Talk turned to the current state of cartel defenses. Estrada, the man they met at the door, had his hands full protecting the bosses. The other security chief was a retired Colombian army officer referred to in impatient tones as "Major Gómez." Clearly, his performance was not measuring up. His intelligence network was woeful. He wasn't aggressive. The no-confidence vote was unanimous, and his absence that night was telling. Jorge still wasn't sure exactly what the Cali drug lords wanted until—

"We want Pablo Escobar dead," said Miguel.

"And we want you and your British commandos to kill him," added Gilberto.

Jorge looked around the room. Everyone was waiting for his response. Mario had obviously told them about his secret contacts with the Brits. Now Jorge understood the summons to Cali. It didn't bother him that the secret had been shared. He felt more flattered than alarmed.

Until that moment, Jorge had never given any thought to avenging the murder of his friend. Law enforcement was a job for police and the courts. Unfortunately, officials who tried to bring formal charges against Escobar all ended up dead. The case remained officially unsolved. If Gilberto's invitation caught Jorge by surprise, it also intrigued him. Maybe justice could be done after all.

Jorge could almost hear the theme from his favorite movie, *The Magnificent Seven.* The notion of riding into town with a crew of foreign gunfighters to rout the great villain Escobar stirred fantasies of patriotic heroics. It also appealed to the same passions that had prompted his enlistment in the army reserves—a yearning for action and adventure . . . all in the service of God and country. He wanted to hear more about the godfathers' plan.

They had already selected the target—Hacienda Nápoles, Escobar's seventy-four-hundred-acre tropical estate along the Magdalena River. It was a fantasyland with man-made lakes for water sports, huge swimming pools, its own airport, and a zoo with elephants, lions, zebras, and rapidly procreating hippopotamuses. It was also Escobar's first choice for serious wining, dining, and partying. Gilberto, who had been a guest there, said that when Pablo was at Nápoles, it could be assumed he would be drunk every day.

Jorge asked about transport. He would need helicopters. "You will have them," Gilberto said. Jorge asked about pilots. "We have pilots who know the area," Gilberto said. Jorge raised the importance of good intelligence and top-quality communications gear—radios reliable even in remote, rugged terrain. "Whatever is necessary will be done— and you can count on the eternal gratitude of everyone in this room."

It was obvious that cost was not a consideration. Jorge was struck by the contrast: the Colombian army sometimes had no fuel for its helicopters, but the Cali cartel could fund an armed invasion. And he was struck by another contrast: with all their money, the four billionaires in the room were terrified of Pablo Escobar.

It was a heady moment for Jorge. He felt important—handpicked for a big job, a great adventure . . . and a public service. He also welcomed a chance to be reunited with his British commando friends. As for prospects that four of the nation's richest men might be indebted to him—that was priceless. Yet he hesitated.

Another extended delay could jeopardize his nascent motor oil recovery business. He was hoping to start construction on a small refinery early in the new year. And what about Lena Duque? She was Jorge's love, his companion, and his fiancée. The Escobar mission could delay their wedding.

The godfathers assured him that preparing the assault would take no more than a few months. After Escobar was dead, Jorge could return to Bogotá "with more money than you will ever need," as Gilberto put it.

The meeting ran well past midnight. Jorge knew he would have to declare his intentions. He would be working for major crime figures—

returning to the Devil's table. But he reasoned that it would be brief and he would have nothing to do with the drug trade. He considered that he might lose his refinery business—but the trade-off could be new and powerful friends and even better business opportunities in the future. Then Jorge considered his family. Maybe working so closely with cartel godfathers wasn't worth the risk to his reputation. That's when Jorge thought about declining.

At various times that evening, the bosses shared stories about their families, their wives and ex-wives and multiple households, and their fears for everyone's safety. The personal information wasn't so detailed that Jorge could, say, track down Miguel's third wife, but it was provided in an atmosphere of trust that would make it uncomfortable for Jorge to back away now.

For a moment he fantasized about making his apologies, about saying, *Thanks, but no thanks.* What then? Would he be seen as a security risk? He had, after all, worked closely with Escobar's partners, financiers of the Brits' Casa Verde plot. No doubt the Cali godfathers knew about that part of the mercenary project, too. If he said no, would they take it as personal rejection . . . or worse, as a sign of loyalty to the Medellín bosses? Would Jorge end up in the trunk of one of those parked cars? He stifled a shudder.

Jorge realized that he was afraid to say no. And thank God for that. Because, deep down, Jorge also knew that he really didn't want to refuse. He felt relief when he announced, "Yes, I'll do it."

A TERRIBLE NOISE

I T IS THE OLDEST DEMOCRACY IN LATIN AMERICA, A REGIONAL CEN-ter of higher learning and an economic power. But beneath a veneer of sophistication and modernity, twentieth-century Colombia was one of the most violent places on Earth.

Civil strife, personal vendettas, and criminal gangs spread mayhem. Colombia was the murder and kidnapping leader of the Western Hemisphere even before it became the center of international drug trafficking. The world's biggest, richest, and most dangerous cocaine cartels operated out of two of its largest cities—Medellín in the north and Cali in the south. Leftist guerrillas and right-wing death squads terrorized cities and rural areas. In one presidential campaign, four candidates were assassinated.

Jorge Salcedo was born in 1947, when Colombia was better known for coffee than for cocaine. Even then, it was hardly a tropical paradise. Jorge's earliest years coincided with one of the deadliest periods in Colombian politics. It was as if, in the United States, Republicans and

Democrats had taken up arms to slaughter each other. Between 1946 and 1957, as many as 300,000 Colombians died in the political strife, an era known as *La Violencia.* The military seized power for a time. Democracy resumed with an agreement between Liberal and Conservative parties to alternate the presidency.

During the worst of *La Violencia,* Jorge's military father was targeted by a hit squad and ambushed in his front yard. A gun battle raged on the doorsteps of the family's Bogotá home. Inside, Jorge's mother protected her crying baby, terrified by the terrible noise. Army colleagues rushed to the father's rescue and routed his attackers. It was the young Jorge's first brush with Colombian violence.

He started school in his mother's hometown of Neiva, where he shared a kindergarten desk with Rodrigo, the future justice minister. The boys' friendship was interrupted when the Salcedo family moved to a safer neighborhood—Fort Leavenworth, Kansas. Jorge's father, on track for high-level promotion, would spend two years with future generals from around the world attending the U.S. Army's Command and General Staff College. While his father learned the ways of command, Jorge learned English. He attended a little brick Catholic school near the fort and very nearly lost his native Spanish.

He was seven when his father gave him his first gun, a Winchester .22 rifle. He bagged his first deer on a hunting trip when he was twelve. For high school graduation, his parents gave him a treasured, U.S.-made High Standard Olympic competition pistol. His fascination with weapons became the foundation for Jorge's keen interest in the design and mechanics of precision machinery. He studied mechanical engineering at the University of the Andes and graduated with a degree in industrial economy. One of his earliest jobs was designing forklifts. He moved to Cali to take a partnership position with a battery manufacturer. He also developed interests in radio and communications systems. He became an avid tinkerer and amateur inventor.

His marriage to María, a university sweetheart, foundered, and Jorge suspected another man. He put his skills to use wiretapping his wife's telephone. It was a terrible breach of marital trust, but it confirmed his worst fears. They separated and shared custody of their four-year-old daughter—until María abruptly moved back to Bogotá and took the girl. A custody battle in the Cali courts gave Jorge his first taste of preferential justice. The ex-wife's new boyfriend was politically connected. After losing custody of his little girl, Jorge never forgot how it felt to be a victim of corrupt power.

With his wife and child gone, Cali seemed cold and empty. He pondered military service. Earlier, while weighing his university options, Jorge considered following his father into an army officer's career. But General Salcedo counseled strongly against it. His own sterling military career had ended prematurely in 1966 when a rival became minister of defense and bypassed the general, promoting an officer with less experience to commanding general of the Colombian armed forces.

"I have many friends who will do anything they can to help you," he told Jorge. "But I've also made enemies, and they will find ways to hurt you . . . to hurt me. Go to school. Get another career. Then think about it."

Now in mid-career, Jorge decided he would join the army reserves. He petitioned for an officer's commission in the Cali-based Pichincha Battalion. On the weekend before formally joining, Jorge was boating on Lake Calima north of town. He rescued a stranded party boat of young women, one of them a striking twenty-four-year-old in a black swimsuit. She seemed barely to notice him despite his heroics. Two days later, Jorge was standing in a group of about forty volunteers as a general welcomed them into the reserves. The officer's remarks were interrupted when a door burst open and a late-arriving recruit joined the crowd next to Jorge.

It was Lena Duque, the girl with the black swimsuit. Jorge stared. Her quick smile nearly knocked the wind out of him. The general's welcoming address faded into an indecipherable drone. All of his senses focused on the woman at his elbow. She was young. She was beautiful. And she was military. They stood there, almost touching, joining the army reserves together.

Courtship bloomed after another chance encounter a few days later. Jorge was bringing dozens of books and technical manuals to the army reserve administration building at the request of a military friend of his father's. He tried to carry too many at once and dropped an armload—just as Lena happened by.

"I'm so sorry. I don't know what happened," he said, scrambling to pick up the volumes strewn at her feet.

"You're the guy from the boat," she said, smiling.

Jorge seized the opportunity as she helped him recover his books. Dinner was arranged. Lena was a banking attorney. Like Jorge, she was formerly married and had a child, a young son. She smoked, but he tried to overlook that. Financially, they were both comfortable and independent, if not wealthy. And Lena was a Cali girl who introduced him to her parents, siblings, and a network of close friends. For Jorge, Cali was starting to feel like home again.

COLOMBIA'S VIOLENCE REACHED a frenzied pitch in the 1980s as antigovernment guerrilla gangs stepped up their attacks. FARC was the largest and had operated from Casa Verde, its mountain hideout south of Bogotá, since the 1960s. Its popular roots were in animosities left over from *La Violencia.* A relative newcomer was the 19th of April Movement, or M-19, born in the aftermath of a controversial 1970 election that critics said was stolen by the Conservatives. M-19 evolved over the next decade into a nationalistic group with Marxist inclinations.

Both guerrilla groups engaged in terrorism and raised funds with kidnappings. But headline-conscious M-19 marauders often upstaged the older FARC. The newcomers arrived in the mid-1970s with a spectacular museum heist of Simón Bolívar's sword and spurs, intended to symbolize M-19's claim to be a citizen uprising against an unjust regime. In 1980, it seized fourteen diplomatic hostages at the Dominican Republic's embassy. It held them for weeks until Cuba mediated their release.

Jorge encountered the violence firsthand when M-19 raided a small industrial town north of Cali. He grabbed his Thompson submachine gun and scrambled to join his reserve unit. Approaching Yumbo, they came upon the still-smoldering remnants of a bullet-splattered Renault. Inside were the bodies of a girl and two teenage boys. It appeared to Jorge that they stumbled into an M-19 roadblock. He felt stirrings of rage. He hated any kind of politics that could justify three dead kids.

The killers had disappeared; there was nothing Jorge could do. He hated that, too.

WHEN RODRIGO LARA BONILLA was appointed Colombia's minister of justice in the summer of 1983, it was a proud moment for Jorge. He had maintained a distant friendship with the rising political star ever since they shared that desk as schoolboys. While their career paths took them to different worlds, their families remained neighbors in Neiva.

The new minister was a reformer who immediately picked a fight with Pablo Escobar, then a member of the Colombian congress, and with the other drug barons of Medellín. He threatened them with the one thing they feared the most: extradition to the United States, where trafficking indictments awaited most of them. The U.S. justice system was not vulnerable to bribes or intimidation, no doubt prompting Escobar's oft-repeated declaration: "Better a grave in Colombia than a jail cell in the United States."

Lara Bonilla became a target of constant death threats but vowed, "I will never again refuse the extradition of one of these dogs." Once in office, he approved and sent to the president a U.S. request to extradite Carlos Lehder, a pioneer of Colombian trafficking. He also canceled the flight permits of fifty-seven cartel-linked aircraft.

On Monday evening, April 30, 1984, the justice minister left his Bogotá office as usual in a government-issued white Mercedes-Benz. He shoved aside a bulletproof vest on the backseat. Despite pleas from his family, he rarely wore it.

The ministry driver eased out into traffic, the Mercedes escorted front and back by Toyota Land Cruisers with armed bodyguards. They were in stop-and-go traffic when a red motorcycle dipping in and out of lanes approached with two men aboard. As it pulled alongside, the man on the back of the bike pulled out an Ingram MAC-10 assault pistol. Before anyone in the escort vehicles could react, a burst of automatic fire shattered the passenger window. More than a dozen .45-caliber rounds blasted the man in the backseat.

Two hundred miles away in Cali, Jorge Salcedo was returning home from his battery business. It was raining, but Jorge lowered his driver's side window to greet the parking lot guard. The man did not look up, fixated on his transistor radio and a voice announcing, "The minister of justice has been shot. His condition is unknown."

Jorge was in his apartment monitoring radio and television when the dreaded news was confirmed—his friend was dead. Rodrigo Lara Bonilla had been hit by seven shots, three to the head. The vest would not have saved him. Jorge skipped the big public funeral. He mourned alone in his apartment. The attack on a government minister was a first for Escobar. It was a first for Jorge, too—the first murder in Escobar's bloody rampage that Jorge took personally.

Assassinations soared through the late 1980s with Escobar's professional hit men, or *sicarios,* sometimes competing with guerrilla gangs for the most sensational headlines. In Bogotá, a superior court judge investigating the Lara Bonilla murder was himself gunned down. The next year, a Medellín judge was shot to death after signing a warrant tying Escobar to the 1976 murders of two Colombian federal agents. A pro-extradition supreme court justice was ambushed and killed on a busy street. Gunmen on a rural highway intercepted and killed the head of Colombia's National Police antinarcotics unit as he and his family were returning from vacation.

In November 1985, an M-19 raiding party seized Bogotá's Palace of Justice and took three hundred hostages. They destroyed vast amounts of criminal records, including extradition files, raising suspicions in Washington that Escobar might have supported the attack. It was never confirmed. More than one hundred hostages, among them eleven high court justices, were killed when government troops stormed the building.

Outrage over the spreading violence was fueled by aggressive news coverage, especially in the pages of the country's oldest daily, *El Espectador.* Its editor and publisher, Guillermo Cano, the silver-haired eminence of Colombian journalism, had earlier that year won a national prize for his columns and editorials condemning the drug mafias. He endorsed extradition to rid the country of its most violent traffickers. Nine days before Christmas 1986, Cano was interviewed about the dangers of provoking Pablo Escobar and his cohorts. "The problem with our business is that one never knows when one won't return home one night," he said. The next day, Cano was shot and killed on the street in front of his newspaper office.

Amid the calculated mayhem, an intimidated supreme court ruled that the country's extradition treaty with the United States was unconstitutional. It was almost immediately reinstated, under Colombian law, by presidential decree—but Escobar's campaign of violence against the government clearly was working.

Then, in late 1987, with Medellín drug bosses already at war with the Bogotá government over extradition, Pablo Escobar picked another fight—this one with his Cali cartel rivals.

EL DOCTOR AND
THE GENTLEMEN

I T ALL STARTED IN NEW YORK CITY. A PAIR OF MID-LEVEL TRAFFICK-
ers had a falling-out over a woman. One trafficker killed the other.
Back home in Colombia, blood demanded blood. The dead man's
friends were allies of Pablo Escobar's, and they turned to the Medellín
boss to avenge their loss. The shooter was a dead man, Escobar vowed.

This sent the frightened killer to another drug boss—Hélmer
"Pacho" Herrera—seeking sanctuary. Pacho and the doomed man had
shared a U.S. jail cell for a time, and they remained good friends. At
thirty-six, Pacho Herrera was a highly successful cocaine dealer from
southern Colombia with long-standing ties to Chepe Santacruz and the
other Cali godfathers. He ran currency exchanges that were highly efficient at money laundering. With his connections to Mexican smugglers
and his distribution networks in the United States, Pacho was a rising
star—and a billionaire in the making.

Until that time, cooperation between the Cali and the Medellín
gangs was common. In 1984, the Cali boss Gilberto Rodríguez Ore-

juela was arrested in Spain along with a Medellín cartel partner, Jorge Luis Ochoa. The two men were scouting trafficking opportunities in Europe. They had previously been joint owners of a Panamanian bank used by all the cartels to launder cash. But that spirit of cooperation died when Pacho blocked Escobar's execution order in the case of the deadly New York love triangle.

The two cartels were already starting to compete more aggressively over the New York cocaine market, and to Escobar such defiance was an affront to his power and authority. El Doctor, as he was known among the peasants of Medellín, regarded himself as the don or czar of all Colombian traffickers. Pacho's insolence was more than disrespectful— it was a personal insult. And it had to be avenged.

Escobar declared that if Pacho Herrera insisted on intervening, then he would die, too. At that point, bosses of the Cali cartel intervened. They took Pacho under their wing and encouraged their friends in the Medellín camp to urge Escobar to cool off. A single death in Queens did not justify a bloodbath in Colombia, Gilberto argued in a telephone conference with Escobar. But neither side backed down. Pablo finally cut off the conversation, declaring, "Then this is war— and I'm going to kill every one of you sons of bitches."

The Cali bosses struck first. In January 1988, they dispatched Andrés "El Pecoso" Vélez to Medellín with a carload of dynamite. El Pecoso, or "Freckles," was one of the Cali cartel's most loyal hired guns. He parked his car beneath the eight-floor Monaco Building, where Escobar's family slept in the penthouse. The blast left a sixteen-foot crater, shattered windows all over the neighborhood, and killed two night watchmen. It also caused permanent hearing loss to Escobar's four-year-old daughter, Manuela.

In retaliation, Escobar launched a series of bombings against Drogas la Rebaja, the national drugstore chain owned by the Rodríguez Orejuela family. The pharmacies were easy targets, but the chief victims of Escobar's attacks were customers, neighbors, and passersby. The drugstore chain served its primary purpose—laundering money for the cartel—whether or not fearful customers stayed away. What really worried the Cali bosses was the threat of violence against their families.

The war escalated. Cali dispatched a seven-man team of assassins to hunt down Escobar. About a week later, boxes of body parts were delivered to Cali—the remains of all seven. Late in 1988, an explosion devastated three houses in an upscale neighborhood of Cali. Miguel Rodríguez Orejuela heard the thundering blast. It was a half mile from his residence and was intended for him. Two Medellín spies were making a car bomb that would detonate when Miguel's car passed taking him to his office. A premature explosion killed the spies.

ON THE NIGHT that Jorge Salcedo joined the fight against Pablo Escobar, the four Cali bosses who recruited him operated the fastest-growing criminal enterprise on the planet—the Walmart, or the Google, of narco-trafficking. The chief of U.S. drug enforcement would declare it "the most well-organized and well-financed crime organization in history."

The partnership of Cali and north Cauca valley traffickers grew out of the longtime criminal association of old friends. Chepe Santacruz and the Rodríguez Orejuela brothers started out as car thieves and kidnappers and moved into cocaine in the 1970s—about the same time as Pablo Escobar and his Medellín associates. Chepe spent considerable time in the United States establishing distribution networks, while the brothers developed coca-processing labs in Peru, southern Colombia, and the Amazon jungles. By the late 1980s, they had moved into smuggling refined cocaine as well. Cali specialized in mass shipments, moving unheard-of quantities—up to ten- and twelve-ton loads hidden in all manner of false cargoes, from hollowed-out lumber and cement posts to frozen fish and broccoli.

The organizational genius behind the Cali cartel was Gilberto, eldest of three Rodríguez Orejuela brothers. Affable, ambitious, a visionary with a keen business sense, Gilberto was known throughout the trafficking world as El Ajedrecista, "the Chess Player." His approach differed fundamentally from Escobar's. Pablo sought attention and ran for, and won, congressional office. Gilberto preferred to buy politicians and to keep a low profile as a gentleman businessman. Pablo put a bounty on the heads of police and judges; Gilberto paid them off.

Seldom was the Cali cartel's cunning and clout more apparent than in 1986, when Gilberto and Jorge Luis Ochoa—still locked up in a Madrid jail since their 1984 arrest in Spain on drug charges—faced transfer to Florida on a U.S. extradition petition. The cartel appealed to Colombia's Ministry of Justice to intervene. But since Gilberto wasn't wanted in Colombia, the ministry had no grounds to seek legal custody. So, a faux felony was concocted: "trafficking in fine cattle." Bogotá's extradition petition trumped Washington's, and Gilberto was sent home. A Cali judge acquitted him. And a grateful cartel paid its friends in the Colombian Ministry of Justice $1 million.

During Gilberto's extended confinement in Spain, management of the cartel's daily operations fell to Miguel, a workaholic who seemed to relish long days. The younger brother proved much better suited to such detail work, and Gilberto happily surrendered the job permanently. There was never a power struggle, nor any serious contention, between the brothers. They seldom disagreed openly. Moreover, they shared a dream of market conquest: total control of the cocaine trade, from production to street sales, from Colombia to the ends of the Earth.

Pablo Escobar stood in the way of that dream, but the cartel war that El Doctor started was going to settle the question one way or another.

THE CALI CARTEL was a labyrinth of compartmentalized responsibilities. Its jungle labs operated independently, and the labs' managers reported directly to Miguel. Each distribution cell—and at one time there were as many as a dozen in New York City alone—reported directly to Miguel. In the transportation arena, separate individuals were responsible for "the broccoli route" and "the coffee route" and "the Brazilian tile route." Each responsible person reported directly to Miguel. There were regional bosses for areas including southern Florida and New York, Panama and Guatemala. They coordinated and confirmed drug shipments, deliveries, and payments. And, of course, each reported directly to Miguel. Warehouse storage, money laundering, cartel security, intelligence gathering, insider tips, snitch reports, it all came through the boss of bosses—a micromanager who worked the phones and held meetings into the early hours.

More than a dozen traffickers in Cali and the Cauca River valley made up what amounted to a federation of small- to big-time drug operators. A management committee was composed of Miguel and Gilberto, Chepe Santacruz, and Pacho Herrera, but the cartel had at least thirty major players.

The partners managed risks on the smuggling side of the Business much as the Medellín cartel did—by pooling narcotics shipments. But the bosses also allowed friends, associates, and businessmen, including some of Cali's social elite, to invest in individual shipments. Small sums could return profits a thousandfold. For locals who dabbled in such investments, it could be like winning the lottery. And like participants in an office betting pool, they didn't feel like criminals. The practice fostered a live-and-let-live attitude in the community, and the Rodríguez Orejuela brothers were widely welcomed in Cali society.

Drug money was a boon to the Cali economy. Unlike Escobar, who was known to stash large amounts of cash in bunkers where rot and rodents literally ate away some of his profits, the Cali cartel specialized in rapid reinvestment. They laundered their drug proceeds as quickly as possible into legitimate investments—purchasing real estate, developing property, buying inventory, and converting cash into financial instruments. The bosses held extensive commercial interests—radio stations, the national chain of discount pharmacies, grocery markets, apartment buildings, office towers, and a professional soccer team.

They owned so much property in Cali that Gilberto was known to send agents out to acquire some attractive piece of real estate only to find that he or his partners already held title. At the end of the 1980s, they were responsible for nearly 40 percent of the city's commercial development.

Prompt reinvestment was calculated to legitimize the Rodríguez Orejuela family holdings. The godfathers appeared determined to spare their children and extended families the dangerous life they had chosen. Both Gilberto and Miguel sent their children to top U.S. universities such as Stanford, Harvard, and Boston College.

When Gilberto's eldest son, Fernando Rodríguez Mondragón, ended up in the Cali jail on local drug charges, his father went to see him. It wasn't to bail him out. Gilberto pulled out his belt and lashed him for several minutes in front of the other inmates. The elders were trying to buy their children a better future.

THE BOSSES AND THEIR FAMILIES lived like captains of industry. Their homes were walled compounds the size of small housing developments, usually with private soccer fields, tennis courts, and swimming pools. Some of their country houses, or *fincas,* included bowling alleys, discotheques, stables, cockfighting arenas, and private beaches.

The Cali brothers could afford to drive Maseratis. Instead, they owned a fleet of Mazdas. The few luxury cars, mostly Mercedes-Benzes, were on constant loan to politicians and civic leaders. They wore minimal jewelry, not even watches as a rule. Miguel adhered to a daily uniform mostly of long-sleeved blue shirts, black slacks, and black Bally loafers, sometimes with gold buckles.

Chepe Santacruz was comfortable in bib overalls and almost never wore socks. He suffered from a skin disorder on his arms that he hid with long-sleeved shirts. Otherwise, he rarely seemed to care about appearances—except when, in the early 1980s, he was denied membership in Club Colombia. Santacruz, who once had a Spanish-language journalist in New York City shot and killed for writing critically about him, took on the Cali country club with an architect instead of an assassin. The billionaire obtained precise dimensions of the clubhouse and built a replica, complete with pool and tennis courts, on his own property.

He wanted it; he bought it. That, too, was the cartel way. In January 1989, the godfathers wanted a private army to eliminate Pablo Escobar. So they arranged to buy Jorge Salcedo and his team of British commandos.

WELCOME TO THE CARTEL

J ORGE THREW HIMSELF INTO HIS NEW ASSIGNMENT, EAGER TO COR-
rect some of the obvious security flaws he saw everywhere. During
those first few days in Cali, even as Jorge prepared to fly off to London
to recruit the British commandos, he and Mario del Basto recommended a number of new safety measures that seemed to please the
bosses.

One obvious problem was the man at the top of Hercules Security,
Major Gómez. He ran one of the cartel's several legitimate businesses,
supervising about one hundred legally armed guards—most of them
working for the family-owned drugstore chain. But Hercules also supported protection teams for the godfathers and their families and had
become increasingly important in the year since the cartel war erupted.

In those early days, Jorge also pieced together the story behind the
boxes of body parts returned from Medellín. It was a matter of personal
and professional curiosity—that, and an instinct to learn from the mistakes of others.

Major Gómez had directed the mission, sending a team of former army sergeants after Escobar. After tracking Escobar to the Medellín suburb of Envigado, the team's cover unraveled. The men had traveled north as a group, seven strangers arriving as a pack. That was the first mistake. None of the sergeants was from the Medellín region, so their Cali accents gave them away. And they drove around Pablo Escobar country in cars with Cali license tags.

Inexcusably stupid intelligence work, thought Jorge.

Before his scheduled departure for London, Jorge had to rush home to Bogotá. Lena was seeing her doctor, and she wanted Jorge along. Tests confirmed that Lena was pregnant. She noticed Jorge's eyes welling with tears. "It's not that bad," she joked. He embraced her. "I've never been happier," he said. They were about to leave the clinic arm in arm when Lena stopped and opened her purse. Pulling out a half-used pack of cigarettes, she handed them to the doctor. "It's over," she said. "For me and for our baby." Jorge knew she would never smoke again.

Lena's tenacity was a source of pride and strength for Jorge. So was her trust in his judgment. She had been supportive, if not enthusiastic, when Jorge brought in the British commandos to take on FARC. He was hoping for a similar response when he told her about his Cali mission.

"Mario and I—we need the Brits again, this time to protect some people in Cali," Jorge started to explain. He did not name "some people." He didn't have to. Lena knew who in Cali needed protection and who had the resources to hire Jorge and Mario. He was trying to assure her that he would be in no danger when she buried her face in his chest. They both fell silent for a long moment.

"Make me one promise," she said.

"Of course—anything."

"Don't ever tell me what you're doing. Please, do that for me. I don't want to know anything. Do you understand? I don't want to worry constantly."

Jorge gave her a reassuring hug and a nod.

"Besides, you know what you're doing," she said. Jorge did not respond.

*   *   *

THE NONDESCRIPT HEADQUARTERS of Hercules Security was in a booming section of southern Cali. The company itself was not growing. It catered to one customer—the Rodríguez family, which owned it. Major Gómez arrived at his office every morning at about seven o'clock, delivered by a driver in a bulletproof car.

One morning, the driver encountered a dump truck partially blocking the entrance. Gómez had to walk a few extra steps from the protection of his armored limo to the front door. He was midway between the car and his office when five men with M16s rose up in the truck bed and opened fire. Gómez crumpled in a bloody heap.

Jorge and Mario were on their recruiting trip to England when they heard about it. Jorge shook his head. "What have we gotten ourselves into?" he said to Mario. It was a purely rhetorical question at the time, but Jorge found himself pondering the subject repeatedly in the weeks that followed. It struck him that the bosses weren't all that bothered by this high-level loss. There were no expressions of sorrow. Rather, the general attitude seemed dismissive. And the bosses wasted no time advising Jorge and Mario that they would assume the major's duties.

Jorge was never quite sure who killed Gómez, but the more he learned, the more troubled he was. The shooters disappeared without a trace, a neat trick if they really were out-of-towners using a dump truck for a getaway vehicle. The hit almost certainly required help from a Cali insider who knew the major's habits. There was no question that Gómez had become expendable with Jorge and Mario about to take over many of his responsibilities.

Jorge and Mario joked that maybe an M16 firing squad was the Cali cartel's cure for poor job performance. They laughed about it, but for Jorge the humor masked an uneasy feeling.

DAVID TOMKINS WAS JORGE's connection with the world of British mercenaries. He agreed to meet Jorge and Mario at the Sherlock Holmes hotel in London to discuss a new proposal. Jorge had been necessarily vague in arranging the meeting over a transatlantic phone call.

Tomkins, an arms dealer in his late forties, was a giant of contradictions—a Rambo character with a touch of old English class.

His military experience was entirely extracurricular. He was a soldier of fortune who never got closer to regular military service than a brief stint as a merchant seaman. His gentlemanly manner concealed a hard past. He was a self-taught explosives expert who had first used his skills as a safecracker. He spent eight of his early adult years in prisons. Even his tattoos were in conflict. On each finger of his right hand, just below the knuckle, were the letters *L-O-V-E;* on his left fist were *H-A-T-E.*

While Tomkins handled explosives and the mercenaries' business side, it was the burly Scotsman—Peter McAleese—whom Jorge had to sway. McAleese was the field leader, a soldier's soldier, and a brilliant tactician. Fighting men would follow him anywhere—even to Colombia, if Jorge could make the case.

"We're going after a terrorist. He's one of the world's most wanted outlaws—a drug trafficker, a killer, a threat to my country—Pablo Escobar," Jorge said.

McAleese had the physical profile and stubborn will of an American football noseguard—and what Jorge figured was a personal grudge against communists. He had fought one leftist guerrilla group or another around the globe. But there were no communists to slay at Hacienda Nápoles. Jorge had to wait for Tomkins and McAleese to confer privately.

The two Brits were predisposed to join any mission with Jorge Salcedo. The FARC mission, though unfulfilled militarily, had worked out well financially. They trusted Jorge and enjoyed his company. McAleese had taken to calling him "our gallant colonel Ricardo"—though the rank was as fictitious as "Ricardo," or "Richard," his cartel code name. Jorge's suspense was brief. McAleese quickly declared that Pablo Escobar was "a big enough villain" to justify his services.

In late February 1989, Tomkins and McAleese landed in Cali for contract talks with the cartel godfathers. Their first meeting with the bosses was similar to Jorge's—delayed until after 10:00 p.m. and held in Pacho Herrera's all-white compound. Again, all four godfathers were there, along with Jorge, Mario, and two of Pacho's brothers, William and Alvaro Herrera.

Gilberto presided over discussions that again continued past midnight. Jorge translated for both sides. There was quick consensus on strategic goals and basic tactics. Just as Gilberto originally imagined, the commandos would lead a daylight raid on Hacienda Nápoles, arriving in helicopters with army and National Police markings. McAleese would work up a detailed battle plan, but the fundamental scheme was set.

It came time to talk pesos. Financial negotiation was Tomkins's theater of operations. He reached into his pocket for a cigarette. Seeing no ashtrays, he asked politely, "Mind if I——?" All eyes turned to Miguel, who scowled and shook his head. Jorge explained, "El Señor is very sensitive to smoke—an allergy." In fact, no one smoked in the presence of any cartel boss—nor did they drink much, or use drugs. The godfathers enforced zero tolerance for indulgences of any kind during work hours.

Unfazed, Tomkins continued. He cited the several challenges of the plan, the manpower needs, and the estimated training time.

"We can do this, make no mistake, but——" He paused for dramatic effect and looked each godfather in the eye. "It will cost you gentlemen one . . . million . . . dollars."

If Tomkins expected the Cali bosses to blink, he was surprised. Gilberto shrugged and said, "That's no problem. We'll pay you two or three times that—plus, if things work out, a bonus." It seemed to Jorge that it was Tomkins who blinked. But it wasn't until later, when the Brits were alone with him in the car, that they let their excitement show.

"This could be worth three . . . maybe five million with bonuses," Tomkins raved. "It's incredible. It's historic!" McAleese reached from the backseat as Jorge drove and clamped a beefy hand on his shoulder. "Ricardo," he said. "We won't let you down."

TOMKINS LEFT COLOMBIA to round up men and equipment. Jorge arranged for McAleese to see Hacienda Nápoles from the air. They flew together in a six-seater Cessna 210M Centurion with a motor-driven Nikon F-1 camera mounted in the belly.

The British recruits began arriving in Cali one or two at a time. Some had been part of the unfinished FARC project. All were experienced mercenaries, most of them previously trained by McAleese in the South Africa Forty-fourth Parachute Brigade. Among them were men who had also served in the French Foreign Legion, the Rhodesian Light Infantry, the Scots Guards, and the SAS, the British special forces. Each new arrival shared space in two luxury apartments set aside for McAleese and Tomkins. None spoke Spanish. They were told to stay close to the apartment, try to act like tourists, and mind their manners. That proved a challenge, especially after visits to the Great American Disaster, a bar run by a U.S. expatriate. The men mixed their scotch with politics, leading to lively debates that too often devolved into brawls.

Worried about mission security, Jorge moved the men to Miguel's mountain estate west of Cali, a ranch called Pennsylvania. It was just off the twisting main road to the Pacific coast and the port of Buenaventura. The spacious grounds had resort-like accommodations at a comfortably cool elevation. There was also a gym and weight-training room, a five-lane bowling alley, a steam room and sauna, and two cooks who provided twenty-four-hour meal service.

One day Jorge and Mario received a small truck courtesy of Pacho Herrera. The shiny aluminum box van was a mobile armory filled with automatic rifles, pistols, grenades, antitank rockets, and detonators. McAleese called it "an Aladdin's cave" of the finest military gear—new weapons, ammo, and explosives, most of it superior to anything provided during the previous year by the Colombian military.

McAleese's attack plan anticipated encountering as many as one hundred Medellín gunmen defending Hacienda Nápoles. To face that potential challenge, each Brit would be equipped with two machine guns, a sidearm, grenades, and other explosives. The commandos would carry enough combined firepower to kill more than three thousand Escobar defenders.

Since the FARC project, Jorge had been impressed by the commandos' training regimen. They ran and worked out daily, drilled tenaciously, were constantly tested on details of their battle plan, and went to bed exhausted most nights. When Jorge was away, they sometimes broke into Miguel's fine wine collection. The boss didn't like that, but killing Pablo was more important to El Señor than any of his Bordeaux.

What weighed most on Jorge's peace of mind was unfinished family business. With Lena expecting their child, he very much wanted to get married. That meant a trip out of Colombia, where, by law, a couple was permitted only one marriage per lifetime. Second marriages were typically performed in Panama. Jorge wasn't concerned about social convention. Marriage would guarantee that if anything happened to him, Lena and his unborn child would inherit his modest estate.

One night, Jorge tossed and turned, trying to sleep. In dreams, he was stalked by a man with a gun, a faceless stranger who kept getting closer. Finally, the gun was in his face, its enormous muzzle inches away. Jorge lurched awake, drenched in sweat.

Jorge would never tell Lena, but it was the nightmare that drove him to force the issue with his bosses. He needed time off, he insisted. He said he was flying to Panama for the weekend with Lena—to get married. The godfathers erupted in laughter and good wishes.

"I thought you were smarter than that," joked the twice-married Chepe Santacruz. Pacho Herrera was first to shake Jorge's hand, prompting Chepe to bellow that the homosexual mobster was "the only smart one in this room. He has no women!" Miguel, the man with four wives, did not join in the banter, but he approved the leave—insisting that Jorge "hurry back."

TARGET: PABLO

THE BRITISH COMMANDOS HAD BEEN TRAINING FOR ABOUT TEN weeks and were physically and mentally ready. It was May 1989. All they needed was for Pablo Escobar to pay a visit to Hacienda Nápoles. The edgy tedium was interrupted one morning when Jorge was summoned from camp. It sounded urgent.

He arrived in Cali to find Gilberto pacing. Miguel was on the phone—as usual. He wasn't often invited into the inner office while Miguel conducted business on the phone, and that was just fine with Jorge. He wasn't curious about the drug trade and figured he was better off staying as far away from it as possible. Although it didn't bother him to protect drug lords from assassins—nor, for that matter, to plot the death of Pablo Escobar—Jorge drew the line at trafficking. He wanted no part in the Business. It was his way of isolating what he did for the cartel from what the cartel partners did for a living. As Jorge saw it, he was not a drug dealer; therefore, he was not one of them. He was not a criminal.

When Miguel finally hung up, an impatient Gilberto thrust a piece of paper into Jorge's hands. The brothers waited as he scanned numbers scrawled on the white page. It was obviously a phone number, but it was unfamiliar. Jorge waited for an explanation. Gilberto grinned.

"Pablo's mobile phone," he said, almost gleefully. "What can you do with that?"

Since joining the Cali organization nearly four months earlier, Jorge had continued to work on cartel radiophone systems, even as he managed day-to-day needs of the British team. Along with Mario, he was pressing to equip all family bodyguards with upgraded equipment—preaching that ease of communications was the key to security.

Jorge had gotten to know a local electronics expert named Carlos Alfredo. Jorge trusted his technical skills completely, but his business connections might be of concern to the Rodríguez Orejuela brothers. He handled radio repair and maintenance work for the Colombian National Police.

"But he works for God and the Devil," Jorge assured Gilberto.

Carlos Alfredo went to work fabricating electronic scanning and locating devices to track the radio signal of Escobar's mobile phone. The cartel was soon equipped to intercept calls, record conversations, and pinpoint the phone geographically from an aerial listening post. Jorge and Carlos Alfredo outfitted a cartel-owned Cessna 210M with the electronic gear, including four directional antennas. The plane was transformed into an airborne surveillance platform.

On the ground, Cali spies were able to intercept Escobar's mobile phone signal from a hideout overlooking Medellín. While the Medellín boss was eluding police and Colombia's entire national security apparatus, the Cali cartel was lurking within earshot. The biggest concern for Jorge remained keeping secret the existence of foreign commandos. A dozen Brits, no matter how fiercely they fought, were not going to overpower four to six times as many armed guards without the help of confusion and chaos—the side effects of surprise.

After an afternoon of training exercises in the mountains, the commando team stopped at a roadside café for a round of Coca-Colas. The pale-skinned Brits in white T-shirts and combat boots caught the eye of a passing motorcycle traffic officer, who stopped to investigate. When the visitors spoke no Spanish, he demanded to inspect their vehicles—one of which was the weapons-packed "Aladdin's cave." Mario del Basto flashed his retired army major's identity card. The policeman was unimpressed. Mario denied him access to any of the vehicles. Jorge noticed a pair of commandos edging toward their weapons. "Tell them to back off," Jorge whispered urgently to McAleese. "Don't do anything stupid."

Mario made a call on his radiophone, and he and Jorge stood between the traffic policeman and the commandos for the next twenty minutes—until a motorcycle courier arrived with a small bag. Del Basto took the bag immediately to the policeman, who considered its contents and finally roared off up the road, his curiosity bought off by a bag of cash. It was hardly a shock to Jorge, who, like many a Colombian, had slipped pesos to traffic cops. But never before had the stakes been so high.

After that near miss, commando training was moved to a jungle camp on the western side of the mountains. It was a flat and reasonably dry expanse in otherwise swampy terrain. In exchange for all that privacy, the commandos had to coexist with giant spiders, poisonous frogs, and snakes, some venomous. At night they listened to the chirps and barks of giant rats—the skittish *guaguas* that look like thirty-pound guinea pigs. "They're delicious," Jorge assured the commandos. But the men stuck with traditional fare: beef and eggs, beef and eggs . . . and more beef and eggs.

The Brits dubbed their new home La Guagua. Jorge called it "Nowhere, Colombia." The men slept in a wooden bunkhouse to avoid snakes and insects. It was also the classroom, the infirmary, and an assembly hall for team meetings. It was papered with photographs of Pablo Escobar.

Jorge had moments of doubt—not about the Brits or their fighting abilities or the battle plan. But he sometimes worried that Escobar would never return to Hacienda Nápoles. The fact that the Cali bosses saw it as a perfect trap meant that El Doctor might have similar instincts.

*   *   *

SOCCER CAME TO THE CALI cartel's aid on May 31, 1989. The Club Atlético Nacional of Medellín defeated Paraguay to become the first Colombian team in forty-one years to win the Copa Libertadores de América, a prestigious South American tournament. Pablo Escobar was a jubilant team owner. Word came from Cali spies in Medellín that a party was scheduled—at Hacienda Nápoles.

"Let's go," Gilberto ordered.

A few loose ends remained, most significantly a missing helicopter. A second Bell 205 Huey was undergoing renovation and repairs in Brazil. The plan called for a pair of Vietnam-era Hueys painted like police choppers to do the heavy lifting of commandos and munitions and deliver the strike team to the drop zone. The much smaller Hughes 500, a four-seater with military markings, would be the aerial command post for McAleese. Without the second Huey, the Hughes 500 would have to fly at or beyond its maximum weight.

Both pilots were reluctant to risk overloading, as was McAleese. But Gilberto didn't want to hear it. After the long wait for Pablo to show up, the godfather was not inclined to waste the first good opportunity to strike. Gilberto pressed the pilots: "You can handle the extra load, can't you?" After discussing redistribution of passengers and cargo, the pilots agreed that it was doable. Gilberto was delighted. "We have to go—now," he insisted. "It could be our only chance." McAleese relented.

At that point, the Chess Player announced another last-minute adjustment, an insurance policy of sorts. Once the commandos were on the ground and the invasion under way, a Cessna 208 Caravan with a dozen or more cartel gunmen would land at the opposite end of the ranch. These were Pacho Herrera's killers. The Cali godfather whom Escobar had vowed to kill was sending in his own team to settle a personal score—and to increase the body count. There were no objections.

D-DAY CAME ON SATURDAY, June 3, 1989. McAleese addressed his commandos, assembled near the helicopters in their Colombian army camouflage uniforms, their tactical vests stuffed with ammo and grenades.

"Whether we shall meet again I know not," McAleese began, quoting Shakespeare's Brutus in *Julius Caesar*. "Therefore our everlasting farewell take. For ever, and for ever, farewell . . . If we do meet again, why, we shall smile. If not, why then this parting was well made."

Moments later, to the scream of surging rotors, two overloaded helicopters lumbered into cloudless skies. Operation Phoenix, as McAleese called it, was under way—two and a half hours of flying time from the staging and refueling site near Hacienda Nápoles.

In Cali, on the other side of the Cordillera Occidental, Jorge was in the co-pilot's seat of the Cessna 210M, code-named Telstar, the attack's airborne communications center. He signaled Irma, the cartel's only female pilot, who powered the plane into an easy takeoff and climb, heading north for the Magdalena River valley. If speed and distance calculations were correct, they would arrive over the staging area just ahead of the helicopters flying up from the coast.

A radio technician in headphones worked a set of electronic receivers. One of his instruments could listen in on Escobar's mobile telephone. Another could pinpoint within a few yards where the phone was being used. Already, the equipment had confirmed that Escobar's mobile phone was somewhere on the ranch grounds. That was enough to launch the commandos. But the final piece of intelligence needed before invading was proof that Pablo was there, too.

The Cali godfathers had arranged for someone to place a call to Escobar's phone at precisely 11:00 a.m., when Telstar would be close enough to intercept the signal. The radio technician had to hear Pablo's voice, or the attack was off. Irma held the plane on a steady course. Jorge checked his watch. At eleven o'clock, he turned to watch the radioman. The technician pressed his headset against his ears, until finally looking up. He grinned and flashed both thumbs up. Jorge activated his radio and announced in Spanish, *"Va a haber fiesta."*

In Cali, an office full of anxious drug lords cheered the news. All four of the Cali godfathers had settled in to monitor live reports from the scene. *"Bueno! Bueno!"* Gilberto responded over the radio.

In the Cessna, Jorge switched to a second radio and repeated the message in English: "There is going to be a party. Repeat, there is going to be a party." He waited for a response. It came from McAleese: "That's confirmed."

In the Hughes 500, McAleese raised a triumphant fist, signaling three men crammed into the back. The four-seat helicopter carried five big men, with the trio of men in back sitting on boxes of munitions. Two standard backseats had been removed to accommodate them. The seat belts were gone, too, but no one sitting on boxes of explosives complained about the missing safety devices.

PHASE ONE OF THE OPERATION was the nearly three-hour lift over spectacular Andean mountain ranges to the staging and refueling area codenamed Kiko. It was a deserted farm secretly purchased by Gilberto to store fifty-five-gallon drums of JP4 aviation fuel. Kiko was eight minutes' flying time from Hacienda Nápoles.

Phase two, the assault, would open with an attack on perimeter guard towers—starting with heavy machine-gun fire and explosives drops from the Hughes 500. Tomkins would man a powerful M240 machine gun mounted on a tripod that Jorge designed to be clamped to the helicopter's skids. The gun had been loaned with great apprehension by a National Police colonel. Gilberto kept reminding Jorge to take special care of it.

McAleese expected that the attacking helicopters would look to those on the ground like a government invasion force. Amid any uncertainty in the hacienda about how to respond, the commandos would move quickly to seize the residence, take out the armed guards, and capture or kill the drug baron. Phase three was reassembly, and phase four was withdrawal. McAleese and the commandos planned to hit and run—to leave Colombia as quickly as possible, stopping first in Panama.

In the command chopper, McAleese looked back frequently to check on his three comrades squeezed into the space for two. He was relieved that takeoff had been uneventful, despite the excess weight. Along with Mario del Basto and David Tomkins, the third man in back was Omar Sánchez, a hired gun. He was one of Chepe's *sicarios*. Omar was the envy of the commandos, showing up for training sessions driving his fully loaded Porsche 911. Omar had learned English dealing drugs on the streets of Los Angeles. He came along on this flight to help with the translations—and the killing.

Their pilot was Tiger, a twenty-nine-year-old police lieutenant from Bogotá. McAleese admired his daring and swashbuckling style. Mario complained that he was reckless. He was the son of a retired police general but had an anti-authority streak that made him a favorite of the Brits. To Mario's dismay, the commandos encouraged Tiger. On the eve of battle, McAleese draped the pilot's seat with the tigerlike skin of an ocelot, the Colombian *tigrillo.*

In the air, they followed a course north, roughly along the Cauca River. The Bell 205 Huey with its ten commandos and a veteran pilot, code-named Toyco, flew alongside in a two-chopper formation—the Bell 205 painted in the green and white National Police colors and the smaller Hughes 500 in army green. If any legitimate agency inquired, they were working an undercover drug case.

After nearly three hours in the air, the helicopters approached Kiko out of the west. A buildup of clouds obscured the last ridgeline between them and the staging area landing site. The aircraft encountered strong, buffeting winds as they flew in and out of cloud patches. Neither helicopter was equipped for flying on instruments, so the pilots climbed for clearer skies.

In his seat aboard the Cessna 210M, Jorge had an excellent vantage point. He could see both helicopters. They were skimming the clouds, sometimes disappearing briefly into the blanket of white. Circling high above, Jorge could see better than the chopper pilots where the cloud bank ended. They were nearly through it.

"Good news, Tiger. Open skies are just ahead," Jorge radioed.

But the call was not received. Tiger had jumped on the radio frequency himself to report an alarming development: the Hughes 500 was low on fuel. "Milk bottles are nearly empty," he said. Climbing while overloaded had only consumed more fuel. Now Tiger wanted to get lower. Both helicopter pilots spotted a break in the clouds.

"You see the hole?" Toyco radioed.

"I'll dive to it," Tiger said.

Jorge lost sight of the helicopters. The next radio transmission came from Toyco in the Bell 205. He was just touching down at Kiko. "Where's Tiger?"

In the Cessna cabin next to Jorge, Irma groaned in dread. Jorge responded, "We don't see him. I'll go back—have a look."

Irma banked hard and swung back toward the ridge. There had been no distress signal, no report of an emergency landing—and there were no signs of fire on the mountain. But the Hughes 500 still had not come out of the clouds.

PRISONER OF THE CLOUDS

JORGE SALCEDO PEERED DOWN FROM THE CESSNA 210M, FLYING LOW along the edge of a cloud, searching the rugged terrain below him. The mountainsides were covered with endless folds of green, what McAleese had called "a broccoli forest." Jorge held his breath, hoping to find the tough Brit leader and his companions in a clearing among those giant green stalks. He saw nothing but green. A familiar voice suddenly boomed through the radio receiver.

"Jorge! Jorge! Do you see us?"

"Mario, thank God! What happened?"

"We crashed. Can you see us?"

"I'm looking. Are there casualties?"

"Yes, one," said Mario. "You can guess who."

"Tiger?"

"Yes. And Peter is hurt. Can you see us?" Mario pleaded.

Jorge could see nothing but the green blur of uninterrupted forest. He told Mario to help guide the plane to their crash site. As Irma brought the Cessna around, Mario relayed what he saw and could hear from the ground: "You must be close. Yes, now I see you. Come right slightly. That's it . . . now straight. You're getting close . . . closer . . . you're almost—there! Did you see us?"

"No—sorry," Jorge radioed.

"No? You flew right over our heads!" Mario sounded furious.

"Calm down, Mario. Calm down or you won't make it out of there," Jorge said.

As the Cessna circled around for another pass, Jorge switched radios to report the bad news to Cali. He decided to blurt it out: "Tiger crashed. He's dead. The command ship is down in the mountains. Peter is injured . . . we have to abort the mission." Jorge waited for the news to sink in. Finally, a disappointed-sounding Gilberto acknowledged the news. He agreed there was no alternative but to call off the attack.

The Cessna made another series of passes. Jorge finally got a glimpse of the crash site. There was no way to land—too many trees and an impossibly steep slope. The Bell 205 had refueled and joined the rescue effort. Toyco reported a flat open area down the hillside. A mountain stream ran to the spot.

"Can you find that stream and get down to the clearing?" Jorge asked Mario.

"Yes, but not Peter."

The series of overflights had allowed Irma to make a precise navigational fix. The stranded team was 16.4 nautical miles southwest of the VHF omnidirectional radio tower at Abejorral near the village of Sonsón, about sixty miles from Medellín. All the aerial activity was sure to be noticed. Jorge had to be careful not to lead unwelcome strangers to the crash site. The rescue had to be private: no search teams from Sonsón . . . no crash investigators . . . no media coverage.

If Jorge could pull off a secret rescue, maybe he could still salvage the secret mission. Maybe later, in a few months, they could try again to kill Pablo.

ON THE GROUND, it was devastation. When Tiger dived into that hole in the clouds, he ran smack into a fog-shrouded forest. He had no chance to pull out before the bubble windshield shattered against a tree. The Hughes 500 twisted violently and careened down the forested slope on its back—being ripped apart by ancient trees and the fierce power of its disintegrating rotors.

His shoulder harness kept McAleese from being ejected, but he felt a wrenching pain in his back. The scream of the doomed engine rose above the sickening screech of rending wood and metal. Finally, the battered helicopter stopped, its skids pointed skyward. McAleese dangled a few feet above the ground, still strapped into his seat. He glanced up to see the forest floor.

The three men wedged in the back came through the crash with little more than cuts and bruises. Omar, Tomkins, and Mario scrambled out through gaping holes in the airframe. Tiger moaned and barely moved. McAleese released his own straps and dropped hard to the ground. He had five broken ribs and a badly sprained back. He was covered in blood. It was Tiger's. The young pilot was alive as Mario and Tomkins eased him to the ground. It appeared that a broken rotor blade had partially amputated his left arm and taken off his left leg at the hip.

McAleese rummaged through wreckage until he retrieved the chopper's medical kit. He jabbed a needle into Tiger's one good arm, delivering a humanitarian dose of morphine. There was no way to stop the bleeding. No one knew how to administer last rites. Minutes later, Tiger was dead.

The survivors rested on a ledge jutting out from an otherwise sheer slope and took stock of their predicament. It could have been worse. Trees had softened the initial impact, and the dense jungle had prevented the crippled aircraft from tumbling hundreds, if not thousands, of feet farther down. They were stranded somewhere above sixty-five hundred feet on the side of a mountain ridge aptly named Cuchilla del Tigre—"Ridge of the Tiger."

They were deep in the heart of Escobar country. For four guys with a corpse, clinging to the side of a mountain, the only thought was rescue. They could hear the distant engine whine of the Cessna 210M. That's when Mario grabbed a radio from the wreckage and called Jorge.

* * *

MARIO, OMAR, AND TOMKINS headed down the mountain, intending to meet the other commandos and lead a rescue team back to the crash site. The linear distance was not far, but it was treacherous landscape. The trek down turned into an overnight ordeal. Inadvertently, they took along the only working radios. McAleese was left unable to communicate, alone with Tiger's body and the eerie grinding noises of the Hughes 500 still caught in the swaying trees.

Toyco and his commando passengers took cover at the makeshift pickup site below the ridge and waited for the descending survivors. Jorge withdrew to Cali. The three crash survivors finally stumbled into the arms of Toyco and the anxious Brits some time after first light. They discovered that in all their fighting gear no one packed a machete, essential for hacking their way back up the mountain. Still, they tried. It took hours to advance a few hundred feet. Then they heard shouts in Spanish. After ducking for cover, Toyco waved everyone back to the partially camouflaged helicopter.

"I don't like it," he said. "We're getting out of here."

Jorge proposed sending a small rescue party that would not risk drawing attention. A cartel lieutenant, assisted by a team of local peasants, could carry McAleese to a safe evacuation site. Jorge was encouraged that the crash had not made news two days later.

The bosses agreed to notify Tiger's family. They would show their regrets and sympathy with a substantial financial gift to Tiger's father, the retired police general—enough to assure continued secrecy about the circumstances of the pilot's death. But what the godfathers seemed most anxious about was the condition of their borrowed M240 machine gun. In all the excitement and concern over life and death, Jorge never thought to ask if the big gun had been damaged or destroyed. He understood the importance of getting it back to the anxious lender, but he was surprised by the intensity of concern.

Jorge had a lot to learn about cartel priorities.

THE ANDEAN MOUNTAINSIDE where McAleese spent the first night alone is part of a microclimate typical of high elevations in tropical and subtropical regions. They are called cloud forests—notable for surprisingly cool temperatures and for clouds that form and linger and drizzle.

McAleese used the last hints of twilight to struggle back to the wreckage. He was cold, and shivering spread intense pain across his back and chest. He noted that Tiger's body was tinged in blue. The Scotsman rooted around in the strewn cargo of the Hughes 500 until he found several packs of C-4—the powerful plastic explosive known to the Brits as Demex. It had been intended to destroy Pablo's guard towers. The claylike explosive is a favorite of saboteurs and demolition workers for its explosive wallop, but it can be burned as fuel without risk of detonation. Back on his ledge, McAleese warmed his hands over a small C-4 campfire.

When no help made it up the mountain during the second day, McAleese took care to ration his supplies. He had no way of knowing how much longer he might have to wait on the slope.

In the chill winds that swept the ridge the second night, he drifted in and out of sleep. By morning the mountain was silent. The mist settled low in the trees, and McAleese knew the poor visibility would delay any chance of a rescue. He painfully returned to the wreckage for medical drip bags, candies, and a loaded Uzi machine gun. If Pablo Escobar's men found him first, McAleese intended to make a fight of it. The morning mist turned to drizzle, and then to rain. McAleese was soaking wet and cold as he braced for another day in agony—a prisoner in the clouds.

After three nights on the mountain, McAleese was starting to talk to himself. He was running low on drip bags. He would have to capture drinking water from the rains. He considered trying to work his way down the mountain. But he had neither radio nor compass. Then he heard sounds—a machete hacking through brush and limbs, voices speaking Spanish. A group of men was coming up the steep slope. McAleese grabbed his machine gun. Looking over his ledge, he caught sight of someone and shouted a warning that needed no translation: "*Alto!* Stop right there, you son of a bitch."

One of the rescuers saw McAleese's Uzi and threw up his hands in horror. "*Amigo! Amigo!*" he screamed. "*Capitán Ricardo. Amigo Ricardo!*"

McAleese lowered his weapon and welcomed his rescuers. The men stayed only long enough to get McAleese out of his boots and into lightweight athletic shoes. One of the men found the M240 machine gun still clamped to a helicopter skid. It no longer looked like new, but at least it could be returned in one piece. They left Tiger's body on the mountain.

None of the five rescuers spoke English. For much of the descent, they followed the stream that led Tomkins and Mario to safety. McAleese, with his wrenched back and broken ribs, needed help down the face of every waterfall—and there were several. Each time he was lowered by rope tied around his waist. And each time he was left gasping in pain. He came to hate waterfalls.

They hiked late into the night, aided by flashlights, and slept by the river. At dawn, they resumed. About six hours later, the rescuers led McAleese to a grassy hill to meet a helicopter. The tough Scotsman stood to board—but the prop wash knocked him flat on his back. Mercifully, McAleese was delivered minutes later to a nearby airfield where Jorge waited in another Cessna to fly him to a doctor. McAleese climbed aboard with great effort. He dropped into the seat behind Jorge, who could not recall ever being more relieved to see anyone. The two men reached out to shake hands. The injured Scotsman still had the grip of a steel vise.

SOME UNFINISHED BUSINESS REMAINED. Tiger's father wanted his son's body. Ten days after the crash, Jorge sent the same crew of rescuers back up to retrieve the remains. The general was grateful and kept his silence. Chance discovery of the remote crash site was about as likely as finding Amelia Earhart's. Pablo Escobar knew nothing about what had very nearly hit him.

MATERNITY AND MARTIAL LAW

THE COLOMBIAN DEPARTMENT, OR STATE, OF ANTIOQUIA WAS THE center of Pablo Escobar country. Medellín was its capital. And Governor Antonio Roldán Betancur was fed up with all the killings. He urged police to crack down. On July 4, 1989, the popular official had prepared a speech denouncing political violence, whose effects he knew only too well. He needed a team of armed bodyguards just to get to the luncheon where he could express his outrage.

Three security men met Betancur at his front door that morning and escorted him to a chauffeur-driven car. Two blocks from the governor's residence they passed a parked car rigged to explode at that very moment. Only the badly injured driver survived. Pablo Escobar was blamed, and political violence continued unabated.

About two weeks later, three motorcycle gunmen intercepted the car of a judge riding through Medellín. They riddled it with two hundred rounds of machine-gun fire. The thirty-eight-year-old judge,

María Elena Díaz Pérez, had recently signed a warrant for Escobar's arrest. The warrant expired with her life.

For Jorge Salcedo, the killings only added to a profound sense of regret over the failed commando attack on Hacienda Nápoles the month before. He and the Cali godfathers were eager to try again, but the team still needed helicopters. Peter McAleese was nearly recovered from his broken ribs and sprained back. David Tomkins had recruited a couple of British helicopter pilots to replace Tiger. The commandos continued to live well, waiting in relative luxury in Panama, financially supported by the drug bosses. But by the end of July most of the Brits were getting restless.

Jorge was restless, too. He was doing a lot of what he regarded as babysitting—keeping the idle commandos fed and housed and out of trouble. The move to Panama was made to help maintain their low profiles during the interminable wait. It was also keeping Jorge away from his pregnant wife for weeks at a time.

He finally sent for her. Lena stepped from the plane in Panama City looking radiant in a pearl necklace and maternity clothes. She was seven months pregnant. Two British commandos who accompanied Jorge greeted her like Buckingham Palace royalty.

Driving back into town, Lena sat by an open window, her hair blowing in the fresh breeze. Jorge kept stealing glances at her in his rearview mirror. At a traffic stop, a street thief lunged for her necklace, ripping it from her body. An instant later he was sprinting for his life ahead of the two angry Brits. He didn't get far. The commandos were beating him enthusiastically when Jorge caught up. It was essential to avoid attracting the attention of local police, so at Jorge's urging they released the thief, retreated to their car, and sped off—with Lena clutching her retrieved pearls.

Jorge worried constantly about mission security. Panama City was full of agents loyal to the dictator Manuel Noriega. The Panamanian strongman's ties to Pablo Escobar and the Medellín cartel made Jorge especially wary.

With Panama-U.S. tensions rising, Jorge was also concerned that his English-speaking commandos might be mistaken for American spies. Jorge decided to get them out of town for a while. He arranged for group instruction in scuba diving off Portobelo on Panama's northern Caribbean shore.

There, among the stone ruins of sixteenth-century Spanish forts once plundered by British privateers and pirates, the commandos worked long days to earn individual scuba certifications. The interlude marked a welcome return to military discipline. There was no drinking before diving, so for weeks there was no fighting either. Things were going so well that Jorge decided he could sneak away for a rare weekend back home.

JORGE LANDED IN BOGOTÁ on Friday evening, August 18, intending to stay one or two nights. He arrived unannounced in a rented car, delighting his pregnant wife. Lena tuned her radio to upbeat salsa music, and the happy couple settled in for some welcome time alone. But a news bulletin interrupted radio programming.

The presidential candidate Luis Carlos Galán had just been shot at a campaign rally southwest of Bogotá. The Liberal Party candidate was the undisputed front-runner in the 1990 elections. He strongly supported extradition and was running as a crusader against Pablo Escobar and the drug cartels. Frequent news updates followed. Galán, forty-five, had been rushed to a hospital. Galán was in critical condition. Galán was clinging to life. Galán was dead.

President Virgilio Barco appeared on national television. He declared martial law and imposed a national curfew, ordering army reserve units to mobilize. Jorge reluctantly headed for the door, planning to report for reserve duty. He lingered, kissing Lena good-bye—then she gasped. Her water broke. She was in labor.

By ten o'clock that night all of Bogotá had been shut down and travel banned, but Jorge had to get to a hospital. He used his military identity papers to pass through a series of roadblocks, rushing Lena to a clinic. Only one nurse was on duty. Jorge used the clinic's telephone to summon her doctor. Then he waited, roaming the empty halls. At three in the morning his son was born—a month earlier than expected, but "little Jorge" and his mother were healthy. With his infant son in his arms, Jorge barely noticed reports that César Gaviria, the interior minister, had replaced the martyred Galán in the presidential race.

Galán's assassination set off nationwide police and military sweeps of suspected trafficking operations. Federal antidrug agents flooded the countryside, detaining or arresting nearly ten thousand in their hunt for Escobar and his partners. President Barco accepted the first in a series of pledges from the new administration of George H. W. Bush to provide major financial, military, and intelligence assistance to fight the cartels.

Escobar regarded the crackdown as a personal attack, but government fury was aimed at all traffickers. To the chagrin of the Cali cartel, authorities seized more than eighty planes from its fleet, sharply curtailing drug operations for weeks. Jorge stayed three extra days with his wife and newborn son before heading back to Panama.

TROUBLE AWAITED IN PANAMA CITY. The hotel manager was so angry he could barely speak. Jorge followed him in silence from the front desk to the elevator lobby, then up to the penthouse suite. The finest apartment in the establishment was in shambles, and the enraged hotel manager was bent on eviction. Everyone out immediately, he demanded.

Jorge had a pocketful of Cali cartel cash—U.S. dollars mostly. Nine hundred covered a week in the penthouse suite. Fifty dollars a day went to each commando. It was cartel small change but enough to satisfy British appetites for food, booze, and whores. So, when the door opened on the debris-strewn penthouse, Jorge calmly examined the damage—a shattered lamp here, a table and chair reduced to firewood over there, nasty stains on a carpet, a cracked sliding glass door to the balcony, and other assorted nicks and gouges. Five hundred dollars should cover it, Jorge suggested. The manager softened slightly. Jorge peeled off an extra fifty for the manager's inconvenience and tried to be sincere as he said, "It won't happen again."

Time dragged on. Escobar had not returned to Hacienda Nápoles since the failed raid nearly four months earlier. The police crackdown triggered by Galán's murder made such a return increasingly unlikely. Some of the commandos had given up and gone home. The others spent hours drinking and whoring and getting on each other's nerves.

The final blow came when the Colombian National Police seized Escobar's ranch. Pablo could not go home. All the training and preparation to invade the compound were useless. Jorge had to come up with a new plan. But keeping the Brits waiting in Panama while a new scheme was hatched became impossible.

Some of the men who went home told their stories to CNN and other media outlets. Their colorful accounts included photographs of Colombian training sites. McAleese was furious over the breach of security, but it was too late.

Yet the Rodríguez Orejuela brothers seemed sanguine. The publicity at least sent a message to Escobar that he was being hunted. Maybe it would cause some indigestion, Gilberto joked. At a last supper over lobsters in Panama City, Tomkins and McAleese agreed that it was time for everyone to step back, get some rest, and, as Jorge suggested, "wait for better times."

It was clear by October 1989 that the Pablo Escobar project, once expected to take only a few months, would take more than a year— possibly much more. Jorge realized that there was no going back to his neglected Bogotá business interests. But he was most alarmed by press coverage of the stymied plot.

How long would it be, he wondered, before Escobar learned about Jorge's role? How long before the man who murdered policemen, judges, and a presidential candidate learned that Jorge Salcedo was trying to kill him?

He decided it was time to get Lena and the children to Cali, where he knew security was better than in Bogotá. It wasn't supposed to happen this way. The job was supposed to be temporary. His family was supposed to be unaffected. But now he had put those he loved most in such jeopardy that they needed Cali cartel protection.

THE WITCH KNOWS BEST

P ABLO ESCOBAR WAS UNDERGROUND AND ON THE RUN, MAKING IT extremely difficult for Jorge and the Cali bosses to mount another military-style assault. Still, the godfathers watched for another opening— and the British commando leaders pledged to drop everything and rush back the moment a fresh opportunity arose. Meanwhile, Jorge focused his day-to-day attention on security, determined to keep Escobar's henchmen from doing harm to his employers. This brought Jorge closer to the Rodríguez Orejuela family, personally and professionally.

He and Lena moved into the same Cali high-rise apartment building as Doña Rita, the eighty-year-old mother of Gilberto and Miguel. The matriarch fussed over Lena and her baby at every encounter in the lobby or elevators. And she always greeted Jorge like family. He came to be recognized as a guardian of the clan's women and children. He was also the wizard of radiophones, the technological precursors of cell phones and something coveted by each wife, ex-wife, and teenage offspring of the godfathers.

The communications network that Jorge devised allowed the cartel to relay messages without fear they would be intercepted by the authorities or Escobar's spies. Showing the instincts of a spy—or a professional criminal—Jorge hijacked the radio signals of legitimate businesses all over the Cauca valley. They were ambulance services, sugarcane-processing plants, paper mills . . . anything with twenty-four-hour operations. The cartel could use their frequencies at all hours without suspicion.

Motorola radiophones were Jorge's favorites. They worked off low-power transmitters—preferably a single watt, making them almost impossible to pinpoint with electronic directional locators. Jorge mounted repeaters on tall buildings in town and hid others on mountainsides and hilltops to extend the network's range. It was a marvel of ingenuity and chutzpah.

His elaborate code system further disguised the cartel's unauthorized presence on the radio channels. When it was stealing the ambulance signal, for instance, all cartel messages were couched in medical terminology. A security team waiting for Miguel to arrive at the Inter-Continental hotel might be alerted that he was entering by way of Avenue 3 North with a call: "Patient en route. Please have a specialist meet us at the north entrance." If using the frequency of the sugarcane processor to report the presence of a roadblock on Ninth Street, the caller might say: "We have a problem on boiler number nine." If further information were required, reporting that the problem was a "broken vapor hose" would indicate that the roadblock was an army checkpoint. A "broken water hose" signaled police checkpoint. "We've got eight inches of water on the floor" meant that eight officers were on the site.

Jorge also made certain that the phones—and their transmitters and antennas—were hidden. He fabricated hands-free radio systems for motorcycles and found ways to conceal antenna wires in car upholstery or molding. For a middle-aged engineer who had spent most of his life following the rules, Jorge was showing a remarkable facility for breaking the law. He had a gift for covert operations. He was very good at secrets.

* * *

THE RODRÍGUEZ OREJUELA BROTHERS and their extended family required a full-time security staff of about 150. Jorge's radiophone system could grow only as fast as he could install new repeaters and transmitters. There was constant pressure from cartel insiders clamoring for the limited number of devices. Miguel, the micromanager, personally dictated who got the newest Motorolas.

The brothers had the most relatives to protect. Three of Miguel's four wives lived in Cali and had a total of eight children. The eldest was William Rodríguez Abadía, a law student, then in his mid-twenties. The youngest was three-year-old Andrea Rodríguez Echeverri. Gilberto had eight children, mostly older, and three wives. The brothers also protected their elderly mother, three sisters, and a younger brother named Jorge Eliécer, known with apparent affection by the nickname Cañengo, or "Good for Nothing."

Two of Miguel's wives competed for the boss's time and attention. Amparo Arbeliaz, whom Jorge called Wife No. 2, was the mother of three of Miguel's children. She had her own private residence that required security, but she also spent considerable time with Miguel at his primary home in southern Cali. Marta Lucía, Wife No. 4, was a former Colombian beauty queen, the mother of little Andrea, and Miguel's apparent favorite. Her private quarters needed round-the-clock protection, and she stayed with Miguel when Amparo was not sharing his bed.

It fell to Bertha, the family's perpetually cheerful cook and chief housekeeper, to regulate boudoir traffic and avoid embarrassments. She did this aided by a Polaroid camera. After each wifely visit, Bertha photographed every angle of the bedroom and restored it to exactly the same state the next time that wife returned. She once missed Marta Lucía's fuzzy pink slippers, which Amparo was shocked to find under her bed. That didn't happen again.

Jorge never met William's mother, Miguel's first wife. The son seemed closer to his stepmother Marta Lucía, who was also a favorite of the bodyguards. She was beautiful and elegantly mannered and treated her drivers and bodyguards with uncommon respect. Marta Lucía once asked Jorge to bring Lena over for tea. "I hear that your wife is a lovely person. I'd like to meet her," she said. Their subsequent meeting went well, but Lena had her own social circle and preferred to keep a distance from the crime families. She made no effort to befriend any of the cartel wives, and she rarely joined Jorge at cartel social functions. Jorge preferred it that way. He was always on high alert at social events, too focused on security to have fun.

To Jorge, Miguel's Wife No. 3 was especially intriguing. Fabiola Moreno was a practicing witch. Jorge investigated security needs at her residence and found charms and talismans everywhere. Aloe plants hung from the doors, and water-filled drinking glasses were behind doors and under tables—each with a raw egg floating in it. A musky Asian incense smoldered in rooms heavily decorated with red ribbons and red glass balls—all of it for luck, Fabiola explained.

"If you need any kind of special energy, you come to me," she insisted.

"Thank you," Jorge said. "I've always been blessed with good fortune."

"You never know," Fabiola said, smiling. "Luck can change at any moment."

ON THE MORNING OF November 27, 1989, Avianca flight 203 took off from Bogotá on its regularly scheduled trip to Cali. Five minutes and about thirteen thousand feet into the jetliner's climb, a bomb in the passenger cabin ripped apart the Boeing 727. Early suspicions pointed to *sicarios* employed by Pablo Escobar, and evidence quickly mounted against the Medellín cartel. The apparent target of the attack, the presidential candidate Gaviria, wasn't even on the plane. Among the 110 dead was a mid-level Cali cartel man, a retired army captain, recently hired to manage Hercules Security. Two other victims were U.S. citizens, giving Washington grounds to designate Escobar and his Medellín partners terrorist threats to the United States.

A few weeks after the bombing, Jorge received a slightly scuffed-up Motorola radiophone. It had belonged to the new guy at Hercules Security and was recovered from the wreckage. Jorge opened it with apprehension. He could not help but imagine its owner's horror in those final moments over Bogotá. He also could not help thinking that—but for Tiger's reckless dive into a mountaintop—the Brits might have killed Pablo that day in June and saved 110 lives in November. It was the sort of thinking that reduced Jorge's moral dilemma to engineer-friendly numbers and equations. He had been trying to save lives by killing Escobar. And 110 victims of Escobar's terrorism merely reinforced Jorge's personal calculation that Pablo's end would justify whatever means.

Pablo Escobar's bloody terrorism continued in the days and weeks after the Avianca jetliner bombing. A truck with a half ton of explosives was detonated in downtown Bogotá, outside headquarters of the Departamento Administrativo de Seguridad (DAS)—a combined FBI, CIA, and Secret Service. The rush-hour blast killed more than fifty, injured nearly one thousand, and shattered windows seven miles away near the U.S. embassy.

"How can the man be so insane?" Miguel fretted during a weekly security meeting. He was in a constant state of worry about his family. His wife Amparo pressed him to let her take the children for an extended stay in the mountains at the Pennsylvania Ranch. Miguel was afraid it might be an inviting target for Escobar. No one but the heavily armed British commandos had stayed there since the cartels started fighting. He told Jorge to investigate all his mountain neighbors and make sure none were Escobar spies or Medellín-linked people.

A formal census was arranged to identify the owners and tenants of about two hundred residences in the hills surrounding the family's mountain estate. The Cali godfathers paid local police to help. Uniformed officers rode along to lend authority to cartel questioners.

It was on this project that Jorge first became acquainted with Andrés "El Pecoso" Vélez, one of the Cali cartel's top hired guns. El Pecoso, or "Freckles," strongly resembled the American film star Nicolas Cage and had an actor's flair for the dramatic. Jorge tagged along one day to satisfy himself that the information being gathered had real intelligence value.

A caravan of two police cars and a cartel SUV made its way up a long, winding driveway to an isolated hillside house. No one came to the door to greet the visitors. Freckles pulled out his Smith & Wesson .357 Magnum, released the safety, and approached the house. He warned Jorge that any house could be a trap. The uniformed officers stood back. So did Jorge. Freckles held his .357 in one hand and tested the door handle with the other. It was unlocked. He motioned for everyone to wait, and then he put his shoulder to the door and burst through.

Freckles landed in the entry hall in a crouched position, both hands on his weapon, ready to fire.

"Freeze!" he shouted. "This is a census."

AT THE TURN OF the New Year 1990, Jorge approached his first anniversary in the Cali cartel feeling pretty good about himself. Despite the failure so far of the anti-Escobar campaign, there had been successes. He enjoyed security work and took pride in the fact that no one under his and Mario's protection had been harmed. He especially liked working with radiophone communications. Devising such a sophisticated clandestine network with off-the-shelf equipment won him plaudits and another nickname. Cartel admirers called him MacGyver.

For the most part, Jorge also liked the people he worked with—the Brits, the bodyguards, the cartel families, and the godfathers. He was comfortable in the organization, and why not? He witnessed neither violence nor illicit activities. During his first year in the cartel, it had become the world's fastest-growing drug organization, but Jorge saw not a gram of cocaine, no stores of cash, and no obvious trafficking activities.

Furthermore, Cali godfathers—unlike Escobar and other crime bosses—didn't shun police. Instead, they financed construction of neighborhood police stations and attended parties with police brass. Mayors, congressmen, and important business leaders were regular visitors. Jorge had never been a criminal and had no experience judging such matters, but to him the Cali cartel didn't feel like a crime syndicate at all.

HOW MANY DID YOU KILL?

I N COLOMBIA CIRCA 1990, SOCCER WAS THE SPORT OF DRUG KINGS. Just as Pablo Escobar owned the Medellín team, the Rodríguez Orejuela brothers owned the rival América de Cali. The Cali godfathers didn't smoke, drink to excess, or use drugs. Soccer was their addiction. They built their residences around soccer fields. They bought large-screen televisions and the world's biggest satellite dishes to capture foreign soccer telecasts.

Pacho Herrera, the youngest and most fit of the godfathers, was an avid amateur player. He organized regular games with his brothers and bodyguards. Jorge suspected, in fact, that Pacho hired some of his teenage bodyguards for their soccer skills. The godfather also financed and supervised construction of some of the finest playing fields in Colombia—some of them strictly for his private use. One of those was at a ranch just east of Cali called Los Cocos, or "the Coconuts." The field was carved out of sugarcane acreage and equipped with professional lighting for night play. It was Pacho's very own "field of dreams."

The remoteness of Los Cocos was its biggest security asset. Otherwise, the powerful stadium lights made the soccer field an island of virtual daylight in the black of a rural Colombian night. It became the site of weekly games—visible for miles around, talked about in ever-widening circles, and anticipated with the reliability of a scheduled tournament. The field was just off a public road and easily accessible. There were no gates, no walls. Friends and spectators—many of them armed members of the cartel—sprawled on the grass along the sidelines.

Neither Jorge Salcedo nor Mario del Basto was responsible for Pacho's security—or for his security mistakes. They served the full-time security interests of Miguel, Gilberto, and the extended Rodríguez Orejuela family, while Pacho took care of his own protection, as did Chepe Santacruz. All four of the cartel godfathers maintained their own stable of personal *sicarios*—killers more than bodyguards. None of the cartel *sicarios* worked for or took orders from Jorge or Mario. They reported directly to the bosses.

Pacho's security detail was made up entirely of *sicarios,* all young toughs and many from the same slums of Medellín that produced Escobar's killers. They looked and acted differently than other cartel security operatives. They wore jewelry, drove big fast motorcycles, and stood out in any crowd. They were flashy thugs and made no effort to soften their gangster image. Jorge and Mario marveled at their intimidating manner.

"I'm just glad they're on our side," Jorge said more than once.

Pacho's men and their powerful Harley-Davidson motorcycles were the envy of bodyguards working for Miguel and Gilberto. The more conservative bosses assigned their men modest Yamahas. One member of Jorge's crew, in a rare reference to Pacho Herrera's homosexuality, told him, "I would gladly spend a night with Pacho if he would give me one of those Harleys."

Generally, Pacho's security was aggressive. His men, many of them from the Medellín area, maintained around-the-clock surveillance at the Cali airport and bus depots, watching for strangers—particularly those with distinctive Medellín accents. Pacho Herrera remained the primary target of Escobar's personal grudge, for daring to protect the

New York love-triangle killer. Three years later, Pablo still sought re-venge.

In September 1990, none of the Cali security teams noticed a gather-ing of strangers who straggled into the area individually or in pairs. They traveled by bus over a period of days and passed through Cali en route to the colonial city of Popayán eighty miles south. There, they transferred to local buses and worked their way back north to within a few miles of Cali. Eventually, they numbered twenty—some as young as sixteen, none older than twenty-one. They assembled at a small farm just outside the village of Santander where a young farmer had rented his place to the strangers. He took his fee and closed his eyes. Over two days, the farm received a series of shipments: police uniforms, two trucks with canvas-covered cargo beds, and twenty AR-15 automatic ri-fles.

On the night that Pacho and his gangsters gathered at Los Cocos for their regular weekly game of soccer, the two trucks rumbled north on a twenty-minute drive toward the island of light. Hidden under the canvas were twenty heavily armed young thugs in mismatched police uniforms.

Pacho and his brother William Herrera were on the field, locked in spirited competition, when the first truck pulled off the highway. No one paid any attention. Even with the arrival of a second truck and dis-mounting armed policemen, the teams played on. Police in the area were well-paid allies of Pacho and his brothers, friends stopping to watch the game, perhaps. Then the shooting started.

The men in uniform fanned out from the two trucks and opened fire on spectators. The players—most of them in shorts and T-shirts, many of them shirtless—were caught with their guns out of reach. Everyone still standing after the first blast of gunfire raced for the cover of darkness and cane fields. Pacho and his brother didn't stop running until they were deep in cane foliage. When the sounds of gunfire ended, survivors ventured back to the field. It was littered with nineteen bod-ies of friends, brothers, and colleagues. The pursuit of vengeance and Pablo's raiding party began that very night.

*   *   *

CALI POLICE SCORED the first break in the case. Two young men on an isolated stretch of highway near Santander prompted a passing patrol to stop and ask questions. The men had Medellín accents. They had been visiting friends in the area . . . they were waiting for a bus . . . they were headed to Popayán . . . they were on their way home to Medellín. The policeman was confused—they were traveling south to catch a bus headed north? A bus out of Cali would save them several hours. Their tale began to unravel. In a Cali jail they spilled the whole story. A friend of Mario's in the police department allowed del Basto to question the prisoners, too. They were kids, and they confessed everything without threat or inducement.

Police swooped down on the farm where the attackers had mobilized for the assault. They found abandoned uniforms, weapons, and trucks—but no gunmen. The owner of the farm had also disappeared. None of his brothers and sisters knew where he was. They seemed genuinely surprised and said he left without saying good-bye.

In the village of Santander, about a week later, police found three bodies—a sister and two brothers of the farmer. They had been killed in their homes, execution-style, each with a bullet in the head. It was a lesson in cartel justice: the family paid for the sins of the brother.

The two confessed Los Cocos shooters awaiting trial in the Cali jail were next. They were killed by fellow inmates on orders from Pacho. The drug lord also sent a team of killers to scour the country for the missing farmer. He could not hide forever.

It had been very important to Jorge throughout that first year in Cali to believe that his bosses were different from Pablo Escobar—that they didn't sabotage jetliners or target the innocent. Such a distinction made them morally superior to the Medellín gangs. Jorge had from the start found comfort in Mario del Basto's words: "They are not violent people." But that perception was shaken after Los Cocos.

The massacre was shocking. But it was the calculated reprisals—the cold-blooded murders of the farmer's innocent relatives—that kept Jorge awake the next few nights. The killings were the work of Pacho's men, but Jorge knew that major decisions required a consensus of all four bosses. It was obvious that the Gentlemen of Cali, when properly provoked, could be just as ruthless as Pablo Escobar.

JORGE SET UP TRAINING sessions to dissect the lessons of Los Cocos. He emphasized the necessity of altering routines and varying travel routes. "Never be predictable," he preached. Regular night soccer games violated that rule. An early-warning system could have changed the outcome, something as simple as sentries on roads approaching the field. He also focused on improving observation skills. There had been clues galore that the raiders were not real policemen. First, their uniforms were all different—similar shirts but mismatched pants, some shirts tucked in, some not. And their shoes—many wore sneakers, and none wore polished police boots. Finally, the Medellín gunmen had attacked with AR-15 assault rifles, Escobar's favorite, but not the distinctive Israeli-made Uzi used by Colombian police.

Among those eager to learn from Jorge was Freckles, a *sicario* with ambitions to move up in the organization. He came to regard Jorge as a mentor. On one occasion, he questioned Jorge about his military past.

"Don Richard," he asked. "In the army, how many guerrillas did you kill?"

Jorge shrugged. He could have invented a number. In the world of *sicarios,* a kill was a good thing. But Jorge replied honestly.

"I don't know. It was combat," he said. "I can't be sure I ever hit anyone."

Freckles considered the answer in silence and then said, "Once, I had to kill one of my brothers."

"Your own brother? But . . . why? What do you mean?" Jorge thought maybe he had misunderstood.

"He betrayed Don Miguel," Freckles said without emotion. "Of course, I had no choice."

Jorge nodded, but said nothing. He thought of Lena and the baby . . . his mother and father . . . his belief that family was sacred. *My God,* he thought. *I can never belong here.*

IN THE CARTEL'S SECRET SERVICE

EARLY IN 1990, THE GODFATHERS MADE A DRASTIC LIFESTYLE CHANGE. They moved their families into high-security luxury apartment buildings and took separate living quarters for themselves in easily protected residential compounds. The cartel bosses, targets for gun and bomb attacks by Escobar hit teams, didn't want their wives and children hurt in the cross fire. Jorge endorsed the strategy. But he was caught by surprise the first time he was summoned to Miguel's new compound, called the Wall House.

The cartel chauffeur, who knew Jorge well, greeted him with customary familiarity—but then handed him a pair of wraparound sunglasses. The lenses were painted black on the inside. Wearing them was like putting on a blindfold. Jorge immediately pulled them off.

"What is this?"

"Orders of El Señor," the driver said, shrugging. He waited until Jorge put them on again.

Jorge felt ridiculous in the glasses. Worse, he felt distrusted. Instinctively, he worried. In his dual role as a cartel security adviser and standby Escobar hunter, he enjoyed uncommon access to the Rodríguez Orejuela brothers. He had started sitting in at private meetings between the godfathers and U.S. defense lawyers, providing translations during legal strategy sessions involving cartel traffickers facing charges in the States. The sessions were rich in cartel secrets, a sign of trust in Jorge's loyalty and discretion. But in an organization with enforcers like Freckles, Jorge had to be sensitive to the danger of lost trust. The "blindfold" bothered him. Did Miguel really not trust Jorge to know where he lived?

Along the drive, Jorge found that he could easily peek around the blacked-out lenses for glimpses of passing neighborhoods. They were heading north into the hills. His concern about lost trust gave way to wonder at who conceived of such a lame security idea. At the destination, Jorge removed the sunglasses only after the car was inside a closed garage. He followed the driver up a flight of stairs and into a house perched on one of the highest hillsides in the city. Picture windows offered sweeping vistas of downtown Cali. It was a clear day, and the view across the Cauca valley was forever.

"Do you know where you are?" Miguel was first to greet Jorge. Gilberto and others gathered around to hear his response.

Jorge looked out the windows for a moment. "Yes, I do. We're in the Versalles district." He named a pair of nearby streets.

Miguel scowled. It was obviously the boss's lame idea, and this was simply a test—not a sign that he doubted Jorge. But then Gilberto laughed, and Jorge immediately distanced himself from this mild brotherly ridicule. He defended the glasses. They could be effective for some visitors, he said. But military training had taught him to navigate using key geographic features. He pointed out the window toward sites that helped him pinpoint their location.

Miguel seemed satisfied. Gilberto slapped his brother on the back and said, "We didn't hire Richard because he was stupid." They left, and Jorge took a deep breath.

IN HIS SECOND YEAR with the cartel, Jorge was getting to know the *sicarios,* the paid assassins. One of the most storied was Henry "El Gamín"

Gaviria—one of Chepe's favorites. He was known for an incident in which he came home to find a young burglar in his house. El Gamín, or "the Delinquent," chased the intruder into a wooded area and tackled him. To immobilize the would-be thief, Henry shot him, once in each kneecap, with his pistol. Then he strolled back to his house, grabbed a snack, retrieved an automatic rifle, and returned unhurried to the woods. The thief had dragged himself a short distance. Henry ended the man's agony with a burst of machine-gun fire.

The most important of the Cali *sicarios* was Guillermo León Restrepo Gaviria, known in the cartel simply as Memo Lara. He was the godfathers' chief hit man—low-key, loyal, and reliably lethal. He would sometimes be gone for long periods, usually coinciding with someone's death or disappearance.

Memo had dark hair, dark eyes, and a dark disposition. Some blamed his grim demeanor on a lost love, a girlfriend who left him for a police captain and then compounded the betrayal by trying to set him up for arrest. Memo barely escaped. The ex-girlfriend had the good sense to flee the country. Years later, Memo still seethed. He kept an eye on her family's residence just outside Cali, lurking in her old neighborhood at odd hours, just biding his time—waiting for her to come home.

Jorge and Memo were outside Miguel's office once when Jorge admired Memo's new Walther pistol, a handsome weapon smaller than those carried by most other *sicarios*. Jorge was a top marksman in the army reserves and had been interested in guns since his youth.

"It is beautiful—but only seven rounds," Jorge said. "You must be very sharp with your aim."

Memo shrugged and nodded.

"Where do you target practice?" Jorge asked.

"It's not necessary," Memo said. "I don't miss when I stick it in an ear."

JORGE'S TRANSLATION DUTIES began sporadically in 1990, then soared with a rash of cartel arrests in the southeastern United States. Miguel hired several American lawyers. Jorge liked translating. He was intrigued by discussions about the U.S. legal system. And he found that insider knowledge about pending cases helped him understand Miguel's mood swings. Jorge was learning a lot—though not about drug trafficking.

Miguel delivered the same speech to each defense lawyer in every case: "This man is completely innocent. These charges are an insult. We are honest businessmen suffering from the sins of Pablo Escobar." And Jorge noted that the U.S. lawyers were just as predictable. They nodded in agreement and promised the most aggressive defense possible.

After translating such meetings with the Miami defense lawyer Joel Rosenthal, Jorge was drafted for a special assignment—a chance to play the role of cartel secret agent. Chepe's half brother, a drug trafficker named Lucho Santacruz Echeverri, had been convicted in Florida and faced a twenty-three-year prison term. The bosses hoped to persuade the U.S. Justice Department to give him a break, at least reduce his sentence.

"Then give them something," Rosenthal suggested. He was a former assistant U.S. attorney from Miami and was representing Lucho.

It happened that these were desperate times at Main Justice in Washington. According to press accounts, federal prosecutors were having difficulty building a strong trafficking case against the Panamanian dictator, Manuel Noriega. This was potentially embarrassing for the George H. W. Bush administration since it had, with great fanfare and overwhelming force, sent U.S. Marines into Panama at the end of 1989 to depose Noriega and haul him before the bar of justice.

What if the Cali cartel could help nail down a Noriega conviction? Under Rule 35 of the Federal Rules of Criminal Procedure, it was likely that Lucho Santacruz could be spared several years in a U.S. penitentiary as a reward.

In a private meeting with the four godfathers, Jorge was dispatched to Panama City to make contact with a potential witness against Noriega. Jorge was to assess his potential value. He flew off with the hopes of Lucho and the godfathers riding with him.

THE CALI CARTEL'S CHIEF operative in Panama City was the playboy son of an assassinated Dominican Republic dictator. Rhadamés Trujillo and a partner ran a coffee export business as a front to ship tons of cocaine. Trujillo was a middle-aged country club habitué who had good Panamanian contacts. He knocked at Jorge's hotel room around six in the evening. He described the would-be witness as a former Panamanian diplomat with ties to the Medellín cartel. Most of his wealth was in frozen bank accounts or tied up in a defunct air cargo company.

Jorge followed Rhadamés to the posh Paitilla neighborhood and a Spanish colonial residence set on a hill. Ambassador Ricardo Bilonick was in his mid-forties, affable and cultured. His wife, Nilka, a former flight attendant, was a five-foot-one dynamo. She greeted Jorge with a gust of hospitality. Then her husband launched into a description of how he could help the case against Noriega.

"I am very valuable. I know the law, and I know that the American government is going to be greatly embarrassed without my assistance," Bilonick told Jorge.

The Panamanian was an experienced trafficker. His air cargo business was started with loans from the Medellín cartel. He smuggled cocaine and currency through Panama and paid Noriega millions of dollars in bribes, exactly the kind of witness the United States needed. Bilonick's credentials were extraordinary. He had served as a consultant to Noriega's predecessor General Omar Torrijos during negotiations with the United States over the return of the Panama Canal. Later, he was Panama's ambassador at large to improve relations with Washington. He had been educated at Tulane and Harvard and spoke immaculate English.

If the Cali cartel helped him financially, he assured Jorge, he would gladly share his information about Noriega on behalf of Lucho Santacruz. "Everyone benefits," Bilonick said.

MIGUEL RECEIVED THE NEWS with enthusiasm: "Call Rosenthal immediately."

Jorge was a friend of the Florida lawyer's. He not only translated during Rosenthal's meetings with the bosses but routinely met the lawyer's American Airlines flights from Miami, delivered him to the hotel, and dined with him after check-in. They talked about family, personal interests, and Jorge's plans to go into business someday soon. Rosenthal was a quick wit with a sharp legal mind and a brash American style that Jorge enjoyed. He also had the temerity to mock Miguel—privately, of course.

"He's a nightmare," Rosenthal had complained after one marathon session during which Miguel repeatedly offered his own legal analyses.

Miguel was well-read in the law and even boasted of a law degree. It was awarded by the University of Santiago de Cali after the crime boss donated millions of dollars to the school—and was, in fact, merely an honorary law degree. But Miguel treated it as though he had passed the bar exam.

"The man thinks he's some kind of legal genius; he's a pain in the ass!" the American lawyer confided to Jorge.

Rosenthal received the news about Bilonick with caution. His information had to be absolutely solid, the lawyer said. Anything false or exaggerated could be worse than nothing at all. And he demanded, "I don't want any part of any arrangements involving bribes." No money, no favors, no deals, Rosenthal insisted.

"Yes, of course," Jorge responded.

OVER THE NEXT FEW WEEKS, Jorge arranged for Bilonick to meet Rosenthal, and those initial sessions quickly advanced to negotiations between the Panamanian and U.S. prosecutors. Bilonick's tentative deal with the U.S. government included his agreement to surrender to U.S. authorities, plead guilty to trafficking, and receive a reduced sentence in exchange for testimony. Separately, Chepe's brother Lucho would receive credit too for helping arrange Bilonick's cooperation.

Bilonick's side deal with the Cali cartel remained unspecified, however, until one night he told Jorge, "I will need $2 million—in cash." Jorge had no way to measure Bilonick's dollar value. He assumed that two million was wildly excessive. Even the Brits—with a dozen men invading Pablo Escobar's heavily guarded estate—asked for only one million. And Jorge was right. The Cali godfathers dismissed Bilonick's price tag without serious consideration. Chepe said he didn't have anything close to that amount available in cash—and he wasn't inclined to pull it together. Certainly not before he knew how much gratitude the Justice Department was going to show toward Lucho.

That was a dilemma. Bilonick wanted his money now, before he surrendered. But his testimony was months away. It would be some time before anyone knew how much leniency Lucho would earn. It wasn't that the godfathers distrusted Bilonick. They were following conservative business practice—don't pay for something until you're satisfied that it's what you ordered.

"I have $250,000. He can have that for now," Chepe told Jorge a few days before Bilonick's surrender date. "You deliver the cash."

"I'm afraid he may be disappointed," Jorge said, hesitating.

"Yes, but he has no choice."

Jorge had another idea. While tending to the Brits in Panama City, he had regular contact with the cartel's local banker, who provided funds for the commandos' pocket money and to pay for damages to their hotel rooms. Once, Jorge overheard talk about certificates of deposit in the name of Chepe Santacruz. The CDs would be worth $1 million upon maturity in 1991. Jorge asked if Chepe would sign over those CDs to Bilonick.

It was embraced as a brilliant solution. No large, risky cash transfers were required. The certificates, still short of their maturity date, would go into a safe-deposit box that required two keys—one assigned to Nilka Bilonick, the other to Jorge. It put financial instruments soon to be worth $1 million under partial control of the Bilonicks while giving the cartel a way to hold up payment if the ambassador turned out to be a bust as a witness.

Three days before Ricardo Bilonick flew off to surrender in Miami, Jorge gave the Panama couple a black leather briefcase stuffed mostly with twenty-dollar bills—the down payment of $250,000 in cash from Chepe. It was by far the most money Jorge had ever seen in one place—and his first glimpse of narco-profits. The certificates of deposit were moved from the cartel's bank into Banco Vizcaya, the Bilonicks' preference. And Jorge flew home to Colombia a hero to the godfathers—especially a few months later when Lucho's sentence was formally reduced by nine years.

MEET THE RIVAL

J ORGE SALCEDO WHEELED HIS LIGHT BLUE TWO-DOOR TROOPER
through downtown Cali, turning and backtracking and watching
for tails. The imported SUV's white fiberglass roof concealed hidden
antenna wires, discreetly connected to four different radiophone systems inside. He had finished a second year in service to the Cali cartel,
shifting from managing the plot to kill Escobar to designing a communications system to defend against Medellín hit men. Jorge considered
the radiophone network his masterpiece. Almost everywhere he drove,
from remote stretches of the Cauca valley to isolated mountain retreats,
Jorge was in radio contact with his teams of bodyguards and security
men. That was especially important on this particular drive into the
Andes. His passenger was the boss.

Miguel Rodríguez Orejuela had his own regular drivers, chiefly
Mateo Zapata and Fercho Castillo—who also doubled as receptionists,
clerks, and personal assistants. These two trusted aides did alternating
weeklong tours of duty, during which they slept in the same house as

the boss, worked his hours, and were on call twenty-four hours a day. They usually drove sedans from the cartel's Mazda fleet. Miguel liked the cars because they were reliable and looked ordinary. He had dozens of them parked around the city in at least ten different cartel garages. This day's drive to the mountains, however, figured to encounter some challenging terrain better suited for the high-clearance and four-wheel-drive capability of Jorge's Trooper. Miguel also wanted Jorge along for reasons he had not yet shared.

Private time with the godfather of the godfathers was rare for Jorge. Some in the cartel would fight for such an opportunity, but he was too worried about security to savor the moment. Jorge took a few extra turns to make sure no one followed. Then he accelerated up the mountain highway.

About fifteen kilometers into the climb, Miguel directed him into the parking lot of a roadside Japanese restaurant. When Jorge spotted a man sitting alone in a green Renault 12, he instinctively hit the brakes and checked his mirrors. "No, no—don't worry," Miguel said, and motioned Jorge to pull up near the parked sedan. "The man in that car is Guillermo Pallomari," Miguel said. "Go tell him to follow us."

Jorge had never heard of Pallomari. He was a bespectacled accountant for the Rodríguez Orejuela family's drugstore chain, Drogas la Rebaja. He was clean shaven with indistinct features—a bland man in big square-rimmed glasses.

"Don Miguel would like you to follow us," Jorge told him. Pallomari nodded but said nothing, so Jorge did not immediately detect his Chilean accent.

A few more kilometers up the highway, a narrow rutted road broke off and wound into a wooded area. They reached a small house hidden in the trees. The other three cartel godfathers spilled outside to greet them. Pallomari carried an armful of computer printouts that seemed to be of immediate interest to the bosses. The temperature at that altitude was chilly. To Jorge's relief everyone retreated quickly into the warm house.

THE CALI CARTEL had not abandoned hope of killing Escobar, but by early 1991 pressure to reengage the British mercenaries on that mission had eased substantially. After the Galán killing and Avianca bombing, Bogotá had launched all-out military and police hunts for the Medellín boss. The Bush administration was pouring U.S. dollars and manpower into support of that initiative. So, at least for now, the Cali bosses focused on self-protection and waited for the government to kill the elusive Pablo.

If anything, Escobar's terror campaign seemed to be growing more brazen. He had shifted from bombings and assassinations to kidnappings—an old favorite of criminals and guerrilla gangs, but with a new and confounding twist. No ransoms. His targets were journalists and the social and political elite of Bogotá, mostly women. First to be seized was the daughter of a former Colombian president. Later, it was the sister of Colombia's ambassador to Canada. In the span of a few months, eight prominent women were taken captive, including the journalist sister-in-law of Galán.

Instead of money, Escobar demanded help persuading the newly elected president, César Gaviria, to ban extraditions. Under pressure, Gaviria backed creation of a constitutional assembly to rewrite and modernize the national charter. With millions of drug dollars ready to influence new extradition language, Gaviria's move amounted to capitulation.

Even as the rival Cali and Medellín cartels worked toward the shared goal of banning extradition, they remained at war with each other. And Escobar's new tactic, targeting women, especially troubled Cali bosses, who feared for their families. That nagging fear and the promise of a potent new intelligence tool had brought the godfathers together that morning on the mountain.

Pallomari's printouts were private phone records obtained from an insider at Telecom, Colombia's national telephone company. They revealed all calls made from Cali to Medellín, and vice versa—times, dates, and durations—thousands of them. If there were spies in Cali reporting back to Medellín, they could be exposed. And with a big enough computer, the cartel could monitor the calling patterns of virtually every telephone in Cali—and then listen in on any suspicious lines.

"I'll need a very powerful computer," the accountant told the bosses. Chepe Santacruz promised to get it and pledged the first million-dollar investment.

Jorge was struck by the ambition of the project. It was an undertaking beyond the technological capacities of some national governments. The scene reminded him of his first meeting with the godfathers some two years earlier. This time, Pallomari was being recruited, just as Jorge had been, to help fight Escobar. The difference was that the drugstore accountant already worked for the organization and had come to the meeting trying to impress the drug lords, angling for a promotion. Pallomari even seemed keen to join the trafficking and money-laundering side of the Business.

By contrast, Jorge had lost his early enthusiasm for the Escobar project. It gnawed at him—an unfinished job that had to be completed before he could move on with his life. But there was little he could do to hasten that day. So he focused on protecting lives and taking pride in that and in his communications masterpiece.

Over a span of a few weeks, there were more trips to the house in the woods. The accountant brought increasingly detailed data. Some suspicious phone activity was identified early. The meetings tended to open with eager Cali bosses skimming through fresh reams of phone logs looking for the latest possible snitches. Jorge assumed from occasional angry reactions that someone would soon be suffering the consequences of doubted loyalty. But it was none of his business. He knew only that he never wanted his personal phone number showing up on those lists.

As for Pallomari, the ambitious accountant promptly moved into a key management role assisting Miguel. He began updating the cartel's financial accounting system, loading data onto computers, and setting up traditional business divisions within the organization. Miguel, who admired efficiency and order and meticulous records, endorsed Pallomari's efforts. And Chepe's million-dollar computer became the foundation for Pallomari's empire building.

There was early friction when Jorge tried to suggest that experienced security experts should analyze the raw information. He was concerned that unfounded suspicions might get the wrong people in trouble, while genuine threats were overlooked. Neither Pallomari nor the bosses had any experience in military intelligence.

Jorge clashed with Pallomari when the accountant began to gather and consolidate vast amounts of cartel records on his computer. Overnight, Pallomari became the cartel's chief financial adviser, business manager, and bean counter. He demanded personnel records, began to monitor spending, and assumed accounting control over virtually all cartel operations, including the formerly private preserve of Jorge's radiophone network.

Jorge hated the intrusion on his work. He was also dumbfounded. As a clandestine operation, the cartel should have been minimizing records, not amassing them. One accountant's business report might be a prosecutor's evidence bonanza. Jorge was especially reluctant to record data about his unlicensed radiophone system. He warned Miguel that Pallomari was creating a security hazard—which only annoyed the accountant. Miguel ignored the warnings. He loved Pallomari's weekly and quarterly reports, loved immersing himself in data. The accountant's neatly printed reports were a micromanager's dream.

THE WAR WITH MEDELLÍN was trending in Cali's favor when a Colombian task force of military and police investigators called the Bloque de Búsqueda, or "Search Bloc," set up operations in Medellín. Its sole mission: get Pablo. The Bloque also set up a branch office of sorts in Cali but ignored the Rodríguez Orejuela brothers.

Escobar accused the government and the Cali cartel of working together. And he was right. The government got some of its best Escobar intelligence from Cali. Not only did Cali cooperation hurt Escobar, but it built goodwill with the Bloque.

On the business side, Cali exploited Escobar's expensive and time-consuming two-front war. Cali smugglers took over trafficking routes to the United States once controlled by or shared with Medellín. Cali profits and market share soared.

Cali's trademark jumbo shipments of cocaine to the United States and Europe were fetching as much as $30 million per load, straining its money-laundering pipeline with the sheer volume of currency flowing back to Colombia. Ten million dollars in cash can weigh well over a ton. The cartel had to hire twenty full-time tax accountants to find fresh ways to cleanse drug-tainted dollars.

Jorge was with Miguel and Gilberto one afternoon when they received a visitor from the northern reaches of the Cauca valley, a tough, lawless region. The visitor was crude, uneducated, and proudly self-sufficient. Iván Urdinola was also a man of legendary brutality, notorious for his chain-saw dismemberments and executions.

That afternoon Urdinola brought news that seemed to catch the Rodríguez Orejuela brothers by surprise. He was thinking of getting out of the drug trade. His cattle ranch was generating $500,000 a month, and he loved ranching. If extradition could be taken off the table, he might try to negotiate with the Gaviria government to surrender—do some minor jail time near his home and finish out his days as a legitimate rancher.

After Urdinola departed, the brothers seemed wistful. Gilberto, now over fifty, sounded ready to give up the Business and enjoy life. Miguel still relished his work but appeared to share a longing for life without security worries.

Their exchange prompted Jorge to ponder his own future. One day, Escobar would be dead or extradited—and it sounded as if the brothers wished to retire once the war was over. But what then? Jorge and Lena were happy in Cali, where she had family and Jorge still consulted on the side with his former partners at the battery-manufacturing plant north of town. Looking to the future, Jorge also figured that he could parlay his communications and security skills into new business opportunities—maybe start a security business right there in Cali, maybe even with endorsements from the Rodríguez Orejuela family.

ON A SUNDAY OUTING to the countryside, Jorge and Lena found an undeveloped parcel of land with mountain views. They walked together through grass and wildflowers that perfumed the air. Lena picked a spot for a home. She imagined a small grove of citrus trees and a row of magnificent palms lining a winding drive to the main house.

If Cali would be their long-term home, Jorge agreed that it was time to put down more roots. The couple had just enough money between them to buy the acreage. They called it "the Lot."

Lena started a garden and planted her first trees. Jorge designed a house, then put the plans aside. The family home would have to wait—until Pablo Escobar was gone and Jorge was free to resume life outside the Cali cartel.

STING OF THE DRAGONFLY

THE DIFFERENCES BETWEEN THE CALI AND THE MEDELLÍN CARTELS were clearly evident in the campaign to end Colombia's extradition arrangements with the United States. While Pablo Escobar spread violence, the Cali brothers spread pesos. Both had value in winning the day. But the Cali model had the added benefit of earning long-term debts of gratitude throughout the Colombian government. It was nonetheless a source of private consternation for Jorge, who was something of an egalitarian at heart. His encounter years earlier with a rigged judicial process that denied him shared custody of his first child still rankled.

It may have seemed an odd attitude for a man serving the security interests of a crime family, but Jorge despised corruption—and he saw no irony in that. Slipping a few dollars to a traffic officer to avoid a fine was one thing; paying off judges to influence justice or bribing government officials to ignore the public interest were sins against democracy.

In a country like Colombia with corruption so widespread, selective ethics were widely practiced. Jorge knew that bringing British mercenaries into the country to fight FARC and to attack Hacienda Nápoles had been illegal, but he also considered it patriotic. *Sometimes we have to do what's right, not what's legal,* he would tell himself. The son of a distinguished general was outraged whenever he encountered corruption in uniform—especially by military officers.

In 1991, a constitutional assembly set about drafting the new national charter. Cali agents, determined to kill extradition for all time, opened a joint hospitality and lobbying center in apartments at the Tequendama InterContinental hotel in Bogotá. From day one, the hospitality suite was bribery central.

To help make its case for an extradition ban, the cartel dispatched a full-time public relations man to manage its largesse. Julian Murcillo was a family friend and owner of El Toro Negro, a popular Cali restaurant. He had excellent people skills and a knack for making things happen. Key politicians could count on Murcillo to make almost any wish come true—stretch limousines, Caribbean vacations, beautiful girls. Miguel kept careful records of who got what favor and at what price, and he was never shy about reminding a wavering politician how much was owed.

Miguel turned his private office in Cali into something akin to a campaign war room where he entertained political guests, stroked egos, and wrote checks. Jorge viewed the operation with a mix of awe and anger as leaders of his country lined up outside Miguel's door to accept favor after favor.

After witnessing another day of payoffs, he complained one evening to his wife, "Our constitution—it is being revised by bribes, booze, and whores." And it was so blatant, he said. "Why is it not noticed?" She interrupted, raising a hand to signal for silence. Such opinions were too dangerous to speak aloud. Lena worried: *What if a neighbor overheard?*

From the cartel war room, Miguel also continued to put his honorary legal degree to use reviewing drafts of proposed laws. He consulted lawyers throughout the region and hired U.S. constitutional experts. Cartel attorneys helped draft key language intended not only to end the risk of extradition but also to pave the way for legal forgiveness of traffickers' past crimes—all of it cynically spun as defense of Colombian sovereignty against intrusions by Washington.

Escobar and the Rodríguez Orejuela brothers finally got their extradition ban, over the strenuous objections of U.S. officials. The Colombian Constitution of 1991 would take effect later in the year, but President Gaviria suspended extraditions immediately. In return, the Medellín cartel immediately released its prominent women hostages. And on June 19, Pablo Escobar turned himself in to Colombian authorities.

The crime boss was tied to political assassinations, murders of judges and police officers, terrorist bombings, and kidnappings. *Forbes* magazine had ranked him the seventh-richest man in the world two years earlier—all of that wealth from drug trafficking. But when Escobar surrendered, he admitted responsibility for only one modest shipment of cocaine to Europe. And he entered prison entirely on his own terms.

TIME MAGAZINE WAS QUICK to label Cali bosses the new kingpins of international cocaine trafficking, a designation that irritated Miguel especially. But a few days after Pablo's surrender, Gilberto agreed to meet with two of the magazine's Latin America correspondents. He called it his first and only interview in fifty-two years.

Jorge picked up the reporters at the InterContinental hotel. One of them carried a briefcase. Jorge tossed it on the front passenger seat, where he had a small electronic device about the size of a transistor radio. It was a frequency counter, an instrument to detect radio transmissions. He tested the briefcase and then slipped the car into gear, satisfied that there was no radio signal that would give away their route.

Gilberto served lunch, quoted Colombian poetry, and denied the very existence of a cocaine cartel under his control. He portrayed himself as a family man forced to invest heavily in security measures to protect loved ones from that "sick . . . psycho . . . lunatic," Pablo Escobar. Jorge took a photograph of the luncheon party. It caught the Cali godfather smiling, relaxed, and looking harmless.

On the drive back to the hotel, Jorge told the magazine reporters, "Gilberto's really a good guy, not a nutcase like Escobar."

*   *   *

THE PRISON CALLED LA CATEDRAL was perched on a forested hillside that a century ago provided lumber to build Medellín's grand Metropolitan Cathedral Basilica. As prisons go, it was more like a grand hotel. It was built to Escobar's specifications on Escobar-owned land by Escobar's construction crews. And it came with phones, faxes, hot tubs, satellite TV, and gourmet dining.

The Bogotá government was so eager to get Escobar into prison that it had allowed the world's most wanted man to dictate virtually every aspect of his incarceration. He handpicked his fellow inmates and the guards. No one had access to La Catedral except those authorized by Escobar. And no aircraft—not even police helicopters—were permitted in prison airspace without prior permission from El Doctor.

The Cali bosses began to worry that Escobar could be more dangerous in prison than he had been while on the run. La Catedral was a sanctuary—a government-protected bunker. The bosses could see their old rival going after his lost market share and striking at them without fear of reprisal. Pablo's imprisonment turned out to be a security crisis for the Cali cartel.

Jorge was summoned to a meeting with two of the bosses. At the urging of Pacho Herrera, Miguel wanted to bring back the British mercenaries immediately for a consultation. The godfathers wanted to organize an assault on Escobar's cell block.

"Storm a government prison?" Jorge was incredulous. No way would the Brits agree to armed combat with the Colombian military and National Police, he told them.

"No," Pacho responded. "We'll bomb La Catedral, hit Pablo's cell."

"What? From the air?"

The two godfathers were too excited to notice that Jorge had not joined in their enthusiasm. He was, in fact, stunned. It was such a bad idea that he didn't quite know where to begin. In the silence, Miguel told him to contact David Tomkins.

Cali drug lords, like the rest of the world, had watched the first Gulf War on television and saw Iraqi buildings turned to rubble by coalition bombs. Why not repeat the feat at La Catedral? Pacho reasoned. There were stacks of five-hundred-pound bombs stored at military installations all over civil-war-torn Salvador. They could be carried by any one of several light bombers in Colombia's military fleet. Jorge was to orchestrate everything—find a plane, a pilot, and the bombs.

"But it's a terrible idea," Jorge said, unable to contain himself.

Military planners, he pointed out, rarely target humans with aerial bombs, and for good reason. They're crude, blunt weapons. Aerial bombardments are used to destroy fixed structures—warehouses or weapons depots, rail lines, roads, and bridges—not kill an individual. Unlike the "smart bombs" used in the Gulf War, gravity-guided bombs sought by the cartel were notoriously imprecise. Many innocent lives would be jeopardized. It could be a disaster.

At that time, the Cali bosses occupied a relatively benign place in the Colombian crime world. They quite literally had friends in high places—in national and local governments, in law enforcement, and in the military. The goodwill they enjoyed grew out of generous bribes and favors and from a measure of public sympathy—they were victims of Pablo Escobar's terror just like the rest of the country. All four of the godfathers were wanted in the United States, but they faced no active charges in Colombia. Jorge feared that bombing the prison would wipe out the cartel's favorable image and leave his bosses, like Escobar, wanted terrorists and enemies of the state.

Pacho and Miguel were unmoved. Their rival was a sitting duck. They wanted to rain bombs on Escobar's head, and they wanted Jorge to arrange it. When Jorge again tried to object, Miguel cut him off.

"That's enough! Make it happen," he growled.

Jorge was stung by Miguel's response and deeply frustrated that his expertise was so easily rejected. He considered threatening to resign, but quickly thought better of it. That would be rash—possibly dangerous—and probably not very effective. He decided to go along for now but drag his feet and look for ways to steer the bosses away from such a dreadful scheme.

FIRST STOP FOR JORGE was Guatemala, where he met Pedro Isern, a courtly and affable Cuban. Isern was handling cocaine shipments to the United States hidden in pallets of broccoli and cantaloupes. The Cuban had long-standing contacts in the Salvadoran military. He escorted

Jorge to meet the commander of Salvador's Comalapa Air Force Base, Lieutenant Colonel Roberto Leiva Jacobo.

Introductions took place over whiskey at the colonel's residence. Jorge listened quietly as the old friends laughed about good times, about hunting rabbits along the air-base runways at night, and about the sexual vigor found in eating a favorite soup made from a lizard they called *garrobo*. Finally, the colonel turned to Jorge.

"I want to help my friend," Leiva said with a nod to Isern.

The colonel said he understood that the plan was to acquire four MK-82 bombs—five-hundred-pounders—for the purpose of an air strike against Pablo Escobar. He said he could arrange it. But was Jorge prepared to pay $150,000 each?

"Six hundred thousand seems a bit exorbitant," Jorge responded with a shrug. "But I am just a messenger. I will go to Miguel with your proposal. Would you take $500,000 total?" With Leiva's shrug, it became the final price.

In London, Tomkins was on board. He called Jorge to say he had found an A-37 Dragonfly, a small fighter-bomber capable of delivering five-hundred-pound bombs. A private aircraft collector would fly the plane to Florida for their inspection. The Dragonfly was a Cessna-made aircraft designed for close ground support missions in Vietnam. It was in fairly wide use in the military fleets of several Latin American countries, including Colombia.

Jorge flew to Miami, rented a car, and headed to Opa-locka Airport, where the Dragonfly was waiting in a hangar about ten miles north of the city. If Jorge liked what he saw, the godfathers would send a Colombian pilot to take the plane for a test flight. He found Tomkins standing next to the olive green aircraft with two other men. The one named Fred said he represented the anonymous seller.

Tomkins climbed into the cockpit while Jorge walked around the plane. All of its identification markings had been removed. "Why no markings?" Jorge asked.

"Commercial reasons," Fred said. "If the deal falls through, the owner doesn't want to be identified."

Jorge wasn't satisfied, but he continued to check the fuselage, landing gear, bomb racks, and wings. It was in pristine condition, a beauty. But focusing on the Dragonfly's nose, Jorge suddenly felt ill. There was gunpowder and smoke residue around the muzzle opening of the nose gun.

"This is a working weapon?" Jorge blurted out.

"No worry. The owner has a permit," assured Fred.

Jorge tried not to show his concern. He knew that no private citizen—not in Colombia and not in Florida—could legally own a military fighter jet with functioning combat weapons. This deal was either a scam or, worse, a law-enforcement sting. The anonymous owner most likely was the Florida Air National Guard, and Fred was either an FBI or a U.S. Customs Service agent. Jorge figured that he also had to be wary of Tomkins, in case he was cooperating in the setup to save himself.

Without committing to the purchase, Jorge said he wanted to wait for the test pilot's report. He returned to his hotel and the next morning told Tomkins he was joining a deep-sea fishing charter and would be out all day. Jorge left immediately for the airport and caught a flight to San Salvador. Once out of U.S. jurisdiction, he sent word to Tomkins through a mutual friend in Miami. He had canceled the test pilot and suspected the deal was a sting. Tomkins forfeited a $25,000 fee when the purchase collapsed. He complained that Jorge had been overly paranoid.

Jorge felt he had barely escaped a trap. Based on his understanding of U.S. conspiracy laws—a by-product of so many nights translating legal discussions between American lawyers and the Cali bosses—even the slightest overt act on his part to help arrange an illegal weapons purchase could result in felony charges. The near miss was a reminder of the dangers lurking in what Jorge had come to regard as the plot from hell.

He wanted to come out of the campaign against Pablo a national hero—not a felon. Now he faced a bizarre predicament: he was risking arrest advancing a scheme that he desperately hoped to prevent.

GET ME A FORK

BETWEEN CARTEL MISSIONS TO PANAMA AND SALVADOR, JORGE focused on ways to improve anti-Escobar intelligence at home. With Miguel's blessing, he monitored tips and reports from cartel snitches. He talked regularly with family members and their bodyguards, checking for potential problems. It was during such routine inquiries that a cousin of Marta Lucía, Miguel's Wife No. 4, divulged troubling information.

The cousin was suspicious after a relative visiting from the Medellín area asked a lot of questions—about the schools the Rodríguez Orejuela children attended, about the cars that took them to school, and about Marta Lucía's various residences.

Jorge alerted the godfathers, who reacted swiftly. A cartel-friendly Cali police sergeant was sent to arrest the man. The officer delivered him to a gathering of grim-faced bosses at one of Pacho's secluded country compounds. The relative from Medellín was known as Caliche. He was sweating when he arrived.

The godfathers sat stiffly in a spacious living room sharing fresh fruit juices and awkward family patter for a few minutes. Pacho's young thugs stood around in doorways, looking menacing. Caliche struggled to appear relaxed. Jorge felt his own heart racing. He sensed Gilberto's suppressed rage.

"You ask a lot of questions—about our children," Gilberto said sternly, abruptly ending the pretense of friendly chitchat. "Why?"

"I'm sorry. I don't understand. What do you mean?"

"You asked your cousin—what schools do they attend . . . our children."

"Oh, yes—but I'm just interested in family. It was natural curiosity. Nothing more," Caliche said.

"Natural curiosity?" Gilberto was irritated by the term. "But you wanted to know their drivers, their bodyguards, the cars they ride to school . . . Natural curiosity?"

"Please, Don Gilberto, I'm sorry. It was rude to be so nosy. I'm like that. I—"

"You are working for Pablo Escobar," Gilberto accused.

"No! No, of course not," Caliche protested, now clearly frightened. "I would never betray my family—your family. Never."

"Look, Caliche—I understand." Gilberto took a softer tone. "You live near Medellín. Pablo threatens you. We understand . . . you have no choice . . . you have to protect your own family . . . you have to—"

"No, no—I tell you, I meant nothing. It was harmless curiosity. I was—"

Gilberto jumped to his feet, cutting off Caliche in mid-sentence. "Get me a fork!" the drug boss bellowed. "I'll take out the goddamn liar's eyeballs myself."

There was a great commotion as someone grabbed Caliche and the crowd moved en masse into the next room, to a polished dining room table. Gilberto, at one end, motioned for the ashen Caliche to be brought to him. Two of Pacho's men shoved and dragged him to Gilberto's side. Another handed the godfather a silver dinner fork.

Jorge could barely breathe. He had a clear view across the table from Gilberto. He didn't want to see what was coming. He couldn't help feeling pity for the spy. Mostly, he hoped not to embarrass himself by passing out at the sight of blood and gore. He was standing at the elbow of a silent and scowling Miguel, who made no move to intervene. Almost immediately, the hubbub around the table quieted. Caliche was whimpering.

"Please understand—he will kill my wife and baby. I am so sorry. Don Gilberto, I would rather die than harm your family. I only wish to save my little ones."

After a moment, Gilberto placed the fork on the table and led the crowd back to the living room. With his reprieve, Caliche eagerly spilled all of his secrets. Pablo had offered him money but also threatened his family if he did not inform on the Cali families. The Medellín boss had summoned Caliche to La Catedral on two or three occasions, he said, where the terms of his cooperation were negotiated on the prison grounds. He said he was sorry and ashamed and would do anything to make amends.

Jorge leaned close to Miguel and whispered, "He's been to La Catedral. We need his eyewitness description. It could be very important."

Miguel immediately interrupted. He said that he wanted Jorge to debrief Caliche starting first thing in the morning and that he expected the man to share everything he knew about Escobar and the prison layout and its operation. Caliche seemed relieved.

IN THEORY, THE COLOMBIAN government ran Pablo Escobar's mountain prison. But Escobar controlled everything from its airspace to which guards won promotions. Military police provided perimeter security, supposedly checking all vehicles entering or exiting the grounds. But Caliche reported that certain supply trucks had false chambers and were never inspected, allowing for daily deliveries of prostitutes and other visitors. Sometimes, cartel snitches were smuggled in for beatings or executions.

Down the hill in Medellín, meanwhile, Cali spies worked in a surprisingly hospitable environment. Escobar had placed a price on the heads of local police, resulting in scores of cop killings. Resentful police were only too eager to help his rivals, especially with the added bonus of liquor, girls, parties, and cash in steady supply at the Cali spy house just outside Bloque headquarters.

Cali's on-site operative was Benito Heredia, also known as El Chapulín, "the Grasshopper." Jorge turned to him for help arranging a personal inspection of the prison. It didn't take long. A police helicopter was scheduled to ferry a judge and court reporter to the prison in a few days. Escobar had approved the flight. The Grasshopper bribed the base commander and the helicopter flight crew to let Jorge pose as the co-pilot.

On a beautiful morning in Medellín, the Bell 206 Ranger lifted off from the task force base with a clean-shaven Jorge sitting in the left seat. Sunglasses and a very large helmet with built-in radio microphone obscured his face. He wore a gray-green jumpsuit sporting the three bars of a police captain; his boots were polished, and he looked every inch an officer.

The flight up to La Catedral took no more than ten minutes. Jorge imagined that inmates could hear the chopper's engine noise while it was still in Medellín—a serious problem for a surprise attack. Jorge asked the pilot for a sweeping approach into the landing site, a soccer field just inside the compound. The landing pattern gave Jorge a full view of the grounds.

Just as Caliche had told him in their debriefing sessions, a perimeter fence had not been completed. In fact, along a one-hundred-foot stretch behind the prison, Jorge saw that there was no fence at all. The entire population of La Catedral could have walked through that gap at any time without forming a line.

The helicopter settled on the soccer field only long enough to discharge its passengers. The judge and his recording secretary ducked under the props, and the Bell Ranger lifted off again. Jorge paid special attention to a children's play area installed for Escobar's daughter. Again, as Caliche had described, there was a large playhouse. Caliche said it concealed the entrance to an underground bunker.

Escobar's imprisonment was a grand charade. He could live in high style inside the prison, or he could leave—whenever he wanted. But most troubling to Jorge was Manuela's playhouse. The hidden bunker, if it was there, suggested that Escobar anticipated the sort of attack Jorge was supposed to pull off as a surprise.

IN CALI, JORGE CONTINUED to lobby against the attack even as he worked to set it up. At every opportunity he reminded Miguel that bombs were inaccurate, especially on the side of a mountain. "It will be ten times more difficult than hitting a target on flat terrain," Jorge said. He warned, too, about likely political blowback. The public regarded La Catedral as a government facility. An assault would be an act of terrorism.

"Just do your damn job," Miguel said, again ending discussions.

The Cali cartel bosses used Caliche to launch a public relations assault on prison officials. They wanted Escobar's Catedral sanctuary turned into a real prison, his special treatment exposed and curtailed. They filed affidavits with the attorney general's office describing the drug lord's prison lifestyle. They leaked details to the press. Nothing changed immediately for Escobar, but the prison director lost his job.

The Gaviria government's new choice to run La Catedral was Homero Rodríguez, a close friend of Jorge's. They had cousins in common. As boys, they were playmates; their fathers were friends at the military academy. Homero was a retired army colonel and had been serving as the top aide to the chief of DAS, the Colombian national security agency.

Jorge met with him at the urging of cartel bosses. The godfathers hoped the new man would end Escobar's free rein inside the prison. They met in Bogotá at the home of Jorge's parents. He used the occasion to urge his friend to decline the assignment. "You don't want this job," he said. "Let me tell you, the cook at La Catedral has more power than you will have."

Then Jorge went further. He had years earlier shared with Homero his secret role with the British commandos when they were planning to attack FARC headquarters. This time he confided the cartel's plot to bomb the prison. It might have seemed risky, but Jorge trusted his friend and wanted to protect him. He also believed that as a last resort he could alert Homero and have the attack blocked—without exposing himself as a snitch. Jorge could only guess how soon the plot might come together—so far, there was no plane and no pilot, and the bombs were not yet in hand. But the bosses were determined, and Jorge feared it was inevitable.

Homero thanked Jorge and asked to be kept informed. If an attack was launched, Jorge was to call the warden's mother and say, "Marcella is looking for Homero." That was the signal to take cover. Marcella was an ex-lover, the central figure in Homero's most recent romantic disaster. *How appropriate,* thought Jorge. If the bombing mission went off as planned, disaster was the only outcome he could imagine.

INTO THE BLACK MARKET

O N JANUARY 16, 1992, THE CHAPULTEPEC PEACE ACCORDS WERE signed in Mexico City, ending the twelve-year Salvadoran civil war. A United Nations peacekeeping force was being assembled to take over military and law-enforcement functions throughout the country. Salvador's good news was bad news for the Cali cartel.

Time was running out on Colonel Roberto Leiva's offer to sell the cartel four MK-82 bombs. The half-million-dollar deal would expire on the day the colonel surrendered command of Comalapa Air Base—and by February that day had become imminent. After weeks of half-hearted preparations, Jorge had to move fast.

On his way to catch a flight to Salvador, Jorge stopped at Miguel's house. The boss sat at a desk strewn with red wrapping paper, gold ribbon, scissors, and clear tape. He was putting the finishing touches on a package the size of a shoe box. His gift-wrapping technique was flawless. Every corner was trimmed at precisely ninety degrees. Each fold or scissor cut was perfect. Miguel was a man devoted to detail.

"For the colonel," said Miguel, sliding the red and gold package toward Jorge. "Five hundred thousand U.S. dollars. I counted it myself."

"It's heavy," Jorge said with some surprise, trying to guess its weight. He looked up to see Miguel scowling, so he quickly added, "I'll carry it on. No problem."

Jorge arrived in San Salvador on a night flight via Panama. His brightly wrapped package was in a sturdy shopping bag stowed under the seat in front of him. When the aircraft doors opened at the terminal, a man in Salvadoran army fatigues entered. He was looking for Jorge. Sergeant José Parada was an aide to Colonel Leiva. Jorge waited until most of the passengers had filed out, then met Parada in the plane's forward galley. He handed over the shopping bag and its red-and-gold-wrapped contents.

"I'll catch up to you outside," Jorge said for the benefit of anyone listening. The sergeant, however, disappeared, and Jorge never saw the package again. Later, Leiva complained that his handsome gift contained only $480,000. The $20,000 discrepancy did not, however, spoil the deal.

El Salvador remained a country officially at war, and security was tight. Jorge told passport control officers that he was on a business trip, scouting investment opportunities in Salvadoran orange juice exports. He was carrying brochures requested from the Salvador Ministry of Trade. Jorge decided not to use a fake name when he checked in to the Sheraton hotel in downtown San Salvador. As he had feared, the desk clerk promptly requested his passport and made a photocopy before handing over a room key. Had he used a phony name, Jorge would have had to feign losing his ID papers and almost certainly provoked a visit from Salvadoran authorities. Though many in the cartel carried false passports, Jorge did not.

The bomb-smuggling plan was in motion by morning. Jorge met with the leader of the cartel's local crew—a tall, powerfully built Salvadoran named Nelson Comandari. He was one of Pacho Herrera's operatives. He had lined up a brother-in-law, a nephew, and several associates to help.

The next day at Comalapa Air Base, Sergeant Parada used his lunch break to move into action. He boarded one of the ubiquitous yellow forklifts and quickly loaded four MK-82 bombs into the cargo bed of a small red truck. He covered the military green cylinders with straw. Tail fins and the all-important detonators were packed separately, and the civilian truck rolled out toward the base gate with the uniformed sergeant at the wheel. No one stopped him.

ABOUT TWO MILES AWAY at Pato Canales, a popular roadside restaurant, the lunch rush was in full swing. Jorge was alone at a table that made him easy to spot from the dining area entry. Across the crowded room—alone at another table—sat Nelson Comandari, Jorge's Salvadoran partner.

The red truck pulled in to a parking spot near the restaurant. The sergeant climbed out and strode quickly across the lot. Inside, he spotted Jorge. Without saying a word, he walked past Jorge and left the truck's ignition key on his table. Jorge palmed it like a magician, shifting it to the far side of his table. A moment later, Comandari settled his lunch tab and headed for the door, brushing past the far side of Jorge's table to scoop up the ignition key. He went out to the red truck and drove away. Jorge returned to the Sheraton, but on the way he stopped at a public telephone center.

"*Patrón,* we have the articles," Jorge said in a call to Miguel. It was the signal to dispatch a cartel plane to the prearranged landing site near Salvador's Guatemala border.

Meanwhile, Nelson was transporting the bombs to the rendezvous site, about fifty miles north. A drive of that distance figured to encounter at least an occasional military roadblock, so Nelson and his confederates took time to disguise their cargo. First, they painted all four bombs yellow, the familiar bright yellow of the Caterpillar company's trucks, tractors, and heavy construction equipment in the area. Nelson even obtained official-looking Caterpillar decals and affixed those to each bomb. The changes might not fool everyone, but without tail fins the bombs could be mistaken for harmless canisters. To minimize chances of even casual inspection, Nelson spread more straw and hay in the truck bed and added his final deterrent—four large pigs. Already, military roadblocks were becoming less rigorous as hostilities receded. In such times, Nelson predicted, "no one is going to bother digging through a load of pig shit."

IN EL SALVADOR'S NORTHWESTERN CORNER, the Zapote River emerges from the highlands and meanders to the sea—a broad, crystal clear stream with few bridges and only occasional ferries. Difficult transit helped minimize military patrols in the area. Jorge reached the river after dark and tried to roust a canoe operator on the far bank, honking and shouting. Just when he thought he would be spending the night in the car with maybe a million mosquitoes, a man in a canoe glided to shore and waved him aboard. The canoe delivered Jorge to Nelson's house a short distance downstream.

The good news was that the bombs had made it this far undetected and were in the truck, ready for transfer. The bad news was that Nelson had broken his leg earlier in the day and would be unable to assist in the strenuous loading operation. Jorge was surprised to find that his men had built wooden crates for each of the bombs. Easier to stack them, Nelson said.

Before leaving the city earlier that day, Jorge had talked by phone with the cartel pilot who would pick up the bombs at dawn the next day. Their brief and cryptic conversation included an exchange of radio frequencies they would use to communicate and to confirm that it was safe to land. Thereafter, the loading operation would have to be accomplished quickly, before Salvadoran authorities could react to an unidentified plane showing up in their airspace. Jorge expected the process to take no more than four or five minutes. It was scheduled for first light.

Jorge was waiting at Nelson's house when the pilot called to report the plane was thirty minutes out. Jorge alerted Nelson's crew and headed for the landing strip astride Nelson's red, white, and blue Honda motocross bike. Nelson's men followed with the crated bombs in the red truck.

It was still dark with hints of light in the eastern sky when Jorge wheeled up to the flat stretch of ground. The seldom-used dirt runway was unlit. He scanned the canopy of fading stars, looking for the flashing lights of a plane, and listened for the distant engine drone. The silence broke with the crackle of Jorge's radio. The plane was minutes away and had a navigational fix on the landing site. "All clear," Jorge reported.

The pale light creeping across the field finally illuminated the area enough for Jorge to see something moving on the runway. He coasted slowly forward on the bike until he saw it. "Oh my God!" he cried. The runway was alive with chickens and pigs.

The inbound plane flashed its landing lights. Jorge could see that it was only seconds from touching down. He kicked his Honda into gear and raced down the runway. Any animal in the path of the landing aircraft could do serious damage to the plane—perhaps catastrophic.

Livestock scattered as Jorge revved his engine and spun his wheels, spraying grit and gravel in a desperate, noisy chase down the landing strip. The plane swept past him and set down safely. That's when he had his second fright of the young morning. The plane was not the spacious Cessna Grand Caravan that he was expecting. It was a much smaller King Air 200, a twin-engine executive plane with a cargo hold fit for golf bags.

By the time Jorge caught up to the King Air at the end of the runway, its passenger door was open, and the co-pilot was tossing out mostly empty fifteen-gallon plastic gas cans. Each of them had been full at departure from Cali and rigged to fuel the engines during the twelve-hundred-mile flight north to El Zapote. It was an old traffickers' trick—doubling the plane's two-thousand-mile range by saving every gallon in its wing tanks for the flight home. The passenger compartment had been stripped of all seats to make room for the makeshift fuel arrangement, so when the empties were tossed, the King Air had room to take on cargo—but not easily.

The King Air was wide enough to seat only two across as a passenger plane, compared with the three-seats-across capacity of a Caravan. Also, the King Air's passenger door was much smaller. Crated bombs didn't fit. Nelson's men began breaking down the crates and removing the five-foot-long yellow canisters.

The pilot, a good-natured, bearded man known to cartel regulars as Barbas, kept the King Air's propellers turning. His co-pilot supervised the loading. Even with the crates removed, maneuvering the long, heavy cylinder-shaped bombs into place was like trying to take a couch around a tight corner. The fine wood-appointed galley and bar at the back of the plane took a beating. The four- to five-minute operation dragged to ten minutes, then fifteen, then twenty. Curious neighbors gathered along the airstrip, watching what was supposed to be a clandestine mission.

The co-pilot worried about weight distribution and the plane's critical center of gravity. The third bomb slipped out of place and slid aft toward the galley, setting off grunts, groans, and much cursing. If a couple of bombs slipped like that in flight—especially during landing or takeoff—the sudden shift could bring the plane down. The frazzled co-pilot had seen enough. He would not risk balancing another bomb.

"No more," he hollered from the plane's open doorway. Then to Barbas: "Let's go—now! Get out of here."

Jorge had just supervised removal of the fourth bomb from its wooden crate.

"Wait! One more," he called to the crew. But the cabin door slammed shut.

"Tomorrow—we'll come back," Barbas shouted from the open pilot's window. Jorge quickly handed up a box with bomb parts and accessories, including the fin attachments—and then a box of detonators. "With these, be *very* careful," Jorge said.

Barbas revved his engines and swung around into a dust-churning takeoff roll. Jorge watched the King Air lift off and bank to the south. Left behind, scattered on the airstrip, were a dozen or more of the white plastic fuel containers. He examined one of them more closely. It was stamped: "Made in Colombia."

Between the incriminating white fuel cans, a leftover yellow bomb, and all those local eyewitnesses attracted by the unusual dawn activity, Jorge feared imminent exposure. He doubted they could afford to wait another day to retrieve the fourth MK-82. He advised Nelson to hide it in the river.

"Just sink it," Jorge urged. And he headed back to the city.

* * *

THAT SAME MORNING in Colombia, air traffic monitors picked up an unexpected radar blip inbound from the north. It had the look of a drug runner. Two military fighter planes scrambled to intercept the rogue King Air 200.

Approaching the southern Colombian coast where he would bank east and head for Cali, Barbas noticed that he had company in the air. He could not outrun them. And in broad daylight, there was only one place to hide—in clouds draping the Andean peaks between the coast and the Cauca valley. The pilot radioed the cartel for urgent assistance. Within minutes, a second King Air 200 was soaring out of the Cali airport to serve as a decoy. It worked. The decoy was intercepted and forced to land for military inspection. Barbas and his cargo of bombs emerged from the clouds undetected and turned for home.

The aerial drama had already ended by the time Jorge checked in from one of the private long-distance phone booths at the central telephone offices in San Salvador later that day. "No problem," said a sympathetic Miguel when Jorge reported the stranded bomb. "It's not your fault. We should have sent a bigger plane. I'll send another one to pick it up." They agreed that it might be best to wait a day or two, just to be certain that the operation was still a secret. "Stay there until Monday," Miguel said.

But Jorge decided he needed a safer place to wait. He retrieved his luggage at the Sheraton and stopped at the front desk. He was spending the weekend at a Salvadoran beach resort, he said, but asked the clerk to hold his room. He would be back in two days. Jorge considered offering the clerk two or three hundred dollars to destroy the photocopied pages of his passport—but that could backfire and prompt an immediate tip to security officials. Jorge simply wished the desk clerk a pleasant weekend and left. He flagged the first taxi driver and said, *"Aeropuerto, por favor."*

Jorge flew to Panama. That afternoon he tried to phone Nelson. It was nearly 10:00 p.m. when he connected with the Salvadoran's sister. She was in a state of anxiety. Authorities had found the fourth bomb.

"It's terrible. Everyone's been arrested," she cried. "They must have

been watching." Jorge felt as if he'd been kicked in the head. He struggled to analyze his options. The sister was chattering: "What happened
to you? Where are you?"

Jorge now regarded Nelson's sister as a threat to his own security.
Maybe she was cooperating with authorities. Maybe her phone was
tapped. Jorge was too far from Cali for cartel protection. He trusted no
one. "I'm in Costa Rica," he lied.

It was a Sunday. Jorge waited until evening to call the one person in
Panama he could count on to lift his spirits, the ever-cheerful Nilka
Bilonick. Her husband, now in U.S. custody, had already provided federal prosecutors with evidence against Noriega. Jorge had with him the
matching safe-deposit key necessary to get at the stored certificate of
deposit. It had matured and was worth the promised $1 million. With
Jorge's key, Nilka could use hers to retrieve the fortune. She embraced
him with gratitude and affection. He felt renewed. Jorge loved playing
the hero.

That same day, news broke all over the world exposing Jorge's secret
mission to Salvador. Press accounts reported the arrests of Colonel
Leiva and several others. They described recovery of a five-hundred-
pound U.S.-made bomb linked to a plot to kill Pablo Escobar. Published reports in Panama and Colombia said that a Cali cartel operative
was involved in the scheme and identified him as a Colombian army reserve captain named Jorge Salcedo, also known as Richard.

Military authorities in Bogotá announced an investigation. Jorge
returned home wanted for questioning. He and his family would have
to go into hiding.

THE DARK SIDE

JORGE SALCEDO'S SUDDEN NOTORIETY CAME AS A SHOCK TO FRIENDS and relatives who knew him as an engineer who tinkered with radios, as the good-humored, gentle father. News accounts described him as a narco-trafficker, as an important operative in organized crime. He wanted more than anything to explain, to clear his name. But he could do nothing.

Beyond Jorge's wife and father, few had any idea of his ties to the Rodríguez Orejuela family. Thanks to the modest consulting work he did for his former partners at Magna Battery, most acquaintances outside of the cartel thought Jorge worked in battery manufacturing.

With authorities looking for him, Jorge had to move to new living quarters. His was a family of five now, with Lena and her son, their little Jorge, and a six-month-old baby girl. Jorge also worried about reprisals by Medellín gangs. He had been exposed as the planner of an assassination attempt against Escobar. Since the mid-1980s, hundreds of Colombian officials had been murdered for less.

The Cali bosses put Jorge and family in a spacious safe house behind gated walls. They gave him a new assignment monitoring surveillance recordings gathered electronically in an adjacent building. It allowed him to stay out of sight for months at a time while analyzing a steady flow of intelligence on Escobar.

Jorge appreciated the time with his family, aside from one big scare. It came on an afternoon when both parents realized that neither had seen their toddler for several minutes. After calling his name with no response, they bolted outside to find the two-year-old boy facedown in the swimming pool. He was quickly revived, but mother and father were badly shaken. Jorge dropped everything for the next couple of days to fashion a floating wave detector, another of his "MacGyver" designs. It sounded a loud horn if anything fell in the pool.

Eventually, calls for government inquiries into the Salvador bomb episode subsided. Cartel friends in the military hierarchy saw to it that no formal investigations ever resulted from the scandal, but there were other repercussions for Jorge. The worst news was delivered first to Jorge's father. The retired general was contacted by an old friend in the officers' corps and told, with deep regret, that Jorge would be stripped of his captain's commission in the army reserves. Lena, too, was decommissioned involuntarily. The senior Salcedo understood political realities. He also supported his son. He told his caller, "Someday you will know the whole truth."

Jorge was devastated. The bomb plot had been absurd, a terrible idea from the beginning. He had been frustrated all along that he couldn't stop it. Now his prospects for future business with the Colombian military were dimmed, if not dead. Worse, the public disgrace was costing him something he treasured more than money or high position—his ability to follow in the military footsteps of his father.

At least the original plan to bomb the prison was dead. The yellow MK-82s were put in permanent storage. The hunt for a plane and pilot was called off. Even Miguel had to agree that all the publicity had rendered the plot unworkable.

Jorge found electronic surveillance and his newly expanded intelligence work much more interesting than basic security. "I know everything that's going on—much more than Mario," he confided to Lena.

But he was troubled by a growing estrangement from his friend. Mario never called Jorge during the height of the Salvador bomb scandal. He offered no condolences, expressed no support, and never stopped by the safe house.

During Jorge's extended isolation, Mario consolidated his authority over the cartel's security apparatus. He also started running some of the police and military informants who needed regular cartel payoffs, a move into the illicit side of the Business that Jorge was happy to leave to others.

Of course, Jorge was likely aiding the illicit side too, if only indirectly. His eavesdropping would have helped the cartel to monitor the loyalty of operatives and to look for information to compromise sources and government officials. Eventually, the cartel was listening to as many as four hundred Cali phones at any time, rotating different lines in and out of the eavesdropping queue with help from a highly placed source at the telephone company.

At the same time, Guillermo Pallomari, the ambitious accountant, continued to encroach on Jorge's communications operations. He insisted that Jorge's radiophone dispatch center be consolidated at the cartel's computer center, which Pallomari ran. It was pointless for Jorge to protest. Miguel loved efficiencies. Besides, Jorge was not interested in fighting to preserve any of his cartel prerogatives. Both Pallomari and del Basto were busy building careers with the cartel.

But in 1992, after more than three years with the cartel, Jorge still regarded himself as a short-timer.

As SUMMER APPROACHED, Pablo Escobar's control of the Medellín drug organization was crumbling from the effects of internal strife. Some trusted allies were accused of taking financial advantage of Escobar's imprisonment. Some were killed. Others turned on him as Escobar became more paranoid and violently irrational. News of the Cali plot to bomb La Catedral had heightened tensions among El Doctor's inner circle. There were rumors he might be moved to a more restrictive prison.

The Medellín boss finally decided to use that handy gap in the fence to "escape." Homero Rodríguez, the prison warden, would end up in jail, accused of gross incompetence. Pablo's stay in prison had always been at the inmate's discretion. Still, Jorge's disappointment was personal. After all his efforts to expose the charade of prison security, nothing had been done about it. Homero could have prevented Pablo's escape. He knew everything—because Jorge had told him. He must have been stymied by higher and corrupt authorities, Jorge decided— an assumption to salvage their old but damaged friendship.

Escobar's escape had a marked impact on Cali security fears—they eased. El Doctor as a fugitive was a far less effective terrorist than he had been in prison. He continued to plant car bombs, but they were directed at government targets.

Sensing vulnerability, Cali moved even more aggressively against Escobar, forming a vigilante group that Gilberto dubbed Los Pepes— the Spanish acronym for People Persecuted by Pablo Escobar. The Cali godfathers kicked in millions of dollars, provided a steady supply of getaway cars stolen in Venezuela, and turned over electronic eavesdropping data to the vigilantes. With that support, Los Pepes mounted a campaign of terror against Pablo's assets, his family, and his dwindling number of business allies. They firebombed his car collection, his mother's country home, and other family real estate. Then they started killing Pablo's people—a cousin, a lawyer, a business associate. Authorities were finding as many as six bodies a day.

When Los Pepes violence was at its peak, Escobar's family left the country for safety. For a time they traveled in Europe. They were followed wherever they went. The Rodríguez Orejuela brothers had dispatched one of their most trusted *sicarios* to shadow them. Should any harm come to the Rodríguez family back home in Cali, Bruno Murillo was to assassinate Pablo's family wherever they were hiding.

Jorge had no direct role in the Pepes operations, but from the sidelines he had a disturbingly clear view of its ruthlessness—especially in the case of Guido Parra, one of Escobar's lawyers. Early in Jorge's tenure with the Cali cartel, he chauffeured Parra to a meeting with Miguel and Gilberto. The Medellín lawyer came to explore terms for a settlement of hostilities between Pablo and the brothers. Parra left without an agreement but with the respect of the Cali godfathers for trying.

All that was forgotten four years later. In the spring of 1993, Escobar and Los Pepes were locked in a tit-for-tat exchange of violent acts, a terrorists' game of chicken. One day in April, a Medellín car bomb killed eleven in Bogotá. The next day, a group of Cali-backed gunmen seized Parra and his eighteen-year-old son. Their bodies were found in the trunk of a Medellín taxi with bullet wounds in their heads and a note: "What do you think of the exchange for the bombs in Bogotá, Pablo?"

Washington condemned Los Pepes and feared that Colombian authorities were sharing U.S. intelligence with the vigilantes. There may have been such sharing, but it was the Cali cartel and its friends that got most of the local credit—and in Colombia "credit" was the appropriate description. Los Pepes were a big hit with average Colombians and with much of the Bogotá establishment—a population tired of fearing Escobar. By now, Escobar's romanticized "Robin Hood" persona survived only among the poorest inhabitants of the slums in Medellín and his hometown of Envigado.

To capitalize on domestic goodwill toward Cali, Miguel opened secret talks with the Colombian attorney general, Gustavo de Greiff, who had assumed office shortly before Pablo's jailbreak. It was a particularly odd pas de deux. The bespectacled sixty-three-year-old de Greiff came from academia, smoked a pipe, and drove a 1953 Volkswagen bug. He had no active cases against the godfathers, but even the godfathers knew that was a mere technicality. The cartel was breaking the laws of Colombia, the United States, Russia, and most of Europe pretty much every day, smuggling drugs, laundering money, and obstructing justice. The bosses sought full amnesty from prosecution at home, in exchange for their promise to abandon the drug trade.

One point of contention was whether the Cali bosses would have to do jail time—and how much. De Greiff proved to be a frustrating negotiator, stubbornly insisting on tougher terms than the Rodríguez Orejuela brothers were willing to accept. He seemed immune to favors. Miguel once complained in front of Jorge, "How can I bribe a man who drives an old Volkswagen?"

* * *

AS THE SALVADOR BOMB SCANDAL receded, Jorge began spending more time at Miguel's side. His duties were evolving, and a new role took shape as the boss's personal security and intelligence aide. Whenever Miguel traveled, Jorge arranged for motorcycle escorts to clear the routes. He also handled advance site inspections. Miguel relied on Jorge to signal that it was safe before he ventured into meetings outside his residence.

Jorge was spending increasing amounts of private time with the boss—more than either Mario del Basto or Guillermo Pallomari. In the process, he gained trust and familiarity with all the other bosses. Jealousies festered among his colleagues. Both Mario and Pallomari complained that Jorge failed to keep them in the loop on important matters.

It was no accident. Jorge recognized and came to relish the power of information. Though no longer hunting Escobar with commandos, he was still tracking Pablo by collecting and analyzing intelligence. It was intriguing, even exciting. And it was experience he could use whenever he started his own private security business.

Of course, he was getting a little ahead of himself contemplating a post-cartel future. Jorge was ignoring the dark side of his close ties to the cartel families. He knew too much.

THE HAUNTINGS

Early in 1993, while most of Colombia hunted Pablo Escobar, a team of Pacho Herrera's men pursued another quarry: the long-missing farmer from Santander, the man whose farm sheltered the gunmen who massacred Pacho's soccer mates at Los Cocos.

Jorge Salcedo was unaware of the latest developments in that search when he received an urgent call one afternoon from Miguel's assistant. Everyone was headed to Pacho's ranch, he said. Jorge dropped what he was doing and made his way to the ranch code-named the Desert, to confirm that it was secure for Miguel's arrival. When Jorge reached the main house, he was waved on toward an abandoned dairy another mile or so down a dirt road.

The place was swarming with cartel personnel. The bosses Pacho Herrera and Chepe Santacruz were in the crowd. Jorge recognized their *sicarios* even before he spotted the godfathers. Something had everyone excited.

A stable served as the meetinghouse. It was under a roof that provided badly needed shade from the afternoon sun. There were no signs that livestock had roamed the area anytime recently. The air was sweet, the grass thick and untrampled. Jorge noticed Pacho had come with his brothers. They were glaring at someone sitting on the edge of a table in the center of the stable—a man pensively smoking a cigarette. Jorge did not know the man. A member of his security crew offered a half-whispered explanation. The man had been delivered by helicopter a short time earlier. He was the farmer from Santander, he said: "the poor son of a bitch."

The Rodríguez Orejuela brothers arrived separately. Miguel was the last of the godfathers, pulling up in his Mazda 626 with Mateo at the wheel. As Miguel strode into the stable, the cartel men fell silent. But it was Gilberto who took charge.

The farmer was younger than Jorge expected. He appeared to be healthy, apart from a black eye and a few scrapes on his face. He was not cuffed or shackled, but he was clearly a prisoner—alone with no way out.

Gilberto spoke. "You know, you are in serious trouble," he said. The farmer stared at the ground and shrugged.

"You thought you would get away with it, didn't you?" Gilberto went on. "You were so smart, and we were so stupid."

The prisoner took another drag on his cigarette and said nothing.

"Why did you do this?" Gilberto demanded.

The farmer finally looked up, and with a calm that amazed Jorge, he spoke directly to his interrogator. "I made a mistake," he said. "I was promised some money to take in some visitors. I had no idea what they intended to do from my farm."

Gilberto simply scowled. "You know what's going to happen to you?"

The farmer looked down again and said nothing. The crowd was absolutely quiet. Jorge was barely breathing. Until, finally—

"Let's go." It was Miguel. The farmer's hearing was over. The boss was heading for his car. Gilberto and Chepe also started for their cars—but not Pacho. He and the other survivors of Los Cocos were in charge of justice.

The helpless farmer was stripped of his shirt and boots. His legs were lashed to the trailer hitch of a Toyota Land Cruiser. His calm finally gave way, and he struggled desperately as his arms were tied to a four-wheel-drive Trooper. He was kicked, cursed, and spit upon. Engines revved. The crowd backed away and broke into cheers as the two trucks eased away from each other, slowly stressing, then dislocating arm and leg joints.

Jorge was not there for the screaming. He left with Miguel, eager to be as far away as possible. The grisly details caught up with him a few hours later. One of his motorcycle crewmen stayed to the end. It took about a half hour, he told Jorge. They didn't rush things. As long as the farmer was breathing, they kept re-tying and pulling what was left of him.

Jorge understood vengeance. In Colombian culture, the blood feud has a long history. But this level of depravity was too much. Jorge was haunted by images he had not seen but could not escape. The incident underscored one unavoidable truth: the Gentlemen of Cali were capable of just as much cruelty as any of Pablo's worst thugs. It was getting more difficult to distinguish between them.

Denial was becoming more and more difficult for Jorge. Some time earlier, he had encountered a Cali *sicario* known as El Navegante, "the Navigator." The hired gunman had just exited Miguel's office and was leaning against his car when Jorge arrived. He was obviously troubled, and he unburdened himself to Jorge—after first telling him about his role in a sensational killing that made headlines across Colombia.

A former ally of Pablo Escobar's who had been feuding with the Medellín boss was found dead along a road near his home at Puerto Boyacá. A sign left with the body implicated Escobar in the killing, calling the man "a traitor" for helping the Cali cartel. It was a sham.

The dead man, Ariel Otero, had come to Cali for protection. He was granted sanctuary and moved his wife and two children. Then the cartel ordered Otero killed—and the murder made to appear like an Escobar hit. El Navegante, a Cali *sicario,* told Jorge that he handled the killing . . . under orders.

What bothered the hit man that day was his latest assignment. The

Cali bosses wanted Otero's family to disappear. "I don't know what to do," the *sicario* confided. "I am to kill Otero's little ones and their mother. How can I do this?"

Jorge had no answer. Even worse, he could think of no way to rescue Otero's family without risking his own "little ones and their mother." He wished desperately that El Navegante had kept his secret to himself. But avoiding knowledge about the cartel also was getting more difficult by the day. Realities, from the brutal to the banal, confronted Jorge whether he looked for them or not.

Jorge could admit it only to Lena, but he wanted out. On some level, he still cared for the Rodríguez Orejuela brothers and their families; he liked his job. But he was tired of lying to himself. Yes, he still wanted Pablo Escobar dead, but then he wanted to move on—to start his own private security business, to build a dream house on the Lot.

"That would be wonderful," Lena agreed. "But when?"

A SHOT AT THE FBI

THE CARTEL'S ACCOUNTANT, GUILLERMO PALLOMARI, CELEBRATED his forty-fifth birthday in 1993 with a party arranged by his wife, Patricia. Jorge was surprised that he and Lena were invited. The two men didn't like each other. Months earlier, during the Christmas season, the accountant had accused Jorge of making an improper claim for reimbursement. Jorge was furious. The amount in question was so trivial that Miguel told Jorge to calm down and forget about it. But to Jorge, there was no such thing as a trivial allegation of dishonesty. Proving that Pallomari had erred did not ease the hard feelings.

At the same time, Jorge was fond of Patricia. She worked hard, ran a computer-training business, was a devoted mother to her two sons, and seemed determined to be a peacemaker. Jorge and Lena attended Guillermo's birthday party—but they did it for Patricia.

Pallomari continued his consolidation of the cartel's administrative operations. He created more front companies to distance the godfathers from their drug proceeds. Cartel management was distributed among five corporate-style divisions, each under the supervision of Miguel. They were trafficking, finance, politics, legal, and military. A committee of mid-level managers from each division met regularly with the boss.

Trafficking was the obvious heart of the Business, and thanks to efficiencies in warehousing and distribution the cartel set records for tonnage shipped to the United States and Europe. José Estrada ran the warehouse network and had much of the logistical responsibility for moving cocaine out of the country and bulk currency back in. Estrada had been Miguel's closest security adviser before Jorge and Mario arrived, and he often thanked them for freeing him to get rich.

Finance was Pallomari's exclusive turf. He met daily with Miguel to go over all checks the boss had written in the previous twenty-four hours. The accountant was also responsible for keeping a record of political favors—cash or otherwise. He paid legal fees, made certain that the families of arrested traffickers were supported while their loved ones were keeping quiet in jail, and provided regular cash allowances to the godfathers' wives and families. Fabiola, the witch and the mother of one of Miguel's sons, kept a special talisman in her home dedicated to Pallomari's continued good health.

The political division employed ex-politicians who lobbied congressmen, governors, and mayors. It was their job to bring key leaders to Cali, where the Rodríguez Orejuela brothers used charm and a checkbook to win over new supporters. Jorge sometimes ferried the VIP visitors in and out of those private sessions and saw public officials stuffing gifts into their pockets ranging from a few thousand dollars to $50,000.

The cartel's first line of legal defense was a cadre of Colombian attorneys led by Bernardo González. Cali attorneys often worked with the American lawyers who were defending traffickers arrested in the States. Members of the legal committee weren't particularly concerned with whether the accused were acquitted. They specialized in protecting cartel secrets, using their access to prisoners to deliver messages from the godfathers: *Keep silent and your family will receive financial support; cooperate with prosecutors and your family will be killed.*

Finally, the military division handled both defensive and offensive needs of the cartel, including internal security, communications, intelligence, and enforcement. Jorge's key role was devoted entirely to defense. Besides constructing the communications network, he handled intelligence analysis, supported Mario del Basto's bodyguard unit, and ran his own team of bodyguards assigned exclusively to Miguel. Fully licensed Hercules Security guards protected cartel property. Additional intelligence and surveillance operations were conducted by the staffs of all four godfathers, which meant that almost everyone was running wiretaps—so many, in fact, that no one could be sure who was listening to whom.

The cartel military wing also cultivated paid informants, especially among police and army personnel. Pallomari wrote checks to Cali-based policemen averaging about $20,000 a month and to National Police amounting to about $60,000 a month. By 1993, one-third of the police and military in Cali, Medellín, and Bogotá were on the drug cartel's payroll.

Enforcement was the job of *sicarios,* the paid gunmen and assassins. Each godfather had his own *sicarios,* but some worked for all the bosses. The senior cartel killer Memo Lara was under indictment in the United States for orchestrating two murders. The victims were a key prosecution witness gunned down in Miami going to dinner with his family, and a Colombian journalist in New York who had written about the Chepe Santacruz drug organization in Queens. Such foreign hits carried higher price tags than domestic killings. Memo's U.S. fees were $100,000 each.

For the cartel, murder was an incidental expense. Annual revenues by 1993 had exceeded $7 billion. In Washington, the Drug Enforcement Administration regarded the Cali operation as the biggest crime syndicate of modern times—much bigger than any American Mafia outfit. There was growing frustration in the new Clinton administration that Bogotá seemed focused on Escobar and was ignoring, if not becoming all too cozy with, the Rodríguez Orejuela family in Cali.

To SUPERVISE THE CALI DRUG EMPIRE, Miguel logged an average of two hundred daily phone calls. His personal assistants tried not to schedule more than fifty meetings per day. Jorge built his daily routine around Miguel's, which typically began at noon and extended until two or three in the morning—a time when day was breaking over Miguel's far-flung operations in Europe.

Jorge's day-and-night presence at the boss's side conferred upon him a de facto authority among *sicarios* and staff. He became the envy of others, especially the ambitious Pallomari.

"Where did you go with Miguel last night?" the accountant would ask.

"If I told you, I'd have to kill you," Jorge loved to respond, though his colleague was never amused.

Pallomari's jealousy grew over time, even as the accountant's own power and influence expanded. Jorge was treated like family. But it should have been no surprise. While Pallomari was trusted with Miguel's fortune, Jorge was trusted with his life.

IN 1993, AS CALI dominance over Pablo Escobar grew, conversations in the cartel's legal division turned to whether to explore negotiation with the United States. The godfathers asked Jorge to contact Joel Rosenthal, the Miami lawyer who helped the cartel intervene on the Noriega case. Could Rosenthal, with his U.S. law-enforcement contacts, broker a meeting with someone in the Department of Justice? The bosses assumed that any legal exposure they had in the States could be bargained away, much like they were trying to do in Bogotá in talks with Attorney General de Greiff.

The FBI dispatched an agent named Bruce Batch to assess the cartel's intentions. Rosenthal came along to make the introductions and sit in on the discussions. The cartel sent the head of its legal committee, Bernardo González. Jorge would translate. The group convened at Casa Vieja, a restaurant across the street from the Tequendama InterContinental hotel.

Jorge was hopeful. That an FBI agent was willing to meet cartel representatives seemed to him promising. Rosenthal didn't exactly predict success, but he wasn't entirely negative either. "What the hell. Let's see what happens," the lawyer said with a shrug.

What could happen, at least in Jorge's imagination, was an agreement by the governments of Washington and Bogotá to reward the Cali godfathers for their help stopping Pablo Escobar's terrorism. The bosses could promise to stop running drugs, accept a slap on their collective wrists, and enter retirement with a clean slate and billions of dollars. That was the goal of talks with de Greiff. Jorge saw it as a potential shortcut for his return to private business.

The FBI agent arrived in a crisply pressed suit, wearing dark sunglasses. Jorge thought he looked like a Secret Service agent, but the American greeted them warmly. The foursome of Batch, Rosenthal, Jorge, and González settled into a booth.

"I'm here to listen," Batch said. "Tell me what you want."

González launched into a strident defense of the Cali godfathers. With Jorge translating, González insisted that they were not drug lords but the owners of a chain of drugstores . . . that their war with Escobar had tarred them unfairly as rival traffickers . . . that they were businessmen, former bankers, family men, and victims of smears and misunderstandings. It was more diatribe than diplomacy. Batch rarely said a word. Finally, González excused himself for a restroom break. Jorge was alone with his friend Rosenthal and the FBI agent.

"Mr. Batch," Jorge said urgently. "I would like to convey to you and to the United States government that anytime you need to talk with someone in Cali, you can contact me. Mr. Rosenthal knows me. He knows what I have done to help on the Noriega case. I can assure you that I have no part in drug trafficking or kidnappings—and I will never do anything to harm the United States."

It was an unrehearsed outburst, and Jorge was nearly out of breath when he finished. He scribbled his father's Bogotá phone number on a piece of paper and slipped it to Batch. "You can leave a confidential message at this phone," he said. The FBI agent put the paper in his pocket without a word.

Jorge had spoken impulsively, trusting that it was safe to be open in front of Rosenthal—just as he had been in private meetings and over dinners in Cali with the lawyer whom he regarded as a friend. On those occasions, he had always tried to distinguish himself from cartel operatives. He was different, Jorge insisted. He protected people. He didn't kidnap, torture, or kill them. He didn't use or traffic in drugs. There were other American lawyers in the cartel's employ, but Jorge trusted only Rosenthal. Perhaps it was because the Miami man was always direct and honest with Jorge.

"I'm afraid you've still got a problem," Rosenthal told him. "By simply doing security work for a criminal enterprise, you are—front and center—in the middle of a conspiracy. That's a felony in the States."

As González returned from the men's room, Jorge was having mixed emotions. Had he said too much? Were his signals to Batch understood? On the plane back to Cali, González chided Jorge for keeping the FBI agent's business card. "We'll never see him again," the cartel legal adviser said.

It was true. The FBI never followed up with the Cali bosses or with Jorge. Agent Batch never left a message with Jorge's father. In retrospect, Jorge was relieved. He had no idea what he could have done for the FBI that would not have risked getting him and his family killed.

BACK IN CALI, Jorge did his best to avoid dealing with Pallomari. Confronted with onerous assignments—such as providing serial numbers for an inventory of radiophone transmitters—Jorge resisted by responding slowly, if at all.

In late summer 1993, Jorge was experimenting with a new low-power, high-quality transmitter. He wanted one installed in the Tower of Cali, downtown's tallest building. The cartel owned three floors of the mixed-use office and residential high-rise, including space on the twentieth floor for Pallomari's accounting operations.

Jorge arrived one morning and was busy until midday dealing with technical challenges of the installation. At some point, he looked around to see that he had been left alone. Rows of clerks and accountants had disappeared. It was lunchtime, and the entire floor had been evacuated.

He wandered around looking at rows of desks and desktop computers. There, in stacks of paperwork or on glowing computer screens, he saw one sensitive cartel record after another—bank statements, can-

celed checks to politicians and policemen, production reports that almost certainly referred to cocaine, employee lists. Confidential cartel
information was strewn on desktops from one end of the office to the
other.

Jorge considered his options. He could confront the arrogant accountant or report the security breach to Miguel. He did neither. A secret could be more valuable in the long run than the brief pleasure of a
comeuppance. And ever since reaching out to the visiting FBI agent,
Jorge had been giving much more thought to what might be in his own
best interest.

IN TOO DEEP

THE CALL FROM MARIO DEL BASTO WAS URGENT. HE WAS ROUND-ing up manpower and asked Jorge to spare a few members of his motorcycle security crew. "It's a big mess," Mario explained. "Someone broke into Pallomari's car and stole his laptop computer—the Toshiba. We've got to find it."

Jorge was beginning to think that the cartel accountant was the most careless man in all of Cali. The missing Toshiba almost certainly was loaded with sensitive information. Anticipating the godfathers' outraged response, Jorge almost felt sorry for Pallomari. But by morning the mystery had been solved.

A pawnshop operator called to say he had something belonging to Don Miguel. Mario retrieved the Toshiba and found out who had hocked it—a small-time street thief with no clue about its contents.

"Pallomari wants him dead," Mario told Jorge.

"But he's harmless; he's a nobody."

Mario shrugged. "But he made a big mistake."

"What kind of god does Pallomari think he is?" Jorge fumed.

A few days later the laptop thief was shot in the head by a Cali *sicario.* One bullet: one dead man. The ruthless efficiency impressed Jorge. He hadn't been close enough to hear the shot or see the bloody aftermath, but it felt close. Too close. Approaching his fifth anniversary with the godfathers, Jorge was growing edgy. The threat from Escobar had all but disappeared, thanks to the vicious Cali-funded Pepes. But all that violence was difficult to ignore.

LATE IN 1993, the Bloque de Búsqueda was closing in on Escobar. The drug boss was perpetually on the run, shunned by friends who feared being targeted by Los Pepes hit squads. He was down to his last loyal bodyguard, hiding somewhere in Medellín.

At three o'clock on the afternoon of Thursday, December 2, Pablo Escobar made a phone call to his family. The conversation lasted a few minutes, long enough for authorities to trace its origin. As the line went dead, a heavily armed team of task force officers pulled up outside the apartment building where he was hiding. They hit his locked door with a sledgehammer. A barefoot Escobar and his bodyguard fled for the second-floor rooftop. The streets below swarmed with more armed officers. Pursuing officers opened fire.

In the explosion of weapons fire that persisted for several minutes, Escobar and the bodyguard dropped dead. A task force major approached one of the bodies, turned it over, and immediately radioed Bloque de Búsqueda headquarters.

"Viva Colombia!" he said. "We have just killed Pablo Escobar."

BEFORE THE WORLD heard the sensational news, Miguel Rodríguez Orejuela did. The Cali cartel boss received a phone call from someone at task force headquarters minutes after Pablo fell.

Jorge was having a late lunch with his family when the radiophone sounded. Everyone knew it was a business call. Faces sagged in disappointment. Jorge answered, expecting Mateo to have an assignment for him from the boss. But the voice was Miguel's: "Richard, I've got some great news. Escobar is dead."

The man they called Lemon sounded positively giddy. He was laughing, maybe even giggling. It had been a long time since Escobar posed a serious threat to the Cali families, but Jorge shared Miguel's delight that their fight with Medellín was finally over.

"Oh, that is wonderful news," Jorge said. "When did it happen?"

"Just now—a few minutes ago. I wanted you to be the first to know. You've done so much to protect us—and our families. Thank you, my friend."

At the office, Miguel found Pallomari and embraced him with a bear hug that almost made the accountant uneasy. Then Miguel called Gilberto. As the brothers shared their relief, Miguel choked up.

Then the celebration began. Gilberto's bodyguards took to the streets of Cali in their cars and motorcycles, honking horns, waving their weapons, and shooting into the air. Jorge finally cautioned that such exuberance over a man's death could be seen as bad taste. The parties moved indoors to private discos and other venues where the salsa music throbbed, the liquor tap ran free, and five years of fear gave way to joy and dancing.

Jorge remained at Miguel's side for the next twenty-four hours. Miguel ordered him to join him for a drink, but Jorge barely touched his. He never drank on duty—and when he was with Miguel, he was always on duty. He had never seen Miguel in such a state of euphoria. The boss was talking loudly and openly, spreading credit and thanks everywhere. Camaraderie was in the air. Jorge soberly assessed the situation and concluded that the time was right—and might never be better—to make his move.

BY DECEMBER 4, 1993, the celebrations in Cali had run their course, and hangovers gripped the cartel community like an epidemic. That same day in Medellín, Escobar's body was buried after a wake that attracted thousands of mourners who considered the dead drug boss a hero.

It was unlikely that anyone in Cali or Medellín happened to read that morning's *Washington Post*. But tucked inside, on page 21, was a story by the correspondent Douglas Farah in which the acting DEA administrator, Stephen H. Greene, offered two reasons why Escobar's death was important. "The first is symbolic, because Escobar was . . . thought by many to be above the law, untouchable," Greene said. The second, he added, was Colombia's promise now to "take all the resources used to hunt Escobar . . . and direct them at the Cali cartel."

Pablo's body was barely cold, and the United States was shifting its sights two hundred miles south to the backyards of Miguel and Gilberto. Washington wanted to go after the Cali traffickers immediately, if only to preempt a deal between the cartel and Attorney General de Greiff that might effectively pardon the drug bosses.

The cartel chiefs were not paying attention. They had grossly underestimated the threat from the United States. For all their international business dealings, the godfathers of Cali were unsophisticated, parochial men. They owned vast swaths of Colombian officialdom, but the rules were changing in the rest of the world.

The Cold War was over. Saddam Hussein had been driven out of Kuwait. Noriega was in prison. Escobar was dead. It required no special insight or geopolitical savvy for Jorge to realize that he was working for the next target of American power. Not that Jorge needed additional motivation. He was more than ready to move on.

A FEW DAYS AFTER the hangovers ebbed, but while the glow of good spirits lingered, Jorge approached the boss. He had just emerged from his sleeping quarters, and the phones were still silent.

"Don Miguel," Jorge began. "This is important."

"Yes—what is it?" The boss was surprised and turned to face him.

"We have prevailed over Pablo, thanks to God . . . with our families well and unharmed. Now, with Pablo dead—"

Jorge hesitated until Miguel motioned for him to continue.

"I believe this is the time for me to say good-bye."

"No." Miguel's tone was incredulous.

"I wonder, to whom should I make arrangements to resign?"

"No! No! No!" Miguel had turned adamant. "What are you saying? Don't even speak of such a thing."

"Of course, we can do this gradually, so that—"

"Absolutely not. No, you can't. You are one of us. You are family."

The rejection was so blunt and unequivocal that Jorge was not prepared to respond further. He saw the familiar pinched expression return to Miguel's face. How naive he had been. Jorge hadn't even considered the possibility that his resignation might anger the boss.

"How can you even think about leaving?" Miguel went on. "Good times are coming. Things will be much better, you'll see. And I've got plans for you. No, no—not now. You don't want to leave now. I need you."

El Señor needed him. That was something positive he could cling to. It made Jorge feel important. He still wanted out of the cartel, but he sensed it was time to pull back—to retain Miguel's goodwill and to avoid making him angry. This was no time to press the matter.

"Thank you, Don Miguel. Thank you very much," Jorge said. "Your confidence means a lot to me."

Miguel nodded and waved him away. The phones were ringing, and Mateo said a caller was holding for the boss. Another day in the Cali cartel was under way. Jorge left the room hoping that he hadn't come off as disloyal—that he hadn't made a dangerous mistake.

A new realization haunted him: maybe he could never quit.

PART TWO

The Cartel's Man
1993–1995

A LIFE SENTENCE

WITH PABLO ESCOBAR DEAD AND EIGHT GUYS FROM THE BLOQUE de Búsqueda posing for pictures over the drug lord's lifeless body, Jorge reassessed where he stood. The trophy photo should have been Jorge and his team of British commandos. But the only thing Jorge got out of his assignment hunting Escobar was what now appeared to be a life sentence in service to the Cali drug organization.

Not that Jorge regretted all, or even most, of his nearly five years in Cali. He still prized the time he spent with the British commandos. His intelligence work tracking Escobar—flying into La Catedral prison, designing the secret radiophone system, even the ill-fated bomb-smuggling operation in El Salvador—gave Jorge a dash of adventure and a taste for intrigue. And he felt like part of history for his secret role helping the United States convict Manuel Noriega of drug trafficking.

But there were wounds as well. His lost army reserve commission still hurt. He could no longer count on getting the security clearances necessary to do business with the Defense Ministry. And he still worried about the near miss in Miami, where he was almost lured into a federal sting while inspecting the Dragonfly bomber.

Jorge had little else to show for his efforts and personal sacrifice in the quest for Pablo Escobar—certainly not significant financial rewards. His monthly salary hovered around $1,000 a month, always paid in U.S. currency. It was a modest income, though by Colombian standards of the day equivalent to salaries of at least five times that amount in the States. It supported a very comfortable upper-middle-class lifestyle in Cali. So Jorge wasn't hurting financially—but he wasn't getting rich, either.

He could never seem to get enough cash together to build Lena's dream house. Having invested $15,000 in the Lot—pulling together $7,500 each from Lena's family and his own cash reserves—Jorge had too little left over for construction. He was constantly looking for new low-cost building materials. Jorge designed one version of their house envisioning its support columns made from used oil-drilling pipes.

His hopes for starting a private security business offered tantalizing promise of substantial income. All over Colombia, kidnappings were rampant. The targets tended to be affluent families, the very people who could afford costly security services and high-tech countermeasures. One full year in business, that's all it would take, he figured, to clear $200,000 on his way to his first million—all of it legit.

Jorge had always counted on the friendship and gratitude of the Gentlemen of Cali to endorse, if not invest in, his venture. He could even parlay his cartel contacts into business success, reasoning that being the security choice of the Cali godfathers would give him a major marketing advantage. Plus, with a small severance bonus—something in the range of about $30,000—he could easily launch his new enterprise.

But Miguel's flat rejection of his resignation had scrambled all of Jorge's prior assumptions. He wasn't going anywhere. He broke the news to Lena, who took the disappointment in grim silence.

"You will have to continue with them," she finally said in resignation.

"What else can I do?"

*   *   *

Jorge joined Mario del Basto for lunch one afternoon. They were directed to a table where José Estrada orchestrated the waitstaff laying out a feast for his guests. In the few years since leaving cartel security to Jorge and Mario, the former army sergeant had amassed millions in a personal fortune. He owned and operated not only warehouses used to store cocaine but also fleets of planes and boats used to move the drugs. Now he was branching out—building a multimillion-dollar state-of-the-art health clinic in a venture with several financial partners, including the Rodríguez Orejuela brothers.

The retired army sergeant had much in common with del Basto. They were close friends and godfathers to each other's children. Estrada encouraged Jorge and Mario to think about their families and to look for chances to make "real money." It was common practice for friends of the bosses to put up relatively small sums of money as investments in drug shipments and then to share in prorated returns once the loads were delivered. It was like an office betting pool—except that Jorge never played. Nor was he interested in following Estrada into the trafficking realm. He suspected that Mario dabbled in the Business, but he wasn't sure—and didn't want to know.

"Thanks, José. But I've got other plans," Jorge said again over lunch.

Estrada studied him for a moment, then turned back to del Basto and shook his head. "I don't know, Mario. How can we trust a man who doesn't want to be rich?"

THE NEW DEALS

PABLO ESCOBAR'S DEATH ENDED THE CARTEL WAR BETWEEN MEDEL-
lín and Cali, but not the hard feelings. Even in total victory, the
four Cali godfathers resented the millions they had spent defending
their families and underwriting the costly Pepes offensive. Friends and
operatives had been lost to the violence. It was not enough simply to
have prevailed. The Cali cartel wanted reparations—in blood or dollars.

The grieving and fearful Escobar family was trying desperately to
leave the country. Juan Pablo, the dead drug lord's teenage son, pleaded
with the U.S. embassy for permission with his sister and mother to seek
refuge in Florida. But the DEA chief Joe Toft was unmoved. "Even if
you helped put the whole Cali cartel in jail, we would not give you a
visa," Toft told him, according to Mark Bowden in *Killing Pablo*. The
family was effectively trapped in Colombia when the Cali bosses summoned Escobar's widow to discuss their price for peace.

María Victoria Henao Escobar was waiting in the lobby of the

InterContinental hotel when Jorge arrived a few minutes before ten o'clock one night.

"Good evening, señora," he greeted her, and then escorted her to his silver Mazda just outside the hotel's main entrance. She was traveling alone, without any bodyguards. She wore a simple blue silk dress and carried only a small purse. Jorge, too, was alone. He was also unarmed. After Pablo Escobar was killed, Jorge put away his personal Walther pistol.

Jorge held open the car door as María Victoria slipped into the backseat. He smiled, trying to put her at ease, and said, "The gentlemen are waiting. We will be there in about fifteen minutes." He got behind the wheel and adjusted his rearview mirror.

She appeared tense and fingered her purse nervously. Jorge felt sorry for her. It would have been inappropriate and insincere to offer the standard condolences: *I'm so sorry for your loss.* Instead, he said, "Please sit back and relax."

Nothing more was said as Jorge steered an unusually direct course through light nighttime traffic toward the rendezvous site. Security was minimal. He had made no effort yet to search her clothing or her handbag. Times had definitely changed. Soon, the car was approaching Alférez Real, a street named after the title of a book set in eighteenth-century Cali. The luxury residence at 151 Alférez Real was code-named the Novel. It was an isolated compound on the southern edge of the city with lush gardens behind twelve-foot walls and a massive wooden gate. The heavy door swung open as Jorge approached.

Armed security was more obvious inside the gates. Jorge pulled in to the last of ten parking spots and again checked his mirrors. His passenger was about to meet her dead husband's enemies, the men behind Los Pepes, the ruthless force that had killed friends, family, and business associates—and was even now threatening the lives of her children. She hesitated after stepping out of the Mazda and waited for Jorge to lead the way. She seemed fragile as a beefy guard pawed through harmless contents of her purse.

Jorge then led the way past sentries into the house, past brightly lit rooms to an office deep inside the compound. It was dimly lit, uncharacteristically subdued for Miguel, who typically liked his rooms drenched in light. All four godfathers waited there in leather chairs arrayed around a single empty seat. None of the men rose to greet her. There were no handshakes or polite greetings. Their expressions were stern. After a brief and pro forma introduction, Gilberto motioned her toward the empty chair.

"Sit down there," he said, his gruff manner fitting the mood of the room.

Gilberto recapitulated the costs in dollars and lost opportunity for everyone as a result of Pablo's wasteful and foolish war. The room grew more tense and uncomfortable even for Jorge. No one asked him to leave, but he decided to slip out early. From the adjoining room, Jorge could still hear pieces of the conversation. There were no histrionics and certainly no laughs. The new kingpins of Colombia's cocaine trade were presiding over the terms of surrender.

An hour later, María Victoria emerged, appearing tired but relieved. The widow and her family would not be harmed. What it cost her was never disclosed, and Jorge never asked.

THE WAR'S END MEANT that Cali traffickers could press ahead on negotiations for an amnesty deal with the government. None would have agreed to a jail term while Escobar was alive to hire prison yard assassins. Now they were safe. Talks with de Greiff were top secret, but what little Jorge gleaned raised his hopes for what the bosses were calling "a soft landing." The godfathers would quit the drug business, do a brief jail term, and emerge with their wealth intact, cleansed of all criminal liabilities. Jorge saw it as his own cartel exit plan as well.

The Rodríguez Orejuela brothers considered such a deal close enough that they convened a rare summit of cartel partners, held at one of Pacho Herrera's country estates—a modern dairy operation near Jamundí. Everyone of any rank in the organization attended, including the emerging trafficking heavyweights of the north Cauca valley.

Nearly one hundred bosses and their lieutenants met at a vacant farmhouse on the remote property. Guests were served steaks, shrimp, and lobsters catered by the InterContinental hotel. But spur-of-the-moment planning, which no doubt was good for security, had failed to account for luncheon seating or service. There was only one table with eight chairs. Diners stood around using car hoods and trunks as table-tops while consuming the feast out of cardboard and Styrofoam.

Jorge had been circling the farm property checking perimeter secu-rity, but he entered the farmhouse just as Gilberto climbed atop the lone table to address the gathering. Jorge found a vantage point in the back of the room with men who stood fanning themselves and waiting.

"As many of you know," Gilberto began, "we've been talking to the government for some time about terms for resolving old legal issues. There has been progress. We want to tell you what has been discussed."

He quickly ticked off the highlights: Bogotá would let them keep their wealth, their properties, and their businesses unrelated to narco-trafficking, and the government would impose only token prison terms. In return, traffickers would have to agree to immediately shut down all cocaine-processing labs in Colombia and, over the next six months, abandon the drug trade. "We can't do this alone or individu-ally," Gilberto said from the tabletop. "We do it together, or no deal."

He called on Miguel, who had on several occasions met directly with the attorney general. But as the two brothers exchanged places atop the table, the room erupted in shouts and murmurs.

"Six months? I can't do that. I just bought a new plane," one traf-ficker shouted. Others chimed in with similar objections—they had in-vestments that had to be paid off, major shipments in the pipeline, new business alliances, and financial promises to honor.

"I've got five families working for me. Who's going to take care of them?" another voice boomed over the din.

Miguel was having trouble restoring order. In the back of the room, Jorge caught bits of private conversations.

"Easy for those old guys to get out. They're already rich," muttered one.

"Yeah," replied a man next to him. "Let them go—but I can't re-tire."

If the Rodríguez Orejuela brothers were expecting a groundswell of enthusiasm, they were badly disappointed. Miguel finally had to shout to be heard over the discontent in the room. "This could be a once-in-a-lifetime deal—a last chance," he told them.

But a chorus of critics drowned him out again. "I need at least a year," someone shouted, to general agreement. "Yes, why can't they give us a year—or two, or three?" yelled another. Other voices encouraged tougher negotiations.

Business for the young Turks of the cartel had never been better. They had benefited most from the dismantling of the Medellín gangs, and they weren't ready to walk away. Furthermore, most of the younger drug operatives were unknown to Colombian law enforcement. No criminal charges were pending against them—not in Bogotá and not in the United States. To voluntarily surrender and make incriminating declarations was unacceptable.

In the back of the farmhouse, what caught Jorge most by surprise was the sheer rudeness of the crowd. Before Miguel could step down from his tabletop stage, many in the crowd were already walking out. It was a show of disdain that would have seemed dangerous, except that so many were doing it.

At the same time, Miguel and Gilberto seemed to shrug it off. The Grand Scheme of the entire Cali cartel quitting en masse would have made great theater—which was its primary political appeal. But the bosses had other options, starting with the financial power to buy off authorities and keep legal troubles at bay. The brothers would also continue negotiating their own private "soft landing," which Miguel preferred since he was determined to hold out for no jail time whatsoever.

So when the Grand Scheme collapsed on the farmhouse floor that afternoon, the only person in the room who winced was Jorge.

FAR FROM HEROIC

I N THE DAYS AND WEEKS FOLLOWING HIS FAILED RESIGNATION, JORGE struggled through a wrenching reality check. The notion that he was a cartel short-timer was as dead as Escobar. And after nearly five years working for Miguel, he could no longer tell himself he was an outsider. Jorge was a cartel fixture—and would be for as far into the future as he dared to look.

The only way to minimize feeling trapped was to throw himself into his work, making sure the bosses never lost confidence and hoping that time and patience served up some new options. But he also had to contend with new complications. Escobar's death had emboldened Colombian authorities, some of them eager to take on the Cali cartel. Others, grateful to the Gentlemen of Cali for their largesse and for helping fight Escobar, were nonetheless under mounting pressure from the United States to crack down hard on all traffickers. Inevitably, Jorge's security responsibilities were going to change.

That lesson was driven home by an incident even before the New

Year. Gilberto and about 150 friends were still celebrating Pablo's burial with dancing and music at an all-night party. The gala attracted a passing military patrol when the commanding officer noticed scores of parked cars attended by thugs and bodyguards. It had the unmistakable appearance of a mafia assembly. A quick phone call established that the party also lacked a permit required for such a large and late-running event.

Inside the party house, the music suddenly stopped when the military team burst in. Guards rushed to block all exits, and the officer in charge ordered everyone to line up. Each person was to produce identification and then leave through the front door. Gilberto feared his name would be recognized and he would end up in jail overnight, long enough for prosecutors to draft trafficking charges likely to keep him in custody—perhaps for years. He wasn't going to take that chance.

The godfather slipped into the kitchen and headed for a back door, only to find an armed guard already blocking his escape. At a big pot of vegetable soup simmering on the stove, Gilberto quickly scooped out a cup of the rust-red broth and poured it sloppily down his chin and the front of his white shirt. Bits of vegetables stuck in his beard and clung to his clothes. Again, he approached the back door, this time staggering and belching. The sentry regarded him as a vomit-soaked drunk and tried to turn him away.

"But I have to go—my wife will kill me," the unrecognized crime boss slurred.

When the guard shook his head and tried to ignore him, Gilberto unzipped his pants and began to urinate on the guard's boots.

"Goddamn it!" the sentry exploded. He grabbed Gilberto roughly and, without checking his ID, angrily shoved him out into the night.

For some, Gilberto's narrow escape added to the Chess Player's reputation for cleverness. For Jorge, it was an awakening to the new rules. He would no longer be protecting the bosses from assassins; Jorge would be protecting them from arrest. It was hardly the heroic undertaking he had signed on for.

News accounts reported plans to move the Bloque de Búsqueda headquarters from Medellín to Cali, another sign that legal pressures on the godfathers were about to escalate. Jorge saw nothing but trouble ahead. But—on a strictly sporting level—the challenge of keeping Miguel out of jail meant Jorge was going up against the combined forces of the Colombian government and its U.S. intelligence allies. Any security man skilled enough to frustrate such giants, even for a limited time, could take great pride in his work—and maybe someday end up with a lucrative career marketing his private protection services. It was the one potentially positive development he could see, and Jorge clung to it.

His role as chief of Miguel's personal protection team meant there was no end to Jorge's workday until Miguel retired for the night. During one typically long evening Jorge was waiting in the dark for Miguel to come out of a meeting in downtown Cali when he was approached by Memo Lara.

"Don Richard, how are you doing?" the senior *sicario* greeted Jorge with an uncommon heartiness. He seemed almost jolly. He said he came to wait for Miguel. It was very important. Jorge invited Memo to join him in his parked car.

Sitting with Jorge in the dim reflection of dashboard lights, Memo told a story that explained his good humor. The tale started with the *sicario's* discovery that his long-missing ex-girlfriend had come home— the ex-girlfriend who had betrayed him to her police captain lover, the ex-girlfriend whose family home Memo had been watching for nearly eight years.

"She was hiding in Japan," Memo told Jorge. "But I knew she would come home eventually."

The close quarters of the Mazda 626 began to feel claustrophobic as Memo went on. He said the ex-girlfriend had ventured to a salon in downtown Cali earlier that day, to a place for hair and nails and pampering. It took two hours. She left in a taxi, Memo said, with the hairdo she will wear to her funeral. Memo chuckled at the irony. Jorge tried not to react at all.

"Don Miguel needs to know that it's over," Memo said. "I wish to thank him."

Jorge understood. The godfathers had approved the ex-girlfriend's execution, no doubt a personal favor to Memo Lara. Cartel-sanctioned killings had become almost routine occurrences during the war with Pablo Escobar. But Memo's ex-girlfriend was no cartel combatant.

Neither was one of the accountants from José Estrada's warehouse business. He was gunned down driving away from his office one afternoon. Jorge questioned employee witnesses to the shooting—until Estrada called him into his office.

"Let's not go any further," Estrada said. "Unfortunately, nothing you do can bring him back to life."

"But we don't know why—"

"We don't need to know anything more. Drop it."

Again, Jorge understood. The accountant had been fired . . . at point-blank range. For whatever reason, it had been a sanctioned execution, an internal cartel enforcement action that was no one else's business. Jorge was now part of the cover-up—but that wasn't the only one.

A popular holiday salsa concert sponsored in downtown Cali by the Rodríguez Orejuela family after Christmas was disrupted and very nearly closed down early by a murder in the men's room. The shooter, a mid-level drug trafficker with one of the cartel's north Cauca valley organizations, had gunned down a romantic rival standing at the urinal. Miguel and Gilberto were furious. It most definitely was not a sanctioned hit.

"We don't care why you shot him," Miguel berated the man. "Don't you understand that we have a reputation in this city? You were disrespectful."

The man begged forgiveness, pledged his loyalty to the godfathers, and was spared punishment. For Jorge, it was simply his latest lesson in the baroque etiquette of cartel killings. At the scene, local homicide detectives were persuaded to wait outside the concert so as not to interrupt the music and disappoint the crowd or the cartel bosses. It was six hours after the killing when police finally inspected the murder scene. By then, potential witnesses had disappeared, along with the gunman, who was never identified to police. Covering up, it seemed, was one of Jorge's security duties.

Jorge was becoming more acutely aware of every big and little thing that disturbed him—about his job, about the cartel people around him, about his lack of options. For the first time he was seeing the crimes and corruptions of the cartel in personal terms. Cartel corruption now was Jorge's corruption—not because he committed murder and bribery, but because he lived with the knowledge of who did and who condoned it. Jorge protected the guilty. And he was feeling guilty about that himself.

VERY LATE ONE NIGHT in January 1994, four men working in the shadows removed a manhole cover and fed one end of a long hose down into the black hole. Passersby could have mistaken the men for a Cali utility crew. The other end of the hose was attached to a chlorine gas tank in the back of an unmarked pickup truck. One of the men opened a valve on the tank, releasing compressed gas that hissed into the hose line.

In Colombia, highly toxic chlorine gas was used in a number of industrial processes. Gas-filled tanks like the one in the pickup were imported from the United States on a regular basis, and spent gas canisters and tanks were then returned to the States for refills. Because they were routinely and regularly exchanged, the tanks were familiar to customs agents as legitimate imports and exports. Also, they were unlikely to be opened because of their harmful contents. And drug-sniffing dogs figured to be totally ineffective. Not surprisingly, the Cali cartel considered the tanks ideal for smuggling cocaine.

The big unknown on that January night was how best to purge the dangerous chlorine gas. That's what brought three men and their foreman to the manhole over a Cali sewer drain. It was a test disposal. And it seemed to be working.

The foreman walked the length of the hose line, from the truck to the hole in the street where it disappeared into the city drainage system. He and the others detected no leaks. But a few seconds later, a light vapor mist began to back up out of the manhole. Even in the darkness, it had a slight yellow-green tint and an acrid, throat-burning smell. The men moved back, but the vapor cloud was growing.

"Get away!" gasped the foreman. "It's going to kill us."

All four men bolted for the truck. Someone closed the drain valve, stopping the gas feed. The men clambered aboard the pickup and wheeled away, dragging the hose line for a couple of blocks until it was safe to stop and reel it in. Having dodged death, they drove home greatly relieved.

But as the pickup fled the neighborhood, the gases that had been drained into the sewer system spread silently through the underground pipelines. Noxious odors began seeping into houses where people slept, wafting up through substandard plumbing. In the predawn darkness, families awoke to terror and panic.

Police and rescue workers rushed to the neighborhood. They broke down doors in frantic efforts to drag victims to safety. Three children died in their beds. Adults gagged, retched, and collapsed. Taxicabs were drafted to rush the overwhelming number of sick and injured to hospitals. The Red Cross set up a field emergency center. An entire section of the city was rendered a disaster zone.

More than four hundred people were hurt that night. Twenty-three were hospitalized for severe lung burns, and some of those died in the weeks and months that followed. Press accounts called it an industrial accident. No responsible party was identified. No one suspected the Cali cocaine cartel. Neither did Jorge until the distraught foreman of the night disposal team came to him for comfort.

"I'm sick about it," he told Jorge. "But I can't talk to anyone but you."

Jorge didn't expect any cartel boss to admit a role in the disaster, but he wondered if they might make some sort of civic gesture—a financial gift or medical care for the victims or something. Instead, they pressed to complete the aborted test. Final disposal of the tank's chlorine gas contents was reset for another night, this time in a rural area well outside of town. And this time the team was cautioned by the godfathers to take more care—to protect each other, to dispose of the gases in an open area far from people, and to leave no evidence behind.

"Make sure you don't kill any cows," Chepe Santacruz told them.

* * *

IN THE POST-ESCOBAR DAYS of early 1994, the fifth anniversary of Jorge's association with the Cali cartel, his security assignment quickly evolved to management of what became Miguel's very own Praetorian Guard. A team of about fifteen motorcycle sentries worked in two-man or four-man shifts. Whenever Miguel moved out of his secure compound, motorcycle crews ran ahead of his path, checking for suspicious parked cars, watching for police or military roadblocks, reporting by radio whether or not the route was safe. At Jorge's insistence, they were unarmed.

"You are the early-warning system," he told his men. "You watch, listen, and report. Never engage."

In fact, the last thing Jorge wanted was to have his sentries get into a shooting exchange with police or military authorities. It would be a disaster for them and for the cartel—but especially for Jorge, who was determined to avoid being drawn into acts of violence. So long as Jorge was asked only to keep silent and cover up, he could still tell himself that he had not crossed the line that made him a party to murder. Then Jorge got an urgent assignment.

It was a summons from Miguel to come quickly. The boss had a Motorola radiophone belonging to someone else that he wanted to secretly monitor. Jorge had less than an hour to identify its frequencies. The instrument had to be returned before the owner discovered it was missing. Jorge and Carlos Alfredo, his radiophone expert, beat the deadline. They were not told who owned the Motorola or why the bosses wanted to eavesdrop. Nor did they ask. But Jorge learned a few days later what had happened next.

The radiophone owner was Claudio Endo, a lieutenant in one of the Cali cartel's smaller trafficking groups. He was an unpopular bully of a man whose *sicarios* had murdered a small-time trafficker well liked by *sicarios* employed by Pacho Herrera and Chepe. They complained, and the godfathers sanctioned Endo's execution.

On a Sunday morning in January, Endo used his compromised Motorola to advise his brothers that he was spending the day with his family at the ranch house. At another location, El Gamín—"the Delinquent"— and a team of gunmen were listening to the same message. They immediately rushed to their cars.

Moments later, Jorge received a call from Miguel advising him to monitor the captured Motorola frequency. "There may be something happening," the boss said.

Endo's ranch house was in a rural area. It was private, isolated, and very quiet until the moment El Gamín's team struck with an explosion of gunfire. Outside, Endo's bodyguards fell dead, and the raiding party kicked in the front door. Inside, the unarmed trafficker abandoned his wife and four-year-old daughter to flee for cover at the back of the house. He was discovered, still unarmed, in a bathroom. El Gamín waited until his team was assembled around the now-cowering bully who had murdered their friend. And then, as a group, the gunmen opened fire. It was the *sicario* way, giving everyone a share in the revenge. Investigators would count more than one hundred bullet wounds in the dead man.

Almost immediately after the carnage, Jorge's radiophone scanner picked up despairing conversations among Endo's three brothers. They shared what they knew about his death and agreed on who was behind it. One Endo brother who, like his dead sibling, was a cocaine trafficker, declared that he would round up all the rifles and gunmen he could muster "to teach those Rodríguez brothers a lesson."

But the other Endo boys—one a doctor and the other a lawyer—weren't so eager. "What? Are you crazy?" Jorge heard one shout into the phone. "Do you want them to kill us all?"

Jorge listened to the exchange with mounting anxiety. He saw the Endo family as a new and serious security threat, whether or not they retaliated immediately. But more troubling was Jorge's realization that he had unwittingly played a direct role in setting up the Endo killing. With those Motorola frequencies, he had provided key intelligence used by the hit team. Jorge had gone from covering up crimes to aiding and abetting.

ONE HONEST MAN

JORGE SALCEDO STILL HAD MANY FRIENDS IN THE COLOMBIAN MILI-
tary. One of them, a major at the Marco Fidel Suárez Air Base on
the east side of Cali, called to alert him that two C-130 cargo planes
were in the air, flying down from Medellín with their cargo holds full of
Bloque de Búsqueda equipment. Maybe Jorge would like to see what
came off the planes. "Come watch the show," said the air force officer.

The C-130s were airborne moving vans of the anticartel task force,
transferring the Bloque's headquarters from Pablo Escobar country to
Cali cartel country. Jorge grabbed his 35 mm motor-drive Canon camera and some lenses and rushed across town. As the cargo planes dis-
gorged all manner of sophisticated gear, cars, trucks, and surveillance
vans disguised as ambulances, Jorge was at the end of a nearby row of
hangars banging out photographs. He was especially interested in the
vehicles. If Jorge and his security crew were to stay a step ahead of authorities, they needed to know what the task force was driving. That
day, Jorge got pictures of the entire Bloque motor pool.

The Bloque's arrival came in March 1994 along with a surge in antinarcotics manpower dedicated to investigating and shutting down trafficking operations out of Cali. The godfathers took it calmly, anticipating only that they might have to exercise their checkbooks a bit more frequently.

The original military boss of the Cali Bloque had been a colonel who spent his entire 1993 tour without once leading a raid on any cartel operations, big or small. But the commanding officer did pay an occasional personal call on Miguel. And he once introduced the drug boss to Sergeant Humberto Valencia, the colonel's top aide. Valencia was promptly added to the cartel's secret payroll and code-named Ernesto. After the commanding officer moved on to a new assignment, Sergeant Valencia stayed in Cali as an aide to the colonel's replacement.

Heavy U.S. pressure had finally forced reorganization of the Bloque in Cali as well as relocation of its headquarters to the new heartland of Colombian cocaine trafficking. More money was poured into the effort, much of it provided by Washington. A new army colonel was assigned to lead the rejuvenated task force—and the new colonel was very different. Unlike the predecessor who had a friendly relationship with Miguel, the new man arrived eager to take down the cartel. He was openly ambitious, determined to win promotion and wear the sunburst insignia of a Colombian army general. He wasn't looking for money. He wanted military and political glory. Colonel Carlos Alfonso Velásquez figured to be a particularly dangerous man to the cartel.

Jorge tried to say as much to the boss. He had known the colonel as a boyhood friend. Their fathers were career military men who served together. The sons of generals had not stayed in touch into adulthood, but military acquaintances told Jorge that Velásquez was an honest, by-the-book soldier. He was also obsessive about military procedures, to the point that colleagues sometimes found him insufferable. His leadership style came off as prissy, pompous, and arrogant, compounded by a renowned lack of street savvy. "The man has no common sense," summed up an army friend.

Nonetheless, a man in the colonel's position was a threat to the cartel and to the Rodríguez Orejuela family. Jorge was puzzled by Miguel's apparent lack of concern. He didn't know at the time about Sergeant

Valencia, the cartel's mole on the colonel's staff. The man on Miguel's secret payroll had a desk just outside the new Bloque office of Colonel Velásquez.

A few days after Jorge photographed the unloading of task force equipment at the air base, he received another call from his friend the air force major. The CIA was hiding a strange airplane in a locked hangar. Did Jorge want to see it? The unauthorized inspection would have to be brief—and this time no cameras.

Jorge had never seen anything like it, an oddly proportioned single-engine aircraft that resembled a glider. Its seventy-one-foot wingspan was more than twice the length of its fuselage. Its skin was shiny aluminum with the insignia of Colombia's air force freshly applied to the sides. It was sleek and smooth, and Jorge couldn't help touching it, running his hands over its smooth finish. He peered into the cockpit, scanning the electronics-rich instruments. It was a magnificent spy plane, loaded with surveillance gear, specially equipped to fly missions at night.

The Condor—more formally known as a Schweizer RG-8 Condor SA2–37B—came stocked with night-vision sensors, photo- and video-recording systems, radio eavesdropping equipment, infrared heat-sensing instruments, and more. It was capable of extended flight—up to twelve hours aloft—and virtually silent operations even at low altitudes. In ranges over twenty thousand feet, it could track its prey virtually undetected. Jorge was especially impressed with the night-vision dome mounted under the plane.

It was an aviation-loving intelligence officer's dream machine. Even though the Condor was there to be used against his bosses, Jorge felt more envy than alarm. He wished he could ride along on a night mission. He would have to come up with some operational changes on the ground to counter what the Condor could see from the sky. This was part of the job that Jorge relished, a test of his skills—and against what he regarded as the best intelligence service in the world.

Until that day the Condor arrived, routine cartel security simply required keeping a low profile in public areas. At meetings or large gatherings—especially those involving any of the bosses—bodyguards took inconspicuous positions. Cars were parked out of sight behind gates and walls. But concealing cars and crowds was going to be a lot more complicated with authorities capable of looking down from the heavens—even in the dark. Jorge arranged for someone at the air force base to call and alert him whenever the spy plane launched.

The United States was obviously raising its stake in the Colombian drug war. The Condor in its locked hangar said it all: the Cali cartel had, as Jorge suspected, become Washington's new top villain.

NEGOTIATIONS THAT HAD BRIEFLY envisioned the mass surrender of all Cali traffickers were already abandoned, and secret contacts between Miguel and the attorney general continued at a halting pace—until the Rodríguez Orejuela brothers settled on a more audacious strategy. They would use the 1994 national election to buy the presidency.

Ernesto Samper, Colombia's ambassador to Spain, was the cartel family's pick. Jorge had no idea why or how the brothers selected the ambassador, but the cartel became the Samper campaign's biggest patron. Ledgers kept by the cartel's accountant, Pallomari, tracked Samper contributions from all corners of the Cali trafficking organization— $50,000 each from a dozen different smaller operatives, twice that from various mid-level bosses, $200,000 each from top lieutenants, and an initial ante of $800,000 from the godfathers. Samper's secret campaign fund eventually swelled into the millions, every dollar noted and recorded by Pallomari and his accountants.

As Election Day neared, pollsters said the presidential race would be close. It was razor's-edge close. Barely twenty thousand votes separated Samper from the runner-up, Andrés Pastrana, out of nearly six million votes cast. A runoff election extended the race—and the flow of cartel contributions—into midyear.

Samper's campaign officials became regular visitors to Cali. Sometimes Jorge was the driver who delivered them to meetings with Miguel and Gilberto. Sometimes he was posted outside Miguel's office when the campaign executives passed through. Sometimes the visitors left with gifts in the shape of shoe boxes, festively wrapped in colorful paper—Miguel's signature method of dispensing hundreds of thousands of dollars in cash.

Much of the U.S. currency that went to Samper's campaign came in shipments out of Mexico originating with Amado Carrillo Fuentes, the Juárez drug boss. He declared himself "the lord of the skies" and made prominent use of large aircraft to ship contraband and currency. His cash shipments to Cali were typically made using disposable jetliners.

Obsolete but airworthy Boeing 727s were widely available in the used-aircraft market. They could be purchased legitimately for under a million dollars—sometimes well under. With the cartel trying to move cash by the tons, the old jetliners provided much greater cargo capacity than cars, vans, or small planes and a less suspicious profile crossing borders. Once a shipment of currency was off-loaded at the Cali airport, or wherever, the jetliner was simply abandoned. By the time anyone noticed, the cash was long gone. The jet's owner would turn out to be fictional. Walking away from such planes was cheaper than paying 10 percent or more to overland couriers.

COLONEL VELÁSQUEZ, the new by-the-book task force commander, was settling into his Cali headquarters when the cartel decided to test Jorge's assessment that he was an honest man. The godfathers sent a local political figure, a man well connected with the Colombian military command, to lunch with the new commander at the InterContinental hotel. The test came with dessert.

The emissary talked about the Rodríguez Orejuela family. They weren't bad people, not like Pablo Escobar, he said. They would like to meet the colonel, he said, raising the promise of generous future benefits—as much as $300,000 as a demonstration of friendship. Velásquez jumped to his feet, glared in silence at the man across the table, and then stalked out of the restaurant without saying a word.

Later the same day, the Cali drug bosses were tipped by military sources that Velásquez had returned to his office and, rather than thinking it over, reported their offer to his superiors and to U.S. intelligence agents. Jorge had been right about Velásquez. The colonel remained a prickly and unlikable character, but he appeared to be someone the bosses couldn't buy. Jorge would have to find other ways to counter the colonel's task force.

A first line of defense was assembled just outside the garrison grounds where the Bloque was based. Jorge rented residences just beyond the gates and posted watchers in each home. Needy relatives of trusted bodyguards got free housing in exchange for keeping tabs on all traffic in and out of the military compound. Each watcher reported by radio to Jorge. And whenever Bloque vehicles left the base, Jorge's radio-equipped motorcycles followed them.

Just outside the garrison, on a hillside overlooking Velásquez's office, Jorge established a twenty-four-hour electronic listening post. From an apartment with a view of the office building, Jorge could monitor and record much of what transpired anywhere near the Bloque's military chief. He tapped the colonel's office phone. He had a low-level transmitter installed in the office IBM computer. It picked up any conversations held in the reception area just outside the colonel's private office.

Everything intercepted over the colonel's phone or from the transmitter in the outer office was recorded. Jorge made regular visits to check on the recordings. Many times he sat with headphones and monitored live communications.

Colonel Velásquez ordered periodic electronic sweeps for eavesdropping devices, but the same Cali electronics experts who installed the original devices for the cartel always conducted the sweeps. Jorge left nothing to chance.

He was listening in to a live phone exchange one afternoon when Jorge heard Velásquez receive an intriguing tip about suspicious activity at the airport. Cargo was being unloaded from a white jetliner with no markings. It was parked in an area reserved for private planes.

"Don't let it leave; we're on our way," Velásquez barked to the caller.

Jorge took off his headset and reached for a radiophone. He called José Estrada, who answered in a jovial voice: "Richard, how's it going?"

"Bueno, bueno," said Jorge. "But tell me, José—do you have anything going on with a white plane at the airport?"

"Jesus Christ! How did you know?"

Jorge explained quickly and Estrada clicked off. At that moment he was standing in the shade cast by a big white Boeing 727. A work crew was nearby leaning against a dump truck already loaded with bulky sacks of cash they had just transferred from the jetliner. It had been time for a rest and smokes.

"Get out—move it now!" Estrada bellowed. "The Bloque is coming."

Everyone scattered. The truck lurched into gear and headed for an airport exit road. It cleared the intersection at a perimeter road just as the convoy of Bloque trucks and jeeps slowed to turn in to the airport grounds. The dump truck's cargo: six tons of bagged five-, ten-, twenty-, and hundred-dollar bills.

Two CIA FIELD AGENTS joined the task force and set up living quarters inside the Bloque garrison. Jorge intercepted their order for installation of a cable television system. Cartel technicians posed as cable guys to install a modified transmitter in the cable box. Its signal was very low and difficult to detect. It operated off the cable box power supply, so it never needed battery replacement.

"All we have learned is that they drink a lot of beer," Jorge reported to Miguel some time later. It never produced any useful intelligence, but Jorge always took pride in having bugged the CIA.

The U.S. intelligence operatives soon returned the favor, however, and planted a listening device in the offices of Miguel's sister Amparo. The boss was tipped to its presence and sent Jorge to locate and remove it. Jorge used a signal-detection device to sweep the space for radio waves. As he moved near an office bookcase, the device lit up and sounded a loud, rapid "beep . . . beep . . . beep . . . beep." An instant later it went silent. Monitoring agents must have turned if off. Jorge examined every surface of the bookcase but found nothing. The bugging device seemed invisible. He called Miguel to report his frustration.

Two days later, after Miguel had conferred with a secret source, he had a precise description. The transmitter was crafted to look like a piece of wood mounted under a shelf. It will appear to be an ordinary structural brace, the boss said. "Don't worry about doing damage; destroy whatever is necessary. Just find it," Miguel told him.

It was no wonder that even Jorge's trained eye had missed it. Following Miguel's directions, Jorge took a hammer and chisel to what still appeared to be nothing more than a strip of wood. Once it was dislodged, he studied what was a marvel of design. There were no markings on it of any kind, but "C-I-A" might as well have been stamped on it in big red letters. Jorge wished he could meet the engineer behind it.

Jorge was also in awe of the boss's intelligence information. "How did you know?" he couldn't help asking. Miguel took the question as a compliment.

"Zúñiga," he said proudly.

Zúñiga was General Camilo Zúñiga, the military boss who had assigned Colonel Velásquez to head the Bloque de Búsqueda. Zúñiga was the commanding general of the Colombian armed forces, Bogotá's counterpart to the Pentagon's chairman of the Joint Chiefs of Staff, the job that Jorge's father had been denied nearly thirty years before.

And now Jorge was being told that Zúñiga, of all people, was a friend of the godfathers of the Cali cartel.

SEX, SPIES, AND VIDEOTAPE

THE BLOQUE DE BÚSQUEDA HAD MOVED INTO CALI WITH ONE broad mission—to find and arrest the cartel godfathers and build trafficking charges against them. Years of polite or benign neglect of the Cali bosses were over. And Jorge suddenly had his hands full.

Electronic surveillance of Colonel Velásquez and his office produced hours of recordings that Jorge meticulously logged and stored. He often took tapes home so he could listen to them at all hours. His diligence helped spot the colonel's early use of an informant from Cali's social elite—a woman code-named Diana.

Jorge also detected a rapid evolution in their relationship. Over the span of a few weeks, their brief conversations kept getting longer. Colonel Velásquez often dispensed with business matters and spent more time inquiring into Diana's personal well-being. He arranged to receive some of her reports over dinners. And the married colonel's telephone flirtations often made Jorge groan.

One day, he was listening live when Diana said that a number of armed men were patrolling the third floor of a Cali medical building. "Someone in there must be very important," she told Velásquez. "I don't know who it is, but he has many guns."

Jorge knew immediately that it was Pacho Herrera. The youngest godfather was receiving treatment for a skin ailment or allergy at the upscale Clínica de Occidente. Jorge relayed a warning, and Pacho promptly vacated the clinic. A short time later, the woman told Velásquez about a social function attended by Marta Lucía.

Jorge reported to Miguel that the colonel had a female spy dangerously close to the Rodríguez Orejuela family. "Who is she?" the boss demanded.

"The colonel calls her Diana—probably a code name," Jorge said. "And I may be wrong, but I think she and the colonel are getting close, personally."

Miguel broke into an uncustomary grin. "Really?" he said. It was as if Jorge had just told him that his beloved América de Cali soccer club had won a big game.

"Do you think she would work with us?" the boss asked. Jorge could only shrug. He had no idea who she was or how to reach her. But Miguel was already plotting and figuring that "a few embarrassing photographs might get him to back off."

Perhaps the colonel who could not be bought could be blackmailed. Miguel was confident he could obtain the spy's name. He didn't tell Jorge, but he would shortly call Sergeant Valencia, who was sitting just outside the colonel's private office.

ROMANCE BLOOMED in the Rodríguez Orejuela family early in 1994. Gilberto's eldest daughter, Claudia, announced in April that she would be married in mid-May to the son of a retired general from Bogotá. They sent out notices to friends and family to save the date—Saturday, May 14. Unfortunately for the daughter of a mobster, among those saving the date was a raiding party from the Bloque. Colonel Velásquez planned to crash the formal reception with a company of heavily armed men. Nabbing the father of the bride would be a public relations sensation for the Bloque, a moment of political glory for the wannabe general in Cali.

Gilberto was appalled to learn that Colonel Velásquez planned to invade his family's wedding party. "The son of a bitch," he said, was trying to ruin his daughter's big day. The Chess Player had Sergeant Valencia to thank for alerting the family to Velásquez's wedding day plot. The sergeant also identified Diana—the colonel's spy—as Dolly Buendía de la Vega.

Dolly was in her mid- to late thirties, the ex-wife of a Popayán rancher, and known for her legendary temper. Her marriage had ended in an angry scene still gossiped about across the region. As the story went, she came home to the ranch early one afternoon to find her husband entertaining two or three of his girlfriends in the family swimming pool. Dolly's last wifely act was to jump back behind the wheel, squeal the tires, and steer her fishtailing car into the pool as husband and naked guests fled in panic.

Jorge knew the story—and, coincidentally, he knew Dolly. She had been a neighbor about ten years earlier when Jorge lived alone in Cali's upscale Parque Versalles apartments. They lived on separate floors and occasionally ran into each other in the elevator or by the pool. They were friendly, but not friends.

Perfect, concluded Miguel. Jorge would assume management of Dolly the double agent and direct the blackmail scheme against Velásquez. Dolly had already signed on after a preliminary secret meeting with Chepe Santacruz. They had mutual friends that brought them together. And he offered her a lot of money—much more than Velásquez was paying. The godfather told her that a man named Richard would call.

"Oh, it's you!" Dolly said, smiling in recognition after Jorge introduced himself the next day as Richard. She remembered his face, though not the name. She expressed no surprise that he was an agent for the Cali cartel. Jorge was grateful for that. He was also happy to renew the old acquaintance. Dolly was still a playful, flirtatious, sexy beauty with expressive eyes.

They were meeting for breakfast at the Hotel Dann restaurant downtown. The conversation opened with a decade's worth of catching up. She was now the single mother of a teenage girl, independent, and trying to make it on her own. She took on challenges with a feisty good humor that Jorge found especially endearing. He understood why the straight-arrow colonel wanted to break a few rules with her. Regarding her service to the Bloque, she told Jorge that she had nothing against the Rodríguez Orejuela family, that she only helped Velásquez because he paid her $250 a week, and that she needed the money. It was an impressively generous stipend, they both agreed. Indeed, she was making as much as Jorge. And the colonel was paying her with public money while conducting a very personal affair. Both facts grated on Jorge.

He had grown to dislike Velásquez even before learning about the colonel's private relationship with Dolly. As Jorge listened to all those phone intercepts, Velásquez came off as an officious bureaucrat. Aides to the colonel complained about him to each other and in phone conversations with their wives. Jorge heard it all and decided quite independently that Velásquez was as insufferable as some of the corrupt officers he so despised—which of course made it easier for Jorge to throw himself into a blackmail plot to destroy the man.

"Have you done anything with Velásquez besides eat and drink with him?" Jorge asked, trying not to be too direct. But Dolly knew he was asking whether they had sex.

"Yes," she said. "Sometimes we have drinks, then go to a motel—the Campo Amor." Dolly's tone was matter-of-fact. Jorge just nodded. She went on: "I have to resist him, or I'm afraid Alfonso would go to the motel every night."

To Jorge in his new role as a blackmailer, it sounded too good to be true. But he pressed on. He asked Dolly whether she could arrange for another visit to the motel as early as next week. Probably, she said, shrugging. Jorge suggested Monday. She agreed.

"There will be cameras," Jorge said. "Cameras? Really . . . ?" For the first time, she faltered slightly, but only for a moment. "Yes, of course," she said.

*   *   *

DOLLY AND VELÁSQUEZ ARRIVED AT Tangos y Rancheras, the colonel's favorite bar, on that Monday night sometime after ten o'clock. Their favorite booth was available. They sat close enough to steal an occasional kiss. Dolly made sure some of their embraces lingered an extra breath or two—for the photographer in the shadows across the room. It was Jorge, sitting at another table with one of the cartel's female radio dispatchers as his faux date. His Canon camera and motor drive were concealed in a black bag with an opening just big enough for the lens. He used a remote triggering device to snap off pictures at an ultraslow shutter speed to compensate for the bar's dim lighting conditions. The bar music blared louder than usual that night to cover up the noisy shutter and the whir of his motor drive. Jorge had paid the bartender for that extra volume—and for the perfect table arrangements.

The Motel Campo Amor was a fifteen-minute drive away. Its green and red marquee featured biblical symbols of temptation—the serpent and apple from the Garden of Eden. And lusty temptation was essential to this motel trade. In Colombia, generic motels cater to erotic fantasy more than to a good night's sleep. And Campo Amor was one of the finer establishments.

Management customarily paid special attention to protecting the privacy of its customers. High walls provided the first line of defense. Inside the compound, clients parked their cars in private garages where a personal concierge greeted them and showed them to their suites. The rooms were air-conditioned, came with fully stocked minibars, and had private closed-circuit television streaming free porno movies twenty-four hours a day.

The Campo Amor was owned and operated by mid-level traffickers, good and loyal friends of Miguel's, who were eager to help the cartel. They provided Jorge access to a pair of adjacent rooms.

Earlier in the day, Jorge and his men had rigged the rooms for secret recordings. A camera was mounted in an air-conditioning duct high on the wall. Its lens peered down through louvered slats with an excellent view of the bed. Jorge had taken precautions to cover over the camera's record-indicator light to prevent a telltale red glow from giving it away. He had also walked around the room himself to see if the hidden camera was visible from any part of the suite—even stretching out in various positions on the bed to satisfy himself that it was reliably camouflaged. A trail of cables strung down the aluminum air-conditioning duct connected the hidden camera to a monitor and recording system set up in the next room.

Jorge had double-checked all the equipment. Then his radio hissed with a terse alert from his man Enrique Sánchez: "They're here." Jorge activated the video camera in the next room. The television monitor in front of him flickered on. And Jorge was watching an empty king-sized bed in a vacant, silent room.

In the adjacent private garage a second cartel agent dressed in the Campo Amor uniform—black slacks and a white shirt—received the couple, checked them in, and escorted them to their room. Watching his monitor in the next room, Jorge could hear the couple's door open, and then Dolly and Velásquez stepped into the frame.

The colonel was eager, and matters proceeded with unrestrained alacrity. Jorge reported soon after to the godfathers, describing the encounter as "a quickie." It consumed less than forty-five minutes of tape—from the couple's fully clothed arrival to their fully clothed departure. But at the heart of the recording was a blackmailer's dream.

THE NEXT DAY, like adolescent boys watching their first dirty movie, the cartel godfathers gathered to watch the sex tape. As they played it and replayed it, Chepe Santacruz and Gilberto were especially derisive, mocking the colonel's every move and utterance. "Oh, that's terrible," Chepe howled more than once. Gilberto chided: "He should learn how to treat a lady." When the reviews were all in, Velásquez was declared a lousy lover, and Jorge was hailed a hero. The original tape was sent to a cartel video editor who made multiple copies and pared down one version to about ten or twelve minutes—just the highlights, Gilberto ordered.

The secret recordings remained a secret for another ten days—until the morning of Claudia's wedding day, May 14, 1994. The cartel bosses reconvened to draft a letter to Colonel Velásquez. Gilberto handled the typing as the others chimed in with suggested language. The note accused the colonel of going too far and demanded that he mind his own business. Chepe insisted that they belittle Velásquez with a very personal insult, "to bring him down." So, Gilberto tapped out one more sentence questioning the colonel's sexual prowess.

The letter went into an envelope along with one of the edited tapes and twelve still photos from the bar. At ten o'clock in the morning a friendly retired army captain delivered the cartel's package to the Bloque garrison. He told Velásquez that two men on motorcycles had forced him, under threat of violence, to convey the package immediately. The skeptical colonel disappeared into his private office to review the envelope's contents—and he remained alone in his office chain-smoking cigarettes for more than two hours. Sergeant Valencia reported every reaction directly to Miguel.

In the end, the colonel who could not be bought also could not be blackmailed. Instead, Velásquez confessed. He grimly contacted his superiors to report the attempted coercion. He also admitted improper relations—with a woman who not only was not his wife but was also one of his paid informants.

Velásquez was deeply humiliated, but he was still the Bloque's army commander—and he still expected May 14, 1994, to end as a day of personal glory. The wedding was scheduled for that afternoon, and hundreds of guests were expected at a catered reception near Jamundí, at a ranch just south of Cali. The colonel wanted the last laugh, arresting Gilberto at the wedding reception.

"So, they call him the Chess Player," Velásquez seethed in a private moment with Valencia. "Well, tonight . . . he gets a big surprise from me."

THE BLOQUE'S RAIDING PARTY—a company of soldiers decked out in combat gear, sidearms, and assault rifles—rolled out of the military garrison in a convoy of troop carriers shortly after sunset. Tag teams of cartel motorcycles joined them in downtown Cali traffic, darting in and out of the military trucks and making regular radio reports describing locations, speeds, and directions—all of it in code.

Those reports were, in turn, received over a squawking radio on a private patio where Jorge calmly translated the coded messages to three men in tuxedos—the brothers Gilberto, Miguel, and Jorge Eliécer, the youngest known as Cañengo. Each brother sat back, relaxed, nursing a glass of Chivas Regal from a bottle in the blue velvet bag. The patio was quiet except for the clink of glasses and the periodic radio reports. There was no alarm. Jorge and the tuxedoed brothers all knew where the convoy was headed.

At a brightly lit and noisy ranch house far from the Rodríguez Orejuela men, four hundred people in gowns and tuxes were partying to a live band. It was the official site of Claudia's wedding reception—but no members of the family were present.

An army troop carrier roared past the ranch house valet station, followed by the rest of the Bloque convoy. Uniformed men in black balaclava ski masks poured out, assault rifles ready, setting off a chorus of frightened screams among the partygoers. No shots were fired. The raiders secured the perimeter, rounded up the guests, and demanded: "Where is Gilberto Rodríguez Orejuela?"

The fancy party at the ranch house turned out to be an elaborate decoy. Its guest list included political and social elites, but no bride and groom and no godfathers—not even nephews, nieces, or cousins of godfathers. The wedding itself had been changed to a small, private affair held that morning in a village north of Cali. Families and close friends then reassembled for a reception at another secret location in the city, while the faux party went on as planned without them. The Rodríguez Orejuela brothers skipped both receptions to hold their own private Chivas Regal party at a cartel safe house.

Gilberto grinned as Jorge relayed the last radio report from the decoy site. "Maybe I have time for a dance with my daughter," he chortled.

"No, no. Let's go straight home," Miguel countered. And Gilberto nodded. He was only joking. Colonel Velásquez had been doubly humiliated, and everyone agreed with Miguel's final assessment: "We've had a good day."

THE VULTURE ACCOUNT

Gilberto had a favorite saying: "Money buys anything." Proof of that was everywhere. The Cali cartel owned policemen, generals, and politicians . . . jetliners, yachts, safe houses, and mansions . . . accountants, pilots, and professional killers. Its money bought silence, loyalty, murder—even a constitution customized to its needs. But corruption also came in small sizes.

In the spring of 1994, an Argentine soccer agent threw a lavish party for the Rodríguez Orejuela brothers at a mountain retreat outside Cali. The agent's private plane delivered crates of Argentine beef, cases of wine, his personal chef, and a dozen exotic dancers from Buenos Aires. Each of the dancers dressed in América de Cali team jerseys and shorts.

After putting on a rousing cheerleader-style show, the dancers mingled and made clear that they were also available for entertainment services of a more intimate nature. Party guests, however, were more interested in face time with the bosses Miguel and Gilberto than with grabbing a quickie down the hall. The girls ended up bored and under-employed on the party sidelines.

The lead dancer—a woman of about thirty and the oldest of the performers—pulled Gilberto aside for a special request. "I want that girl for me," she said, pointing across the room to the girlfriend of the cartel's publicity chief, Julian Murcillo. Jorge was sent to summon her.

"No way!" she responded moments later to the proposition.

Gilberto pulled a fist-sized wad of U.S. currency from his pocket. As the godfather peeled away individual bills, he asked the reluctant young woman, "How many of these would it take?" Each folded bill was $100.

"Please—" she protested. But Gilberto flashed more bills. She hesitated. "What about Julian?" Her boyfriend was just across the room.

"Julian will be far away." And then Gilberto resumed counting the bills: "You want one . . . ? Two . . . ? Three . . . ?"

Now she was torn. Jorge knew that feeling. On the one hand, he loved his security and surveillance work, he loved gadgets, and he relished challenging assignments. But he was repelled by the violence and troubled by the reach of cartel corruption. Sometimes he felt so . . . owned.

Gilberto was still counting: "Eight . . . ? Nine . . . ? Ten . . . ?"

"That's enough," she almost whispered.

Gilberto dispatched Julian down the mountain on a ruse, to pick up a pair of phantom party guests the boss said would be waiting at the InterContinental hotel. A select group of spectators was ushered into a bedroom suite. Miguel, Gilberto, José Estrada, the Argentine agent, and Jorge stood along the walls as the seduction began.

"You just relax," said the dancer, who touched the girl gently, circled her, and took control of the moment. The older woman was masterful, slowly undressing, caressing, and kissing the girlfriend. Within a few minutes it seemed that neither woman was aware of the men or conscious that they were performing for an audience. Jorge no longer worried about Julian's girl. She clung to the dancer, trembled at her touch, moaned and gasped, and seemed only to want more. When it was over, Gilberto stepped to a nightstand and dropped the ten bills next to the girlfriend. She stopped him.

"Half for her," she said with a nod to the dancer.

Jorge was struck by the transformation. Money had turned the sweet kid into a prostitute, once again proving Gilberto's maxim. But that was nothing compared to the cartel bosses' next trick.

"WE DID IT! We bought a president," declared Miguel Rodríguez Orejuela, banging a triumphant fist on his desk.

It had cost the Cali godfathers millions of dollars, but on a night in June 1994, Ernesto Samper—the cartel's man in the Liberal Party—eked out the narrowest of victories in a runoff election to become Colombia's president-elect.

Vote totals were so close that every contributor to Samper's campaign could take some credit for the win. But the Cali cartel's secret gifts, totaling more than $6 million, vastly exceeded anyone else's generosity. Jorge considered it an unseemly development for a proud democracy like Colombia's, but he hoped such a high-level friend might hasten a negotiated surrender, or soft landing, for the godfathers.

Cartel leaders were so convinced of good times ahead that they requested vacations long delayed by the cartel wars. Mario del Basto, for one, planned to attend World Cup soccer matches in the United States. In his absence, Jorge would have solo responsibility for cartel security—and more.

On the eve of Mario's departure, he arranged for Jorge to meet one of the cartel's key informants inside the elite police antinarcotics command. Captain Efrén Buitrago was attached to the police side of the joint task force. He looked about thirty years old, slim, fit, and about five feet eight. It was Buitrago's self-importance that Jorge disliked immediately. Del Basto felt the same. He called the captain El Buitre, "the Vulture." The man thought far too highly of himself, especially for a crooked cop, Jorge concluded.

The informant handoff was accomplished in broad daylight at a popular farmers' market in the city. Mario warned Jorge to beware of the police captain's irritating gamesmanship. He often stiffed his handler by holding back information and waiting to share his best tidbits directly with Miguel.

"I don't like him," Mario confessed to Jorge, "but he is dear to Miguel."

Buitrago had a corporal with him who stayed so close and was so eager to do the captain's bidding that Jorge dubbed him "the Shadow." He could never remember the corporal's real name.

At the farmers' market, Jorge was given an electronic pager that would signal him whenever Buitrago had information. They agreed that upon receiving such a signal, Jorge would return to the same produce market. Buitrago's alerts were invariably helpful. He reported to the cartel which bank accounts were being investigated, which phones were being tapped, what addresses were to be raided, and who among the cartel operatives was under surveillance.

For his part, Jorge saw to the regular care and feeding of Buitrago. The routine weekly bribes and occasional bonus payoffs were customarily made in person and, in his case, in cash. Even after Mario returned from his soccer holiday, Jorge kept the Buitrago account. It gave him a sweeping intelligence overview. Jorge had eyes, ears, and eavesdropping equipment on both the police and the military sides of the joint task force—yet it accounted for only a portion of the cartel's pervasive infiltration of Colombian institutions. In the organization's strictly compartmentalized intelligence system, Miguel and the other bosses all had their own high-level contacts as well.

It was no wonder that U.S. authorities were impressed. Cartel intelligence was superior to the Colombian government's. A story in *The Washington Post* on Thursday, June 16, 1994, quoted an unnamed U.S. source acknowledging the cartel's advantage, telling the reporter Douglas Farah: "Every operation against [the cartel] has been compromised. It is seemingly impossible to mount an operation in Cali . . . without their knowing about it." American drug agents referred to the cartel security network in awe as "the Cali KGB."

THE RODRÍGUEZ OREJUELA BROTHERS were still celebrating their $6 million investment in the Colombian presidency later in June when a set of police wiretap recordings was leaked to the press. The disclosure was later tied to the outgoing DEA chief at the U.S. embassy in Bogotá.

One of the so-called narco-tapes captured a conversation in which Miguel could be heard discussing a $2 million cartel payment to the Samper campaign. Overnight, political triumph turned to scandal.

The losing candidate, Andrés Pastrana, called on Samper to renounce the election outcome and agree to a new round of balloting. The United States threatened to cut off financial support to the Bogotá government.

Jorge followed the breaking news with apprehension. Samper's ties to Cali traffickers threatened his presidency even before he was sworn in. He denied accepting cartel money, but his own campaign aides finally confessed to receiving it on Samper's behalf. He took office badly wounded, fighting for his political life. The Rodríguez Orejuela brothers tried to help, firing off a letter flatly denying that they contributed to the campaign.

That Samper survived was thanks largely to Liberal Party control of congressional hearings into the scandal. But it was clear immediately that any cartel hopes to benefit from a friendly administration were at best delayed. In fact, law-enforcement pressures on the cartel mounted with Samper desperate to prove, at least to Washington, that he was moving against traffickers. Hopes for a soft landing receded—again.

ONE EVENING IN JULY, Jorge was at his listening post just outside Bloque headquarters going through a day's supply of newly recorded phone taps. One exchange caught his attention. A raid was apparently scheduled for the next day and a site identified only by a number. Jorge realized that it matched the street address of Pallomari's accounting operations downtown. Jorge called to warn him.

"Yeah, we heard something may happen," Pallomari responded, having already been tipped from one of the cartel's inside sources at the Bloque. He assured Jorge there was nothing to worry about, that all the books were in order, and that everything was legitimate. "We're just businessmen. We have nothing to hide."

The next day, Jorge was in Jamundí, south of Cali, when his radio crackled with reports from his motorcycle security crews. "Alert one . . . alert one," came the first coded message signaling an army convoy on the move. Jorge's men were in traffic with the convoy, reporting its every move. They were heading westbound . . . then northbound . . . then proceeding toward downtown Cali. Finally, the convoy stopped outside Pallomari's building. Troopers were pouring out of cars and vans and rushing inside. Jorge ordered his men to back off, to leave the site before they were noticed, and he rushed back to join the godfathers.

Pallomari not only had ignored Jorge's warnings to leave but also had left crates of records vulnerable to seizure. At first, the Rodríguez Orejuela brothers seemed surprisingly sanguine. Jorge learned that a key figure in the prosecutor's office was on the cartel payroll and, as the bosses predicted, Pallomari was released the next day. But not before the Chilean accountant had answered a few simple questions like, who's your employer? Pallomari responded truthfully that he was business manager for the Rodríguez Orejuela family. It was the wrong answer.

The brothers had expected him to deny, deny, deny . . . and lie— whatever it took to deflect all attention away from the family and the cartel. The last thing he was supposed to do was say he worked for the family. Pallomari compounded that mistake by having no glib answer to explain away the vast sums of cash that flowed through his supposedly legitimate business accounts. As a liar, the accountant was a disaster.

Confronted with details about Pallomari's poor performance, Gilberto exploded. He put in the harshest of terms sentiments that Jorge shared. The accountant was "an idiot" and "a dangerous man," especially to his friends, Gilberto complained.

"You know, they say they had to hit him once to get him to start talking," the godfather said. "Then they had to hit him twice to get him to stop."

Gilberto may have been joking, but he was not amused. He declared Pallomari "a big problem," which under certain circumstances might have attracted a visitor named Memo Lara or Freckles or the Delinquent.

But killing the accountant would require unanimous agreement by all four godfathers, and Miguel strongly objected. He still valued Pallomari's meticulous bookkeeping and relied upon the accountant in running daily operations. Gilberto acceded, and Miguel assured his brother, "We'll keep him out of sight; he'll be fine." They also agreed, however, that Pallomari would have to change his statement to the Bloque, sign a letter or swear out an affidavit denying that he worked for the brothers.

Pallomari complied, knowing that the safety of his wife and two young sons hung in the balance. Under the terms of Pallomari's controversial release from Bloque custody, he was supposed to return to resume his interrupted interrogation. Instead, he went into hiding. That, too, was under explicit orders from the cartel.

THE MOTHER LODE OF DOCUMENTS and cartel records scooped up by Bloque raiders at Pallomari's expense finally gave Colonel Velásquez a big victory, his first real measure of satisfaction in what had been a one-sided contest of wits. He immediately parlayed the investigative leads from those records to pinpoint and raid other cartel sites. Pallomari's computer data center was next. It wasn't all of the accountant's records, but the evidence haul was truly sensational. It documented high-level payoffs, complete with names, dates, and amounts. Never before had the Cali cartel's privacy been so thoroughly violated.

Cartel ledgers revealed monthly stipends to police officers ranging from $275 to $1,250. Several hundred policemen were fired or reassigned in the weeks after the raids. Key insiders, including Bloque informants Valencia and the Vulture, remained undetected. Their funding records were kept on separate books. They were not yet in danger, but elsewhere there were signs of unraveling.

With leaked accounting records producing a stream of press exposés, Samper seemed forced into anticartel postures. Colonel Velásquez kept sending out raiding parties, chasing cartel assets and personnel. The ominous developments had Miguel constantly on the verge of migraines and increasingly prone to dark suspicions. He kept Jorge closer than ever, demanded extra security, and fretted about who was taking advantage of his family's difficulties.

And there were fresh problems in Panama. A large drug shipment had been seized. These things happened, of course, but this time Miguel suspected treachery. Jorge couldn't tell if it was overreaction or legitimate concern. Either way, he sensed trouble. Amid escalating fear and paranoia, mere suspicion could be deadly.

HER NAME WAS EMILIA

AUGUST 15, 1994, WAS MIGUEL'S FIFTY-FIRST BIRTHDAY. HE WAS spending it at home entertaining family and a few friends between the inevitable phone calls but a reduced schedule of business meetings. Security demands were lighter than normal, and Jorge anticipated being home for dinner with Lena and the children—a rare treat. Meanwhile, he made his rounds troubleshooting various communications network problems, checking on the needs of his motorcycle security teams, and dropping by the Bloque listening post for the latest wiretap recordings.

Late in the afternoon came the call he dreaded. It was Mateo, the boss's assistant. Miguel had decided to get out of the house after all and was organizing a trip to the Desert. The site was a Pacho Herrera ranch northeast of town with an unlikely code name for a lush luxury resort. It was a favorite party spot with a spacious hacienda surrounded by soccer fields, pools, tennis courts, stables, a cockfighting arena, even a lake

with an imported sand beach. Though disappointed, Jorge left immediately to secure the ranch for what he assumed was Miguel's last-
minute birthday party.

A year earlier, Miguel's elaborate fiftieth celebration was hosted by
Wife No. 4, Marta Lucía, with orchids, torch-lit promenades, and
keepsake silver napkin rings etched with "MRO-50." Such extrava-
gances were definitely out this year—too many troubles on all fronts . . .
legal, political, and business.

Loss of the big cocaine shipment through Panama weighed on the
godfathers. They suspected an insider leak. Miguel had summoned
Rhadamés Trujillo to Cali for a postmortem on the costly incident.
Jorge ran into him by chance at the InterContinental hotel. They hadn't
seen each other since Rhadamés introduced Jorge to Ambassador
Bilonick some two years earlier in the Noriega case.

Jorge's radiophone chimed again. He was still inching his way
through Cali traffic, trying to get out of the city. This time it was
Miguel on the line. Rhadamés was going to be at the ranch, and the
boss wanted Jorge to interrogate him.

"You know him. I want you to ask if he had anything to do with—
with the three letters," Miguel said. "The three letters" was cartel code
for the DEA.

"Of course, Señor—but I know nothing about—"

"Just ask that one question when you see him. I'll be there later."
And Miguel clicked off the line.

Jorge was troubled. He didn't know about the missing drug shipment or the circumstances of its seizure by U.S. Drug Enforcement Administration agents. And Miguel couldn't really expect Rhadamés to
incriminate himself. Suddenly little about the evening ahead was making any sense.

JORGE REACHED THE MAIN GATE to the ranch after nearly a thirty-
minute drive from Cali. One of his motorcycle sentries had already secured the entrance. The hacienda was another quarter of a mile off the
road. Outside the residence, Jorge found a number of Pacho's *sicarios*

scurrying in and out of the house. In fact, he saw only hired guns. This was no party. Jorge put a call through to Mateo as he glanced around looking for someone in charge.

"All clear at the Desert," Jorge reported to the boss's assistant. Mateo acknowledged and clicked off before Jorge could ask about Miguel's estimated arrival time. Based on standard procedures, Mateo would call back and alert Jorge once Miguel's convoy was on the road. They were at least a half hour to forty minutes away if they launched immediately.

"Good evening, Don Richard," said a cold, flat, and familiar voice. Memo Lara had stepped silently to Jorge's side and was looking up the long driveway toward two sets of headlights approaching from the main gate.

"What brings you here?" Memo asked.

It seemed an odd question, but Jorge shrugged and replied as if stating the obvious, "El Señor. He's coming."

Memo didn't respond, because at that moment two sedans swept past and braked to a stop. Armed men piled out, followed first by the familiar figure of Rhadamés. He stepped from the car desperate for a bathroom and rushed off toward the house without noticing Jorge.

The next two men out of the cars were strangers to Jorge. The cartel escorts referred to one of them as "Major." He had the unmistakable bearing of a military officer. The other was a man of average size and appearance whom Jorge barely noticed, because the last of the guests to emerge distracted him. She was an attractive woman in her early to mid-thirties with stylishly short dark hair. Jorge watched the strangers disappear inside the hacienda. Both vehicles were emptied, four sets of suitcases and personal items stacked to one side. Moments later, the two cars drove away. Obviously, Jorge thought, the Panamanians were spending the night.

There seemed no rush to question Rhadamés. Jorge decided to make a quick drive to check his sentries around the ranch perimeter. First, he alerted Memo: "When I get back—Miguel wants me to ask Rhadamés about the DEA." The chief *sicario* shrugged and replied, "Don't go too far."

Jorge was puzzled. He thought he had plenty of time. Miguel

wasn't even on his way yet. Jorge went ahead with his drive and was back in ten minutes. He headed into the hacienda.

Any signs of hospitality had evaporated by the time Jorge pushed through the front door. He found Pacho's men, grim faced, commanding the residence. Jorge encountered the woman in the living room, sitting alone on a leather couch and smoking a cigarette.

"Would you like a drink? Some water or juice?" Jorge asked her. She declined, but smiled slightly at his courtesy.

Then Jorge heard noises—angry voices, loud thumps, furniture breaking. He hurried toward a hallway, following the sounds to a bedroom doorway—where he saw what first appeared to be a brawl. Were the Panamanians trying to seize control of the hacienda? Should Jorge alert Miguel?

"Grab him! Grab him!" someone was shouting as Jorge recognized the major being wrestled to the floor. At least four *sicarios* had all they could handle in the powerfully built military man. The struggle continued as the heaving pile of men kicked, gouged, and slugged it out in close quarters. Jorge was desperate to know what was going on. The major turned out to be the only Panamanian in the room. And if he had initiated the attack, he was getting the worst of the fight. As Jorge watched, the major's situation turned desperate. Memo slipped a rope around his neck, creating an instant garrote by twisting the noose tighter with a twelve-inch piece of broom handle. It was like a tourniquet applied to the big man's neck.

Memo's small hands deftly twirled the garrote stick. Jorge stared at it, mesmerized. For a moment he lost track of what was happening. He had never seen anyone put to death before. What was the etiquette for such a moment? Did he have to watch? *No, of course not,* he decided, and quickly backed out of the room.

Standing for a moment in the hall, shaken and confused, Jorge called to another *sicario* guarding a door across the hall. "Where is Rhadamés?" he asked. The man pointed toward a bathroom up the corridor. Jorge found his man looking anxious, sitting on the floor next to a toilet under the watchful eyes of two armed guards. The man from Panama brightened at the sight of Jorge. "Where is Miguel?" he pleaded.

"Rhadamés, I don't know what's going on here tonight, but I have an important question for you," Jorge said. "Miguel wants to know— did you have anything to do with the DEA?"

"No, of course not," the man cried. "There's been a big misunderstanding."

"Well, he's coming to ask you about that. You need to be ready," Jorge said. "He's on his way."

Of course, by now Jorge knew that Miguel was not coming. It was a mercy lie. Miguel would never visit a crime scene—and there was already one body down the hall. Jorge considered leaving immediately for Cali. That was his first impulse—to flee the mayhem. But procedures first required a coded radio message confirming Miguel's change of plans. And the radios remained silent.

Jorge wandered back toward the kitchen looking for a place to be alone. Everywhere he turned, there was shouting and hyperactivity— loud men darting about, always in haste and on the verge of hysteria. Jorge had never seen it before, but he recognized what surrounded him—it was a killing frenzy. One *sicario* with a black mullet-style haircut raced toward him. Jorge stepped back, and the man rushed by half shouting, "I need a knife! I need a knife!" Jorge found himself sweating. He could hear himself breathing heavily. He decided to make another visit to his roadside sentries, just to get away.

The break gave him time to think, but it also let his paranoia run free. There were reasons why Jorge might be one of the doomed. Maybe his attempt to resign back in December raised doubts about his loyalty. And what about the Noriega case? Was the Panamanian about to be killed to cover up the cartel's involvement? If so, Jorge's knowledge of the case made him vulnerable, too. Besides, Jorge felt as if he had been sent to the ranch on a ruse. He had no role except to protect Miguel, and now it was clear that the boss wasn't coming. Had Jorge been sent to his own execution?

He returned to the hacienda dreading what he might encounter. He avoided the front door and circled the house outside, moving along its wraparound veranda. He stopped at a lit window. The woman was there, sitting at the end of a bed, legs crossed, smoking another cigarette. She seemed remarkably placid, even bored, as if in a doctor's waiting area. Jorge wondered why she didn't open the window and run for it.

"Why do you keep leaving?" said a voice out of the darkness. Jorge jumped as Memo Lara hurried past. "I'm checking security. What's the problem?" Jorge snapped, hoping he sounded more irritated than terrified. He realized as he stood there that he had better start acting like the security boss he really was or risk looking timid and scared—which he also was. Jorge began making the rounds of the hacienda and its grounds.

Almost immediately, he came upon three men in the auto court struggling under the weight of a body wrapped in bloody draperies. The bundle was hoisted into the trunk of a Chevy Sprint that sped off into the darkness. Jorge knew from the direction it turned at the highway that the car was headed toward a Cauca River bridge a short distance up the road.

A few minutes later, Jorge encountered the man with the mullet hairstyle and a kitchen knife. He was covered in blood. Strangulation was only part of the murder ritual playing out in the hacienda that evening. The mullet man's role was disemboweling. Years of experience disposing of bodies in the Cauca River had taught Colombian killers that a slashed abdomen prevented a corpse from bloating and then floating to the surface downriver.

Jorge finally entered the hacienda again. It was quiet now. A strange calm had settled over the scene. Voices were subdued. People moved at normal speeds. The killing frenzy had passed. Instinctively, Jorge knew he had survived. There was no one in the kitchen and no one in the living room. Jorge wandered toward the first hallway—and stopped.

THE NAKED BODY of the woman was lying on its back atop bloody terra-cotta tiles, the same spot where the other three bodies were prepped for disposal. Her death was so recent there remained a touch of pink in her blue lips. Her body was unmarked but for a slight bruise around her neck. He didn't know what device ended her life—the garrote or a plastic bag sealed around her soft neck by the strong hands of her killer. Jorge didn't see it happen. He saw nothing after fleeing the major's room. Murder happened all around him that night, and all Jorge could do was try not to look. He had never felt so helpless or more afraid.

Then the body moved. Not the entire body, just the feet—both feet. They arched and stretched, slowly pointing down until in full *pointe* position. The involuntary muscle action spooked him. Jorge felt a prickly sensation on the back of his neck. She looked like a ballerina doll, like a toy Jorge's three-year-old might have cast aside.

The dead woman had done nothing to deserve this, Jorge was certain of that. It was possible that none of the dead was guilty of treachery. For Rhadamés, mere suspicion warranted capital punishment. This woman's offense? She was a witness, in the wrong place at the wrong time—and she knew too much. Jorge could identify with that.

The silence and Jorge's reverie were disrupted by the return of the disposal crew—the man in the mullet with the large kitchen knife and a second man with a fresh set of draperies. Jorge turned for the door and tried not to run.

A GASOLINE-ASSISTED BONFIRE was blazing in the auto court. Memo was burning the Panamanians' personal belongings—their clothes, luggage, and toiletries. "Everything burns," he declared to the men assisting, "except identity papers . . . I want driver's licenses, passports, airline tickets." Memo held a fistful of documents as Jorge stepped up beside him.

"They will all fly home in the morning," Memo said to Jorge, uncharacteristically amused by his own words. Four cartel people would pose as the dead and fly to Panama. Any search for the missing foursome would have to start in Panama, not Cali.

"Did you speak to Rhadamés?" Memo asked.

"He said he had nothing to do with the DEA," Jorge said.

Memo shrugged and studied Jorge in the flickering light of the bonfire. "You look like you saw ghosts," he said.

Jorge no longer had the strength or inclination to bluster. He didn't care about his macho image. He was tired, very tired, and his sense of vulnerability had passed. He ignored Memo's observation.

"I want to see their papers," Jorge said with a weary nod toward the identity documents that Memo held. There was no hesitation. The *sicario* immediately handed over everything. Jorge sorted through the tickets and passports until he came to the woman's driver's license.

Her name was Emilia. She was from Costa Rica, the wife of one of the other dead strangers. Her hair was shorter in the license photo, but her expression was familiar. It was the same expression he noticed when she sat on the end of the bed smoking a cigarette and waiting to die. That was it—a vision of resignation, not boredom, and it had a jolting effect on Jorge. She never so much as looked around searching for a way to escape. It was an unfathomable acquiescence to fate.

Jorge was determined not to accept the unacceptable. And unlike Emilia, he could still resist. He had time and opportunity to rewrite his ending. He had no idea how to extricate himself and his family from this company of dangerous friends and ruthless killers, but that night at the ranch left him no option but to try. Jorge handed the fistful of papers back to Memo and turned away. "I'm going home," he said.

IN THE AFTERMATH of his close encounter with mass murder, Jorge sensed a subtle shift in his working relationship with Miguel—and Memo, too. They seemed more at ease discussing the business of killing in his presence. It was as if Jorge had been admitted into a secret club, the fraternity of killers.

Within days of the ranch murders, another of Rhadamés Trujillo's Panamanian partners was lured to Bogotá, where Memo Lara was waiting to kill him. As was cartel standard practice in such matters, the body was never found. The missing man's sudden disappearance prompted a frantic visit by his wife or girlfriend, searching through Bogotá hospitals and morgues hoping to solve the mystery. The woman finally telephoned Miguel to plead for help. Jorge overheard the godfather's side of that conversation.

"I'm so sorry," Miguel told the caller. "He must have had an accident." The boss promised that some of his best people would look for the missing Panamanian. Then, after a pause during which she apparently thanked Miguel and said that she was returning home to Panama, "No, no, no—wait there," Miguel insisted. "I'm going to send someone to help you. My associate Memo Lara can assist—whatever you need. And he will be happy to escort you home."

The comment sent a chill through Jorge. Miguel's cynicism was breathtaking. Jorge prayed in silence: *God, make her run . . . make her run for her life.*

NEW KIDS IN TOWN

Miguel Rodríguez Orejuela was not a patient man by nature. He could be plunged into a foul mood by any number of annoyances, then turn around and take out his frustrations on the first unsuspecting aide who crossed his path. It was such a common pattern of behavior that Mateo, his assistant, often alerted colleagues. "Señor is angry today," he might say. More than once he warned Jorge to avoid the office.

By mid-1994, El Señor was angry many days. The cartel was getting nothing but political headaches for the $6 million it invested in the new president. Meanwhile, drug seizures in Florida had exposed major players in the cartel's U.S. distribution network. At least four of the cartel's last five Miami bosses had been arrested. Miguel's Mexican partner, Amado Carrillo Fuentes, was calling in drunk. Pallomari's accounting records had compromised hundreds of valuable informants. Those still in their jobs required bigger bribes. And to top it all off, his América de Cali soccer team had hit a very bad patch with a string of losses. The

owner wanted a word with his players. A meeting was scheduled one afternoon at the team house, a large dormitory-like residence with many
bedrooms and a classroom-sized living room.

Jorge arrived first, as usual, to get an advance look at the security
situation. He signaled Miguel that it was clear. The first to arrive from
the family, however, was Miguel's eldest son—William Rodríguez
Abadía, the lawyer now about thirty. He was being groomed to handle
much of the family business, and Miguel wanted William taking a
greater role in ownership duties related to the team.

Unlike Gilberto, who preferred that his children stay far from the
trafficking business, Miguel increased his son's cartel profile with added
responsibilities. The young lawyer was already trying to help his father
dig out of the legal mess resulting from the seizure of the Pallomari
records. William was also starting to take over accounting and bookkeeping duties, hiring his own staff and gradually assuming various
projects, including money laundering, which had previously fallen to
Pallomari. At the same time, Miguel kept William busy drafting affidavits of dubious legal value for dozens of accused traffickers. Most of
them were patently false. For a new lawyer still learning his profession,
the burden of also protecting a massive criminal enterprise was especially stressful.

Jorge noted the son's weary expression and asked if he was sick.
"No, it's my father," William said. "I don't know how I can do all the
things he wants of me."

The frank response caught Jorge a bit by surprise. He took it as a
sign of trust and ventured a few words of sympathy.

"I know what you mean. Things are getting to be such a mess—and
I don't see it getting easier anytime soon," Jorge said. "You need to look
out for your own interests."

"Right. But you know my father. Who can say no to him?"

Jorge nodded and patted the young man's shoulder. "Whatever you
do, William," he said, "don't inherit the throne."

Their conversation ended abruptly as Miguel's car entered the compound. More than a dozen soccer players, coaches, and staff suddenly
swarmed into the living room, taking chairs that faced a table where
Miguel would hold court. The boss entered the room with a fierce

frown and launched immediately into a verbal assault on the team's physical and emotional performance. "You are an insult to your uniforms," he scolded. Then he fired the team's star player. Through it all, Miguel insisted that William sit beside him. He wanted the players to see his son as an extension of his own authority.

Watching from a doorway at the edge of the room, Jorge felt sorry for William. They shared a dilemma. Like him, the drug lord's son had no way out.

MIGUEL'S PROPENSITY FOR TELEPHONE CONFERENCES with his far-flung trafficking aides finally landed him in legal troubles both in the United States and at home. A conversation discussing delivery of a one-ton load of cocaine was intercepted by a federal wiretap in Louisiana. The United States indicted the brothers and notified Colombian authorities—who filed their own criminal action against Miguel and Gilberto based on the same evidence.

The bosses immediately retained U.S. and Colombian lawyers. Two key witnesses in the case against the brothers were traffickers who had already done prison time in the United States. They were flown to Colombia to testify. But after a lawyer for the Cali godfathers paid the witnesses $50,000, they promptly forgot who the Rodríguez Orejuela brothers were and denied ever working for them. A Colombian judge threw out the charges.

Belatedly, Miguel gave Jorge another mobile phone he feared had been traced back to him. "Take it apart and destroy the pieces," he said. Jorge spent the next half hour shredding its motherboard, hammering memory chips, and scattering the broken remains.

The new cooperation between U.S. and Colombian prosecutors was an alarming development inside the cartel. There were a number of old criminal indictments against the godfathers—some from the early 1980s—tucked away in forgotten files from California to New York. If they were resurrected and shared with Colombian officials, the case from Louisiana would not be the last.

And worse news was brewing. The cartel brain trust didn't know it yet, but four of their former southern Florida distribution managers were secretly cutting deals with the Miami U.S. attorney's office, agreeing to cooperate with a task force of federal investigators in the States determined to help dismantle the cartel in Cali.

A PERSONNEL MOVE at the U.S. embassy in Bogotá that summer had gone unnoticed in Cali. Miguel and the bosses had never heard of Chris Feistl or David Mitchell, a pair of aggressive American drug agents in their early thirties with plenty of youthful energy. What they lacked was Colombian experience. They had been sent from Miami to beef up a team of agents dedicated exclusively to the Cali drug organization. They were tall, blond, and such obvious gringos that colleagues feared for their safety almost anywhere in Colombia. To their frustration, they were barred at first from traveling beyond Bogotá. The U.S. State Department considered Cali too dangerous for Americans.

For agents assigned to break the Cali cartel, such restrictions were hard to accept. Mitchell, a U.S. Army–trained paratrooper, finally pushed embassy officials to ease the ban. They could do little in Bogotá and needed to learn their way around Cali before hoping to develop any new sources and informants. Mitchell's request was granted with a caveat—he and Feistl could fly into Cali, but they had to be back in Bogotá by nightfall. This was supposed to be an American drug agent's dream assignment, but the new kids in town were beginning to feel like schoolboys with a strict curfew. Nonetheless, the two agents managed rather quickly to develop good relations with National Police attached to the Bloque's Cali garrison. Gradually, their restrictions eased, and the agents began spending nights inside the garrison.

Despite their rapport with police, Feistl and Mitchell were wary. Colombian National Police had cornered and killed Pablo Escobar, but it was well-known that the cartel had many friends in the ranks of antinarcotics officers all over the country. To protect the security of their investigative leads, the American agents in Cali worked independently and shared only what was necessary for cooperative efforts. One top officer stood out, however, as something of a nuisance—asking too many questions, acting too friendly, inviting himself into private conversations. After one typically unwelcome encounter, Mitchell wondered

aloud how they should deal with the intrusive man. What they didn't
know, of course, was that the nosy officer named Captain Efrén
Buitrago was "the Vulture"—one of Miguel's best-paid informants.

THE NEW DEA AGENTS in town were of no concern to Jorge. He was
looking at the big picture—and he didn't like what he saw. Washington
didn't trust Ernesto Samper. The Clinton administration threatened to
withhold hundreds of millions in foreign aid from his government. Top
Colombian officials were denied visas by the U.S. State Department.
The director of the CIA refused to meet with his Colombian counter-
parts. Jorge wondered if U.S. Marines might try another Panama-style
invasion. But even if that radical step were ruled out, U.S. pressure was
changing the rules of the game in ways that the godfathers seemed not
to grasp. They still thought they could work out some sort of negotiated deal with Colombian officials.

The cartel had two strategies in play going into 1995. One campaign, through Samper's office, was to arrange for a so-called surrender
to justice. This was the latest iteration of the "soft landing" option. Cartel leaders would turn themselves in, promise to stop trafficking, and
get a slap-on-the-wrist punishment. The bosses wanted treatment at
least as favorable as that granted Pablo Escobar when he volunteered for
prison in 1991. Five years or less of house arrest was probably accept-
able, the four godfathers had agreed among themselves.

The second strategy, promoted through their friends in congress,
was to obtain a legislative amnesty of sorts. They called it "the Argentine model" or "forgive and forget"—a variation on Argentina's military
amnesty laws forgiving security forces for past human rights abuses.
The same mercy should be considered for retired traffickers, they argued. And they backed that argument with an aggressive lobbying campaign.

One afternoon, Miguel dispatched Jorge to a Cali restaurant to
pick up three members of the Colombian congress, two of them newly
elected to the Chamber of Representatives—Ingrid Betancourt and the
former M-19 guerrilla Carlos Alonso Lucio. They represented potential
new votes for amnesty legislation and had agreed to meet privately with

the godfathers at a mountain retreat owned by Pacho Herrera. Jorge was to drive them about eight miles up the steep, twisting roadway to the high-altitude rendezvous.

Betancourt was an attractive thirty-three-year-old from an old Colombian political family and the former wife of a French diplomat. Jorge was looking forward to seeing her. She had run as an anticorruption candidate, handing out free condoms as a campaign gift. She promised to be "like a condom against corruption." Lucio was in congress because the previous Bogotá government had made a deal with M-19, inviting its members into the political system in exchange for renouncing violence. Jorge thought it a bad deal for Colombia. He considered the former guerrilla personally despicable—even before Lucio climbed into the Mazda.

No more than halfway up the mountain road, Lucio pointed out a sun-bathed ridge north of the highway and told his fellow passengers that he had once fought the Colombian army on that distant ridge. He described the encounter in colorful detail, recounting an M-19 incursion into Yumbo that sounded terribly familiar to Jorge. "We were outnumbered, but we took the town," he boasted.

Jorge glanced into his rearview mirror to see Lucio playing the macho guerrilla to an admiring Ingrid Betancourt next to him in the backseat. "We withdrew over the mountain under heavy fire," he was telling her. Jorge felt slightly sick and tried to concentrate on the weaving centerline. But he couldn't block out a long-repressed image—that smoldering, blood-splattered Renault with three dead teens. For the first time, Jorge had someone to blame.

At Pacho's mountain retreat, the three politicians met privately with cartel bosses for about two hours. Jorge finally was summoned again, and he arrived to hear Miguel thank them for coming. "We hope we can count on your support," he said.

Then Chepe Santacruz interrupted what already seemed like cordial farewells with another friendly gesture. "Wait," he said. "We don't want you to leave empty-handed." He opened a checkbook and hastily scrawled a name and a number with many zeroes—50 million pesos, or about $50,000. He handed the slip of paper to Lucio with a jocular admonition.

"It's not all for you, Carlos Alonso," Chepe said. "This is for all three of you." The godfathers laughed. Back at the car, Jorge also kept smiling as he held the doors open for his departing passengers. It was all he could do to conceal his contempt.

Betancourt would later deny any knowledge of Chepe's check. She said she didn't see such a transaction and never received any funds. Her voting record remained staunchly anticartel, a source of continuing irritation and frustration to the bosses.

PRESIDENT SAMPER ALSO REMAINED a disappointment to the drug lords, but they held out hope for the future. Most of the congress owed them favors. Many were on their payroll. The bosses figured they had enough clout to wait out U.S. pressures. At times, however, it seemed to Jorge that Samper had less to say about running his administration than did another president named Bill Clinton. Washington had already forced Samper to fire his choice for chief of the National Police and to appoint the Clinton administration's choice—General Rosso José Serrano. And Serrano had promptly asserted his independence by firing about two thousand policemen suspected of graft, corruption, and ties to criminals.

During that period, too, the cartel watched its extensive investment in negotiations with Attorney General de Greiff go to waste. Under withering U.S. criticism, de Greiff was forced to step aside and was replaced by an ambitious prosecutor and cousin of Galán, the martyred presidential candidate. The new attorney general, Alfonso Valdivieso, immediately declared that unlike his predecessor, he would never negotiate with the cartel. By early 1995, he was issuing scores of search and arrest warrants for General Serrano's antinarcotics teams to execute.

Jorge knew he could not protect Miguel from arrest indefinitely. It was time for some straight talk about the deteriorating situation and about the future of the bosses' security. He asked for a private meeting.

The Rodríguez Orejuela brothers were using office space in the Santa Monica neighborhood of Cali, less than half a mile from Miguel's Wall House compound and Gilberto's personal residence. The office was a seventh-floor penthouse suite with a big-screen projection television. A remote control device lowered the big screen out of the ceiling. The godfathers loved it. Jorge hated the place. Its underground parking garage was a potential trap. The single narrow ramp could be a nightmare if rapid escape was needed.

The meeting took place a couple of days after Jorge's initial request. He would be the last visitor on their meeting schedule. At around midnight, a Colombian senator emerged from the private office, and the godfathers motioned for Jorge to come in. He sat across the desk from Miguel and next to Gilberto. This was the first time he had ever requested such a formal session.

"I have thought a great deal about what I see going on," he began, "and I want you to know that this comes from my heart."

Jorge's personal feelings toward the brothers had become much more complicated over time as he witnessed firsthand violence and corruption sanctioned by his bosses. That night, he focused on their humanity, on what he admired about them—their commitment to family, their work ethic, their friendship. Jorge's message was self-serving—he wanted out—but he also wanted to sound sincere when he said he was only thinking of their best interests. The brothers urged him to continue.

"As you know, I came here to help you, to protect you and your families from Pablo Escobar. And I continue to work for your wellbeing and that of your families. But I am very concerned. I see pressure building but not much progress with the government. And international pressure is only getting worse. That should be a concern."

Jorge shared his opinion that since the fall of the Berlin Wall and collapse of the Soviet Union the United States was alone as a world power, that since it had successfully taken down Noriega and pushed Saddam Hussein out of Kuwait, it had a lot of military resources with little to do. Jorge said he feared one day American forces might even land in Cali to take the cartel leaders.

"My concern is that, rather than waiting until it is too late, would it not be better for you and for your families to surrender to justice now, while you can still negotiate certain favorable terms?" Jorge said.

"My God, don't even talk like that," Miguel interrupted. "It's bad luck."

"No, no, no—Richard is right," Gilberto countered. "We may not have much more time. That's a problem, I agree."

Jorge addressed both brothers as he plunged ahead: "I strongly believe that today you are enemy number one of the United States. And somewhere in Washington—wherever they keep their trophies—there, they are saving spaces on their wall for your two heads."

Miguel scowled. Gilberto, however, thanked him.

"You may not know everything that we're doing behind the scenes," the older brother said, "but you should know that we are still making good progress. Please, don't worry. And I very much appreciate your interest and concern."

Jorge left the office feeling that he had done his duty to his employers. He had warned them about what he saw on the horizon. He had recommended a strategy intended to shield them from the worst of what might be coming. His hope was that a negotiated surrender in the near future might still release him before it was too late—before Jorge got into serious legal trouble . . . and before anyone noticed his waning enthusiasm for the job. Any day now, Jorge feared, his true feelings could become dangerously obvious.

THINGS TOOK A DECIDEDLY BAD TURN early in 1995. President Clinton threatened to decertify Colombia as a reliable partner in the war on drugs—a move that put millions of dollars in U.S. foreign aid at risk. The action was a blow to President Samper's political prestige and forced him to prove his antinarco bona fides. The Cali cartel suffered serious collateral damage.

The former senator Eduardo Mestre, a respected Liberal Party figure, arrived in Cali one night as an emissary for Samper. He had been flown from Bogotá aboard one of Pacho Herrera's executive planes, a Beechcraft 200. Jorge met him at the airport and drove him around Cali, waiting for the godfathers to summon their visitor. Mestre spoke candidly about Samper's political problems.

Jorge asked the biggest question on his mind: "What do you think, Senator, about the prospects of negotiations between the gentlemen and the government?"

Mestre shook his head sadly. "These are difficult times," he said.

Jorge let the silence hang for a moment, then nodded and said, "Yes, I'm very concerned for their safety."

"We are all concerned. That's why I'm here tonight," Mestre replied, staring out the window.

"I have come with apologies and a special message from President Samper. He wants me to tell the gentlemen that his hands are tied, that he can do nothing. For now, the president's only advice is . . . don't get caught."

THE LIMIT

THE CALI CARTEL ENTERED 1995 UNDER PRESSURE, BUT NOT YET under siege. In recognition of U.S. effectiveness breaking up its Florida smuggling networks, the godfathers shifted increasingly to partnerships with Mexican traffickers. And back home, the bosses focused on cleaning up loose ends—and legal liabilities. Non-Colombian operatives were considered extradition targets and therefore cartel security risks.

Jorge spent his sixth anniversary with the cartel pretending to search for Sergio Aguilar, a Miami Cuban who—in the early 1990s—ran a Florida car dealership. Caribbean International Motors was financed by the cartel to supply falsely registered cars and vans to move cash and cocaine. Now Aguilar was avoiding a U.S. indictment by hiding out in Colombia.

By early 1995, Cali had become a way station for refugees from U.S. racketeering indictments. Some of the displaced operatives moved on to new cartel assignments in places like Bolivia, Ecuador, and Venezuela, gateways to drug distribution networks in Russia and Europe. The less ambitious or less versatile among them languished in Colombia. Some got by with financial help from the godfathers, cartel welfare that came to annoy the bosses.

One of those was Aguilar. He also had a playboy reputation—partying, drinking, and womanizing on the cartel dole. The bosses' patience finally ran out when they learned that Aguilar was boasting about his ties to the Rodríguez Orejuela family, taboo for anyone without Rodríguez or Orejuela DNA. Miguel decided that Aguilar knew too much, talked too much, and drank too much.

Instinctively, Jorge knew better than to make a serious effort locating the Cuban. The best he could do, he told Miguel, was to confirm that Aguilar had moved to Bogotá—address unknown. Late in January, Memo Lara came to see Miguel.

"Good afternoon," Jorge greeted him. "I haven't seen you for a while. Have you been traveling?"

"I was in Bogotá," Memo answered. "I had to kill Sergio Aguilar."

To Jorge, the most shocking thing about Memo's report was that it wasn't shocking. It was business. It was only later that Jorge questioned his own lack of reaction and wondered whether his conscience would ever be the same. But Carlos Salvador Ponciano helped restore Jorge's faith—at least in himself.

Ponciano was a low-level Guatemalan operative, a driver and general errand boy for the cartel's regional boss in Guatemala City, Walter Soto. When Soto fled Central America to avoid arrest, the loyal Ponciano tagged along. Soto soon moved on to another cartel assignment in Bolivia. Jorge found Ponciano homeless and hungry on the streets of Cali, and he persuaded Miguel to write a check for the Guatemalan's food and shelter.

After payments of about $3,000, Miguel summoned Soto back from Bolivia. One topic of conversation was the extraditable Ponciano.

"He could be trouble," Miguel said. "One day he will be captured, and that will be bad for all of us. Take him out."

"But, Don Miguel," Soto protested, "Carlos is a good man. He is not dangerous."

"Get rid of him," Miguel insisted.

Alone with Jorge outside Miguel's office, Soto was distraught. "How can he ask this? Carlos is my friend, my worker; he is so loyal to me," he said. "We don't really have to do this—do we?"

"No, we don't," Jorge assured him, sounding more certain than he felt.

Defying Miguel's orders was never safe. And keeping secrets from the boss was hazardous, too. In the case of Ponciano, however, Jorge vowed to do both. Fortunately for all of them, the cartel had bigger problems. Miguel never asked again about the inconvenient Guatemalan.

A STRING OF U.S. law-enforcement successes in Florida grated on Miguel. He was already hypoglycemic and subject to sudden drops in blood sugar that made him feel faint. Stress only made it worse. He also suffered bouts of migraines. His temper was shorter than ever as he found himself dealing with one crisis after another. One problem was the mounting cocaine backlog. The cartel produced more than it could move through its compromised distribution pipelines. Every lost shipment enraged Miguel and created more defendants whose silence had to be ensured—and more lawyers, though not just any lawyers. The cartel needed American defense attorneys who could live by Colombian rules of the game. The first rule: *no one talks . . . ever.*

The primary villain, from the cartel point of view, was Operation Cornerstone—a Miami-based law-enforcement task force targeting the Cali drug lords and their cocaine distribution network in southern Florida. Cornerstone included numerous federal and local narcotics investigators, but the Florida pit bull that made life most miserable for the godfathers was an obscure federal agent named Eddie.

The U.S. Customs Service agent Edward Kacerosky was an obsessive investigator with a chip on his shoulder for the Cali big shots and a pager on his belt that was rarely silent. He passed up promotions, raises, and plum headquarters assignments to work the case of a lifetime. His investigative coups bolstered a series of federal racketeering and conspiracy actions against the biggest criminal enterprise in the history of crime. And his extensive knowledge of the cartel and its methods made him the closest thing in U.S. law enforcement to an expert on the Rodríguez Orejuela empire.

Kacerosky was to law enforcement what Miguel was to cartel operations—methodical, organized, and persistent. His investigations developed leads that fed eager young DEA agents on the ground in Colombia. None of the godfathers had a clue, but Kacerosky was just about the worst thing that ever happened to them.

By 1995, the veteran customs agent had targeted cartel lawyers for fostering perjury, laundering money, and coercing witnesses. His information helped gain court approval for unprecedented wiretaps on several prominent American attorneys. As a result, government tape recorders were rolling when some of those lawyers passed along threats from the Cali godfathers to their clients.

IN CALI, one of the cartel's greatest extradition fears involved Guillermo Pallomari. The Chilean accountant had been charged in a Colombian arrest warrant with numerous corruption allegations based on evidence found in his seized business records. As the highest-ranking non-Colombian in the cartel, Pallomari could do more damage to the cartel than almost anyone if extradited and induced to cooperate with U.S. investigators.

Miguel's son William was gradually replacing Pallomari in key areas of responsibility, assuming daily management of cartel properties, for example, and supervision of accountants. Jorge was slow to recognize the trend and its implications for Pallomari's future. But the displaced accountant sensed his own vulnerability. By the spring of 1995, Pallomari was hiding not only from authorities but from some of his cartel colleagues as well.

William moved into Jorge's security operations, too—installing one of his closest friends as Jorge's second-in-command. Juan Carlos Delgado, known as Dario, had been an army lieutenant but had limited security experience. He mostly liked to party, use cocaine, and sleep late. Jorge never complained. Dario was almost family. Jorge's new number two was engaged to marry a niece of El Señor and Marta Lucía.

Friction sometimes flared, however, between Jorge and Mario del Basto. Jorge routinely refused to attend weekly meetings and share intelligence information with Mario's security team. The two men were equals in the cartel hierarchy, but Mario's security portfolio was much broader. Jorge had primary responsibility for communications systems, for monitoring the Bloque de Búsqueda's military wing, and for the personal security of Miguel. His motorcycle corps also served as the cartel's eyes and ears around town. Mario was chief of cartel security for everything else. They clashed when Jorge complained that the meetings were both a waste of time and unnecessarily risky. At times, the two friends were barely speaking.

Miguel finally interceded. Without taking sides regarding the merits of their dispute, the godfather insisted that they coordinate their security efforts. "I need you both working together," he demanded in one telephone conversation with Jorge.

AT THREE O'CLOCK on Friday afternoon, June 9, 1995, Jorge responded to an urgent message from Miguel. The boss wanted Jorge to call in a tip to police that cartel bosses were meeting at that very moment at an address a mile or so from his brother Gilberto's hideout. It was, of course, a ruse. The Bloque was already at Gilberto's door, and Miguel was desperately trying to draw them away. Jorge hurried to a public telephone and did as requested. When he reported back to the godfather, Miguel's spirits were down.

"It's too late," he said. "I fear they have Gilberto."

"Oh, no. I'm very sorry," Jorge replied.

"Be very careful," Miguel warned. "Keep your eyes open. They are on our necks."

When Jorge made the call, a Colombian National Police helicopter was circling the godfather's secret residence, and a police search team with two American agents was already inside. It would take the raiding party nearly an hour, but the agents finally found Gilberto in a makeshift hiding place, in a closet behind a big-screen television set. The Chess Player was in his underwear, barefoot, and waving two handguns when he was discovered by the unarmed DEA agent Ruben Prieto.

Members of the Colombian search team, responding to a commotion, rushed into the room accompanied by the ominous clattering sounds of automatic weapons being readied to fire. For a breathless moment Prieto stood between the armed police and their armed quarry. But Gilberto eased the tension.

"Don't shoot," he said. "I'm a man of peace." And he laid down his weapons.

The agents had been led to Gilberto's upscale hillside hideout by watching and secretly following a cartel associate known as Flaco. News of Gilberto's capture flashed across radio and television news channels in Cali before ricocheting around the globe. Jorge listened to the reports and made sure that his men stayed far away from the investigative scene. Over the next few hours he learned that the raiding party was not part of the Bloque. It was a team under the command of Colonel Carlos Barragán, a low-key but determined lawman who reported directly to the chief of the National Police, General Serrano. While Serrano was the public face of Colombia's counternarcotics efforts, Barragán was the gloved fist.

Barragán's men were also the favorites of DEA field officers in Bogotá. They were a unit assembled specifically to work with U.S. intelligence agents—and subject to frequent polygraph tests. As successful as the Cali cartel had been penetrating the Bloque, the National Police, and the Colombian army, it had been stymied trying to corrupt Barragán's unit. Miguel told Jorge he was "very afraid of this colonel."

Gilberto's transfer to a Bogotá prison was delayed until General Serrano arrived for his press photo op marching the Chess Player into custody. President Samper issued a triumphant statement about his administration cracking down on the drug mafia. He toasted Gilberto's arrest with champagne. To Miguel, that was no way to show his gratitude for $6 million in campaign gifts from the Cali godfathers.

"Goddamn that son of a bitch," he fumed.

*　*　*

MIGUEL DISPATCHED WILLIAM to meet with Gilberto in prison the next day. It had been Gilberto's opinion for several months that the cartel's most serious problems could all be traced back to the raid on Guillermo Pallomari's offices—and to the accountant's inept and incriminating performance under questioning. Only Miguel's support had kept Pallomari from being fired . . . or worse. William returned from his uncle's Bogotá jail cell with the message that Pallomari's time with the cartel had expired.

Jorge was summoned to the Wall House on Sunday afternoon, two days after Gilberto's capture. Miguel assured Jorge that his brother was doing just fine and moved quickly to the purpose of the meeting.

"This is very important," Miguel began. "You know Guillermo Pallomari. He's a good man. And you know that he is very dear to us—but he has made many mistakes, and he talks too much."

Dear God, no. Jorge started to pray.

"Now he is a danger to us," Miguel went on. "A very serious danger. And I am sorry to say it, but—we have to kill Pallomari."

God, help me. Jorge prayed again. He tried to affect a quizzical expression, as if unclear what Miguel was saying.

"Of course, César Yusti will take care of it. But I want you to help him," Miguel said. "Nobody can know about this, but you need to find Pallomari . . . help make the arrangements . . . make certain the job is done—and done now. Pallomari must go. Do you understand?"

Jorge didn't answer immediately. It was as if there was a great noise roaring through his brain. In his own head, Jorge was in full rebellion. *No, I won't do this. No, no, no!* He was screaming in silence. Yet at the same moment he was nodding to Miguel and telling the boss exactly what he expected to hear: "Yes, of course. Yes, I understand." His first instinct was to buy time. He didn't know what else to do.

Jorge had come full circle. The man who had joined the cartel to help kill Pablo Escobar was being asked to help kill another threat to the cartel. The difference, of course, was that Jorge regarded killing Pablo as an act of patriotism on behalf of his terrorized country. But killing Pallomari was murder on behalf of cold-blooded cartel business interests.

In that moment, despite his uttered assurances to the godfather, Jorge knew he had reached his limit—this was the line that he could not and would not cross.

Now he faced a terrible dilemma: refusing Miguel's deadly assignment could be deadly to Jorge. And he was going to have to risk his life for Pallomari, of all people. Jorge didn't even like the arrogant prig.

PART THREE

The Last Days
Summer 1995

MORE WRONG NUMBER

Cali, Colombia
Monday, June 12, 1995

I N THE HOURS BEFORE DAWN, JORGE LAY AWAKE IN A DARK AND QUIET apartment assessing and reassessing his limited options. Nearby, his wife and children slept peacefully, unaware of his silent struggle. It had been only a few hours since Miguel ordered him to help murder the cartel accountant. That dreadful assignment had already clarified one thing: Jorge had to get out—out of the murder plot, out of the cartel, maybe even out of Colombia. Dawn loomed over the eastern Andes when he rolled over and closed his eyes. He had very little time, but Jorge finally had a plan . . . of sorts.

Through his earlier career as an engineer, Jorge had designed fine, precision machinery. As a cartel security adviser, he had assembled an elegant radio-communications system. But as a desperate man looking for a way out of the Cali cartel, Jorge had come up with a precarious scheme more akin to a house of cards.

Killing Pallomari was so important to the godfathers that Jorge knew he could not safely refuse to help. He would have to resign from the cartel. Of course, no one did that without a funeral. To quit the cartel, Jorge realized that his only hope was to destroy it on his way out. And destroying the cartel seemed impossible. Jorge could begin by helping authorities capture the boss of the bosses. But Pablo Escobar had run the Medellín cartel quite effectively while in prison, and Jorge figured the Rodríguez Orejuela brothers would do the same. If getting Miguel arrested was all that he could accomplish, there was no place on earth Jorge could hide without living in constant fear that Memo Lara or Freckles or some other anonymous *sicario* would hunt him down and execute his entire family.

Jorge would have to inflict an utterly devastating blow. He had to find a way to expose cartel trafficking networks and the billions of dollars in hidden assets. Stripping the godfathers of their wealth also stripped them of power. But Jorge also considered it essential to identify the cartel's vast support system of corrupt public officials—to name, shame, and jail them—in order to end the cartel's indecent influence over the Colombian government.

During his long night of quiet reflection, Jorge saw that bringing down the Cali cartel wasn't impossible after all. One insider could do it—Guillermo Pallomari, the accountant whose records and potential testimony already worried the cartel brain trust. He was also the key to Jorge's escape.

The man he was supposed to help kill was the man Jorge now had to help save.

JORGE LEFT HOME to make his routine Monday morning security rounds as if everything were normal. He didn't whisper a word about his intentions to Lena. It would have terrified her. But he was not keeping silent simply to spare his wife from worry. Jorge didn't want to risk that her fears might be detected and give them away. Lena had an open and direct personality. She was not a good liar, and under the circumstances that was dangerous. Jorge decided he would do the lying for both of them.

Some time after one in the afternoon, Jorge headed for the bustling Cali Telecom offices downtown. They had small private rooms for telephone calls, but what Jorge liked most about them was the fact that he didn't have to worry about cartel wiretaps.

Jorge slipped into one of the rooms, mopped his sweaty forehead, and then reached for the receiver. In Spanish, he asked for an overseas operator. A moment later, in English, he requested the main number in Langley, Virginia, for the Central Intelligence Agency. It was a bitter truth for the Colombian patriot in Jorge, but he could not trust another Colombian. Even honest Colombians were too often surrounded by others who were corrupt. And since Jorge felt he was gambling with his life, and the lives of his family, he trusted only the CIA.

As the electronic beeps and buzzes began in Jorge's ear, he took a deep breath and told himself: *There is no going back now.*

"Central Intelligence Agency," said a woman's voice.

For the next couple of minutes Jorge tried hard to offer his insider services to the U.S. government in its pursuit of notorious international drug lords. Instead, he was ignored, treated like a kook, and dismissed. Jorge had to find someone else to trust.

A KILLER'S BUSY DAY

CÉSAR YUSTI, THE GODFATHERS' DESIGNATED HIT MAN FOR THE Pallomari killing, was a thirtysomething henchman of José Estrada's who did odd jobs around the warehouses, handled phones, and pulled bodyguard duty. He also drove for Estrada and ran errands. Sometimes he would disappear for weeks at a time. But Jorge knew nothing of his *sicario* skills. In fact, Yusti seemed to him a nervous, jittery type—hardly the stone-cold killer Jorge saw in Memo and the others.

At the same time, he had a disarmingly harmless appearance. Yusti was a small man, no more than five feet three, with the demeanor of a clerk or a shoe salesman. He was plain and balding, with a bad combover. In a telephone conversation, Jorge arranged to meet his new partner in assassination.

It was Yusti who promptly clarified their mission: "I have been instructed to coordinate with you the killing of Guillermo Pallomari."

Jorge could barely believe they were talking murder in such business-as-usual tones. He tried for similar indifference. "That's right. I expect it will be a simple matter."

Fortunately, Pallomari had gone into deep cover ever since William Rodríguez took over supervision of cartel financial and bookkeeping operations. The sometimes-clueless accountant was sharp enough to realize that he knew too much for his own good. He did not, however, attempt to flee Cali, where his wife, Patricia, continued to run a computer business.

Jorge knew Pallomari's primary residence. He knew where Patricia worked in downtown Cali. And he even knew where the hunted accountant was hiding out at a friend's apartment. Jorge had visited the friend's place once as a favor to Pallomari's lawyer, who needed some documents dropped off for the accountant's signature. But in his first meeting with Yusti, Jorge feigned complete ignorance.

"I will locate him as soon as possible," Jorge assured the gunman.

Yusti asked if Jorge knew where to obtain an AR-15 rifle. Although Jorge knew exactly where he could retrieve such a rifle—in his own private storage locker—he said he would look into it. The request could buy him at least a day or two. But what ended up buying the most time was Yusti's busy schedule. He disappeared for a couple of weeks.

JORGE WAS STILL PONDERING what to do next and how to safely contact the Americans when his pager beeped. Mario del Basto wanted to see him. He found his friend relaxed, shirtless, and chatty. It was midday and Mario offered Jorge a bowl of homemade soup. They talked about how many hours everyone was putting in since Gilberto's unfortunate arrest. It felt like old times, back when they were partners and pals, before Mario's ambitions made him jealous of Jorge's access to the boss. For that day, and for reasons Jorge could not explain, the hard feelings seemed to have vanished.

Mario confessed that he was tired. He also showed flashes of frustration with Miguel. "He demands that we clean up this mess or that problem. We take the risks—but then he doesn't back us up," Mario complained to Jorge, perhaps the only person in the cartel he could trust with such criticism of the boss.

His latest problem was slow reimbursements. Mario had made a number of cash payoffs to informants, but was still waiting to be paid. With Pallomari underground, the cartel's administrative efficiency was hurting.

Mario advised Jorge of an afternoon meeting scheduled with about a dozen of his security men. He planned to share a fresh batch of intelligence—lists of telephone numbers that the Bloque de Búsqueda was tapping and the license tags of suspected cartel cars that police intended to follow—the latest from Captain Buitrago. Mario had arranged for the meeting at a practice field of the América de Cali soccer team.

"You're welcome to come, but don't worry if you can't make it," Mario told him.

No more than a month earlier, Mario had been demanding that Jorge come to these meetings, prompting Miguel to intervene. The godfather had scolded Jorge and demanded that the two men work together. Now Mario was conciliatory, even apologetic. Jorge welcomed the return of their easygoing relationship, but he still wanted no part of such a gathering. He declined politely and wished Mario well.

"It could be dangerous meeting there in broad daylight. Be careful," Jorge said.

Two HOURS LATER, Jorge's pager and radiophone went off, and a flurry of messages followed. There was some sort of military operation under way at the soccer club training facilities. Jorge knew immediately that a cartel disaster was in the making.

One thing puzzled him: the military team was not from the Bloque task force. It was a unit of the regular army, initially a small squad from the Cali-based Pichincha Battalion. Jorge had been attached to that group in the army reserves. Mario had been its second-in-command in the mid-1980s. The battalion usually had no direct role in counternarcotics operations.

Del Basto and his men had been clustered in the shade of a covered grandstand when the army burst in—a squad of about eight men. They claimed to be responding to a citizen tipster who had noticed the gathering of civilians, some of them appearing to be armed. The small army team arrived outnumbered—and very likely outgunned—but Mario and his men offered no resistance. Instead, they immediately began tearing up documents and stuffing them in their mouths, trying to eat as much evidence as possible—until ordered at gunpoint to stop. Additional troops were called, and together they salvaged plenty of intact, telltale copies of confidential Bloque data.

The cartel security men were charged with espionage and taken into custody. Television cameras rolled as they were led away in handcuffs—all, that is, except for the former major Mario del Basto. As a special courtesy to the battalion's former number two, he was arrested without the indignity of cuffs.

That evening at the Wall House, Miguel greeted news of the arrests by flying into a rage—not over the devastating loss of key security personnel, but over the harm done to the soccer club's reputation. The team's ownership by the Rodríguez Orejuela family was well-known, but arrests on club grounds made the crime ties inescapable.

"Stupid . . . stupid . . . stupid!" thundered Miguel over and over again. "How could that son of a bitch be so stupid?"

Jorge had never seen him so irate. The boss was astonished that so many so-called security experts could be caught off guard so easily—and in broad daylight. "Do they have bullshit for brains?" he stormed. Pressed for his opinion, Jorge acknowledged cautioning Mario about the meeting. It was a mistake he recognized immediately. "You knew about this and didn't stop it?" Miguel turned on Jorge. "I should have been informed. You fucked up. Do you understand me?"

It seemed to Jorge like an opportune time to excuse himself. Mario's mistake might well have trumped all of his successes over the past six years in protecting cartel leadership and their extended families. Others who had disappointed the godfathers met bad ends—beginning with poor Major Gómez, the inept Hercules Security boss who was gunned down just days after Jorge joined the cartel. And now, of course, there was Guillermo Pallomari.

* * *

THE TWIN BLOWS of Mario's arrest and Gilberto's fall prompted calls of condolence and offers of assistance from Miguel's loyal allies. One of them was Chupeta—more formally known as Juan Carlos Ramírez Abadía. At the early age of thirty-two, he had already amassed more than a billion dollars and the reputation of a ruthless enforcer. Jorge considered him the unofficial fifth godfather.

Two days after Mario was seized, Miguel summoned Jorge to arrange a meeting "with Chupeta's people." It was set for six o'clock outside the Unicentro shopping mall. Jorge climbed into the front passenger seat of a car driven by Chupeta's security chief. In back were two men wearing Colombian National Police uniforms. Both were majors.

"We are here to help in any way," said Chupeta's aide. And the two majors pledged their services. The officers in that backseat were further evidence, if such were really needed, that Jorge should never risk going to Colombian law enforcement for help or protection.

There was talk that some of Mario's men blamed Jorge for their boss's arrest. In Colombia, coincidence is seldom accepted as an adequate explanation for anything. The fact that Jorge was invited but didn't attend made him especially suspect to some. And it was amid this troublesome buzz of distrust that Jorge received a pager message from Yusti requesting a meeting.

Jorge felt paranoia well up within him. He knew the familiar pattern. An unsuspecting target gets called to a meeting with someone he knows. He shows up and is never seen again. It happened to Sergio Aguilar and his old friend Rhadamés. On the other hand, Yusti might simply want to talk about the Pallomari job. Jorge slipped a small Walther pistol into his pocket . . . just in case.

His meeting with Yusti would be at a large, parklike traffic circle in the Ciudad Jardín district of town. A stand of bamboo gave Jorge cover from which to watch Yusti's arrival. The *sicario* parked his car on the street and approached alone. It was a good sign—no accomplice or lookout on motorcycle.

Jorge stayed out of sight as Yusti walked to the meeting site, a popular ice cream stand crowded with families and potential witnesses. Finally satisfied that it was safe, Jorge emerged to discuss Pallomari's murder over ice cream. Yusti asked if Jorge had located an AR-15 rifle.

"Yes. It's at a friend's house," Jorge lied.

"Ah, good. Let's get it now."

Jorge stalled. He said his friend was out of town.

"No problem. Pallomari's a sitting duck. We'll get him soon."

As Jorge stalled, paranoia built throughout the cartel, an especially unsettling condition in a community of armed men. Mario's arrest had come as such a surprise that it spawned irrational fears. Was it part of some big military operation with the United States that was secret even from the Colombian government? Did it involve agencies in which the cartel had no informants? For a few days, no one was sure whom or what to fear. Jorge suggested that all nonemergency communications be restricted to pay phones or face-to-face meetings in secure settings.

The Colombian government, meanwhile, had begun running television advertisements offering a million dollars for information leading to capture of the remaining Cali godfathers. Washington was underwriting the campaign. It was enough money to keep the telephones ringing at a police hotline. Unfortunately for many tipsters, there were cartel wiretaps listening in on the same hotline. Some died before their tips were even investigated.

Jorge was among several cartel managers asked to listen to one recorded tipster call. It was the voice of a man who said that he worked on a medical clinic under construction in Cali. It was being built with drug money, the man said. Jorge didn't know who the man was, but there could be no doubt he worked for José Estrada on the multimillion-dollar state-of-the-art health clinic financed by the Rodríguez Orejuela brothers.

The anonymous caller said he was fed up with how organized crime was destroying Colombian society. He was speaking up, he said, because he didn't want his children to grow up in such a corrupt society.

"Who is this guy?" Miguel demanded of Estrada.

In late June 1995, Jorge met Yusti one afternoon in a neighborhood overlooking the residential complex that Jorge reluctantly disclosed was where he thought Pallomari was in seclusion. Jorge could not plead complete ignorance without appearing to be hiding something. Still, he pretended not to know which building was the accountant's.

Throughout their brief conversation, Jorge noticed that Yusti seemed uncommonly distracted and impatient. The *sicario* asked no questions, nodded quickly to anything Jorge said, and kept checking his watch. "Do you have another appointment?" Jorge asked. It was nearly noon at the time.

"Yes, I'm afraid I do," said Yusti.

He had to be at El Rancho de Jonás, a restaurant some distance away. He held a lunch reservation for 12:30 p.m., and he had to be there on time. He was killing another diner, he explained—the architect of Estrada's multimillion-dollar state-of-the-art medical clinic. The hotline snitch had apparently been identified. The man who didn't want his children growing up in such a corrupt society was about to leave them fatherless.

Oh my God. Help him, Jorge prayed silently. But what he said aloud came out as a compliment to Yusti. "You must be a very sharp shooter," Jorge said.

Yusti grinned. He said he was using an automatic pistol with laser-assisted targeting. He couldn't miss. And he couldn't dillydally, either. He had a second assignment immediately after lunch—a two o'clock hit at a bus stop across town.

The orgy of killings was keeping Yusti too busy to concentrate on Pallomari. And that, at least, was a good thing—especially since Jorge had still not figured out how he was going to save the accountant . . . or, therefore, himself.

EL DORADO IN A DESK

AN OUTGROWTH OF MARIO DEL BASTO'S SURPRISE ARREST WAS THE immediate promotion of Jorge Salcedo as the cartel's solo chief of security. All the false rumors about Jorge's suspected role in Mario's capture never gained traction with the bosses. Immediately, the daily leaks from inside the Bloque de Búsqueda came to Jorge. He was looking at a list of scheduled task force raids one afternoon when he saw one planned for the residential neighborhood where Pallomari was hiding at his friend's apartment.

Now that Jorge was bent on saving Pallomari, a central feature of his own cartel escape plan, he couldn't afford to let the accountant fall into the hands of Colombian authorities. He was sure Pallomari would never get out of jail alive. The only mystery would be who got to him first—the godfathers, crooked cops, or compromised politicians.

Jorge arrived at Pallomari's door at about three in the afternoon. The man who owned the residence answered and denied that anyone else lived there. But Jorge persisted, and his tone grew increasingly urgent.

"It's an emergency. Guillermo's life is in danger," Jorge insisted.

Pallomari emerged uncertainly from a back room. "What are you doing here?" he demanded. He offered no gestures of hospitality.

Jorge described the pending raid "somewhere in this area," and since he could not be certain which house, he suggested that Pallomari stay away at least for the next twelve hours. Jorge offered a safe house where he could spend the night and wait out the raid. Still, Pallomari hesitated. His two sons, aged fifteen and eleven, appeared at their father's side. They were frightened.

"Your boys will be safer if you're not here," Jorge told him.

Pallomari agreed. He packed an overnight bag and joined Jorge in his silver Mazda 626 for a ten-minute ride to the safe house, one of the cartel residences code-named the Twins. Jorge had converted the smaller of two similar houses into a listening post where wiretapped lines were recorded, copied, and stored. Only Jorge had routine access, and he tried to assure Pallomari that he would be safe there for the night.

"I'll be back in the morning after the raids to take you home," Jorge said before Pallomari locked the door behind him.

The task force did not, as it turned out, hit the residence of Pallomari's friend, and Jorge returned to collect Pallomari the next morning. Pallomari did not respond to his knocks. He had already left. Jorge considered it a healthy sign that Pallomari didn't trust anyone. For one thing, it minimized chances that he might naively walk into a cartel trap.

And Jorge didn't trust Pallomari much, either—at least not with his life. He dared not tell the accountant about the Yusti murder plot or about his own secret role trying to delay it. Jorge feared that Pallomari, in desperation, might sell him out for the promise of a cartel pardon. He could easily imagine the results: they would both be dead, quite possibly the twin targets of another busy day for César Yusti.

THE PACE OF BLOQUE RAIDS quickened throughout June 1995, a by-product of new evidence developed out of the Pallomari records and out of the still-secret cooperation of cartel operatives in Florida. One of the unexpected consequences was to drive a number of cartel lieutenants to voluntarily surrender. Some found it intolerable hiding out and living the life of hunted criminals. But Miguel seemed to relish the forced isolation. It meant fewer distractions from his work. He still met visitors, still made phone calls, and still fretted about moving drugs and currency. He had no intention of surrendering.

Anticipating that he might be forced to relocate in the face of Bloque raids, Miguel made duplicate copies of key documents, cartel phone numbers, and lists of friends. On diskettes and computer printouts, he kept records of everyone who owed the cartel for past favors, with many of those favors specifically enumerated. He stashed files in various houses around Cali, along with extra checkbooks and other financial records. Wherever he might be in hiding, Miguel wanted easy access to documents that he considered essential to his political leverage and to the cartel's daily operations.

Miguel had lived undisturbed for about two years in the Wall House until one morning in June 1995. Jorge picked up a wiretapped phone exchange indicating a planned raid on the address. He rushed to inform Miguel, who contacted the cartel's man inside the Bloque police unit. Captain Buitrago responded: yes, a raid was scheduled, but not until about three o'clock in the afternoon.

The task force could always be trusted to keep to its schedule. Miguel had nearly four hours to pack before fleeing his residence. He took a leisurely shower, dressed in his traditional black slacks and blue shirt, and then sat down to a hearty lunch.

When the raiding party arrived, it found the house empty except for the pool boy, a young man named Carlos, who said the owners were on an extended trip to Europe. He had never even met them, he said. After a thorough search, the government team left empty-handed. For Miguel, however, the task force discovery had compromised his Wall House sanctuary—he could never return.

Later that day, cartel wiretaps picked up a man's voice on a call to Bloque police. He was angry. The caller was the apparent tipster, and he berated police for letting Miguel get away. He charged that the raiders seemed to move with deliberate sloth. He accused them of criminal incompetence. There were no real clues to the man's identity.

Miguel's new base was a house on a cul-de-sac in the Ciudad Jardín district owned by Salomón Prado, a friend since their days as school-boys together. Miguel called him Chalo. His friend worked in Bogotá, leaving the Cali house vacant for months at a time. It was spacious and comfortable and featured a large Jacuzzi. The drug boss could pick up right where he left off the night before, running the cartel business without skipping a beat. But first Miguel wanted to know about a new desk he had left behind at the Wall House. His assistant Mateo Zapata contacted Carlos, the pool boy, for a post-raid report.

What did the raiding party do . . . what did it examine . . . how many were there, and in what parts of the house did they snoop around? The questions were routine and casual until Miguel pressed Mateo to find out about the desk. He wanted to know if it attracted any suspicions or special attention . . . did anyone look through it? Was it damaged in any way? The pool boy said it was unnoticed and un-touched.

"It passed the test," enthused a delighted Miguel. But Mateo was not so eager to celebrate. Later, alone with Jorge, he complained to the security chief that the desk was a potential security hazard.

The desk was custom-made of a red wood, possibly cherry, and de-signed with a hollow chamber in its four- to five-inch-thick top. Within that secret space, Miguel was keeping a set of his sensitive cartel records, canceled checks, computer printouts, and diskettes—a treasury of data that documented payoffs to everyone on the cartel dole. Mateo called it Miguel's "ransom demand." Politicians might forget that they owed the Rodríguez Orejuela family for past favors, but Miguel would never for-get. And he kept plenty of proof at hand. The desk had been designed and built by Genaro Angel, the cartel's carpenter, who delivered it to the Wall House barely a week before the raid. Few knew of its existence. It was Miguel's plan to move the desk wherever he went.

"El Señor is kind of stupid about this, I'm afraid," Mateo told Jorge.

Having all those files in one place, and kept in such close proxim-ity, was unnecessarily risky. Mateo seemed to want Jorge to help make that case to Miguel. And Jorge certainly agreed with Mateo's general as-sessment. He nodded but let the matter drop. Miguel had intended to keep the desk a secret from just about everyone, including Jorge. And Jorge wanted to keep it that way. Miguel's secret would be Jorge's secret, too.

It was obvious to Jorge that Miguel's red desk held an intelligence bonanza. Its contents were the stuff of dreams for prosecutors in Bogotá or Miami—the evidentiary equivalent of the treasures of El Dorado, the Sierra Madre, and Montezuma all rolled into one. In the right hands, it could destroy the Cali cartel.

THE CHALO RESIDENCE in Ciudad Jardín, or "Garden City," had always been considered a convenient but temporary stopover for Miguel since he had never been a visitor to the house. It seemed highly unlikely that any Colombian intelligence reports could link Miguel to the random address. The godfather felt so safe, in fact, that he invited one of his wives to join him at the residence.

At the time, Miguel was trying to open a line of secret negotiations with undisclosed government officials using a former leftist priest as an intermediary. The ex-cleric, Bernardo Hoyos, had recently served as mayor of Barranquilla in the north and was a controversial figure in his own right, with ties to radical causes. Miguel wanted support from Hoyos's political allies. But when the former priest arrived at Chalo's house one afternoon, he was followed.

U.S. embassy–based American drug enforcement agents had developed information earlier that Hoyos had been in contact with Miguel. The DEA agents acted on suggestions to keep an eye on the leftist activist whenever he came to town. It led them to the Cali cul-de-sac.

Jorge Salcedo was barely awake the next morning when his windows were rattled by the rotor noise of a low-flying Colombian National Police helicopter swooping past his residence. He lived about a five-minute drive from Miguel's hideout and had a chilling hunch that the Chalo house was ground zero of a raiding party.

He dressed hastily and headed for the safe house. A moment later he spotted the helicopter. It was hovering noisily above Chalo's house. In a vacant lot behind the house, Jorge counted at least ten uniformed police deployed to prevent any escape out the back. He ordered his crew of bodyguards to withdraw from the area immediately. If they were noticed, it might tip authorities that Miguel was nearby.

Jorge never got close enough himself to see a police SUV with heavily tinted windows parked out on the cul-de-sac. Inside the vehicle, the American drug agents Chris Feistl and Dave Mitchell watched the action and listened to police radio reports from the house. Because of efforts to minimize the appearance of U.S. involvement in the raid, only their colleague Jerry Salameh was in the house. He was a dark-haired, olive-complexioned Palestinian-American who looked Colombian.

Inside the house, the raiding party found only Marta Lucía, a maid, and the stand-in driver Carlos Millán, who was working to give Mateo and Fercho some days off. The presence of Miguel's fourth wife and a known cartel aide set off high expectations. But after nearly two hours without finding any trace of Miguel, the raiding party assumed that he had been tipped in time to escape. By the time the Colombian raiding party abandoned the search and left the house, the local media had camped outside. There was no hiding. The front page of *El Tiempo* the next morning carried a photograph of the DEA agent Salameh at the door.

Some time before noon that morning, Mateo paged Jorge. The boss needed a rescue. Jorge drove immediately to the house on the cul-de-sac, where he would pose as a friend of the traumatized Marta Lucía. Jorge pulled in to the residence garage and shut the door behind him.

Miguel was in a sour mood. He was about to move into the residence of another woman, which chilled relations with Marta Lucía. He also had spent two hours during the raid hiding in a cramped space under the hot tub, concealed along with the plumbing and heating systems under the Jacuzzi. Miguel was sufficiently claustrophobic that his confinement had been an ordeal. Jorge escorted him out to the garage and opened the trunk of his Mazda 626. Miguel hesitated before climbing into another confined space.

"It's only five minutes," Jorge assured him.

LOVE IN THE TIME OF CRISIS

RAIDS THAT FORCED MIGUEL RODRÍGUEZ OREJUELA TO RELOCATE twice in a matter of days had one notable benefit for his chief of security: Jorge could set aside his assignment to hunt down and kill Pallomari. It was a welcome relief, and Jorge savored it as long as he could. Then one morning he encountered Dario, his second-in-command.

"Hey, Richard," said the young security aide with conspiratorial glee. "Do you know who's going to be killed?" Jorge shrugged and waited. "Pallomari—and not only that, but his wife, too!"

"What?" Jorge feigned surprise about Pallomari, but his shock regarding Patricia Pallomari was genuine. "How do you know that?"

"William told me. He says Pallomari is dangerous. He talks too much."

Jorge said nothing to acknowledge his own role in the planned Pallomari hit, and it appeared that Dario did not know that part of the plot. But Jorge pressed to learn how much more of the secret had been shared.

"Yes, the accountant, I can understand. I know there was a problem after his arrest last year—but why the wife?" he asked.

"Well," Dario began, as if stating the obvious, "imagine how much she knows."

Jorge had an uneasy feeling. He had to assume that William's inner circle all knew about it. He also worried that his delaying tactics might have worked too well. Maybe Dario wasn't told about Jorge's role in the assignment because the logistics job had been handed off to someone else—maybe to one of William's friends. That would be a disaster. It was an absurd situation, but the only way Jorge could protect Pallomari was to be in charge of setting up his assassination. As soon as he was alone, Jorge paged Yusti to arrange another meeting.

It was also getting urgent for Jorge to make contact with U.S. authorities. A visit to the embassy in Bogotá seemed unavoidable. He considered various disguises—hats, scarves, and, most radically, shaving off his beard. Waiting could not keep Pallomari alive indefinitely. Almost immediately, however, priorities shifted again. Yusti disappeared, apparently off on an extended assignment out of town. Jorge didn't ask questions but figured his good luck was someone else's tragedy.

Miguel's new hideout was in the Cali residence of a beautiful young widow. She was Claudia Escobar Endo, widow of Claudio Endo—the bullying trafficker cornered in his ranch house bathroom and riddled with bullets by El Gamín and his team of vengeful *sicarios*. Her daughter had turned five years old, and Miguel had become a replacement father figure. However, only Jorge and Miguel's two closest aides—Mateo and Castillo—knew the boss was hiding in her house.

Jorge assumed a new role as romantic enabler. At Miguel's request, Jorge arranged for Claudia's visit to a local clinic for liposuction treatment. And since Miguel could not risk a visit to her bedside, Jorge delivered the flowers and good wishes in the boss's place. When Claudia recovered enough for drives around town, Miguel had Jorge take them on house-hunting trips. The godfather planned to buy her and her daughter a new ranch or vacation home.

During one real estate tour, Jorge found Miguel down on the ground on his hands and knees—giving a "horsey ride" to the squealing five-year-old. For the painfully solemn boss, his undignified state at the moment of their encounter was embarrassing. Miguel's scowl told Jorge that he was never to breathe a word of what he had just seen. Jorge immediately backed away and left the little family to its privacy.

The romance between Miguel and Claudia had been growing since the days immediately following her husband's slaying. Jorge found her a mellowing presence on El Señor, who treated her with almost worshipful respect. While Claudia and everyone else knew that Endo's killing was a cartel hit, Jorge doubted that the widow was aware of Miguel's direct role approving the bloody execution.

Their first contact came through an intermediary. Endo's killers had departed the murder scene with hands full of jewelry they found in Claudia's bedroom—some of it with special sentimental value to the new widow. After the intermediary's intercession, Miguel arranged for the jewelry's return. Later, they met—and the fifty-one-year-old godfather fell for her, as Jorge described it, like "a teenager in love." He also became her fierce defender. When Endo's brothers had tried to claim ownership of the dead trafficker's properties, Miguel intervened to enforce Claudia's rights to retain the assets. Duly intimidated, the Endo family quickly conceded.

Miguel's brief encampment at Claudia's residence lasted only about two weeks, but it provided the cartel boss with a respite from cartel business—a sort of forced vacation. Meanwhile, preparations for a new hideout in the Santa Rita section of Cali were stepped up. Miguel was headed next to an apartment previously occupied by his chief *sicario,* Memo Lara. But first it had to be properly outfitted to accommodate cartel business demands. For one thing, it needed a secret escape chamber, or *caleta*—the hidden spaces or panic rooms that the godfathers were having built into the walls of all their hideouts. Tanga Vélez, a brother of Freckles, was one of the installers.

"I've been working night and day on the *caletas*. They're beautiful," Tanga had boasted to Jorge recently. He said the escape vault at Memo Lara's former apartment was especially clever—disguised behind the wall of a small bathroom with quick access from the living room.

The new hideout was also being outfitted with greater telephone capacity. Daily cartel operations required multiple phone lines with conference call capabilities, continuous music while on hold, and various other features not in wide use in 1995 Colombia. Miguel insisted on Panasonic equipment in all of his residences. Callers on hold could count on listening to Scott Joplin's ragtime theme from *The Sting*.

Telephone installation was entrusted to a Cali-based phone company executive named Carlos Espinosa, known in the cartel by his nickname Pinchadito. He wore white shoes, a gold Rolex, and imported men's cologne, and he was one of the cartel's most trusted associates. Jorge considered him one of those most responsible for keeping Miguel a step ahead of Bloque raiding parties. Pinchadito always made certain that phone lines leading to Miguel were routed through a remote switching device that foiled any electronic attempts to trace calls over those lines. As a result, to the Colombian government and its CIA and DEA partners, Miguel's telephones always appeared to be located in some downtown building miles away from his actual location.

Without *caletas* and special phone systems, Claudia's residence was secure only so long as no one noticed Miguel coming and going. The drug boss was forced to leave cartel business to others for several days. He might have grown anxious and frustrated anywhere else, but in Claudia's company Miguel was relaxed and happy—more so than at any time Jorge could remember in his six and a half years with the Cali godfather.

But happy days and carefree times were brief.

The cartel suffered an intelligence blow in the spring of 1995 when Sergeant Valencia was bounced from the Bloque de Búsqueda. He failed a polygraph test administered as part of an internal investigation into task force leaks. That left the cartel with only Captain Buitrago inside the police side of the task force.

Valencia immediately joined the cartel's security team. Miguel told Jorge to put him to whatever use best suited the organization's needs. There weren't many. Valencia was so thoroughly discredited within the military that he was shunned by uniformed colleagues and had no access to useful information. He became an instant rival to Jorge, however, angling for Miguel's attention as an intelligence adviser.

Meanwhile, more cartel lieutenants surrendered to authorities. Meetings of the cartel godfathers were suspended as too risky. Chepe

Santacruz moved to Bogotá, hoping to find greater anonymity in a bigger city. His penchant for good food, however, brought him out of seclusion on July 4, 1995, to dine at the Carbón de Palo, a neighborhood steak restaurant. Someone spotted the notorious diner and notified authorities. A police raiding party arrived before the check to arrest him.

With Fourth of July fireworks going off back home, U.S. drug agents at the embassy in Bogotá celebrated the fact that half of the Cali cartel brain trust was now behind bars. But it was Miguel, the godfather of the godfathers, who remained the most elusive and their most prized target.

By July 1995, the DEA partners Chris Feistl and David Mitchell had observed their first anniversary on the ground in Colombia. They had developed a number of confidential informants and learned their way around Cali, both geographically and politically, but they had yet to land a serious blow against the cartel they were sent to dismantle. They looked to Miami and colleagues in Operation Cornerstone for help.

The customs special agent Eddie Kacerosky had a number of cooperating witnesses, including former cartel operatives indicted in southern Florida. Feistl had worked cases with Kacerosky in Miami, and the two men respected each other's work. In the highly politicized world of major crimes investigations, competition between agencies such as Customs and DEA—and FBI and CIA and Immigration and so on—is a chronic obstacle to law-enforcement and intelligence cooperation. The exceptions often are facilitated by personal relationships that bridge those bureaucratic chasms. Agents Feistl and Kacerosky had that sort of mutual trust.

Feistl made the initial contact. He asked Kacerosky to go back to his cooperating sources and have them make lists of people in Cali whom they knew to be closest to Miguel Rodríguez Orejuela. Feistl and Mitchell would personally tail those most likely to lead them to the big boss.

The result a few days later was Kacerosky's lightly coded, two-part list labeled "Best Leads to Find Mickey" and "Mickey in Disneyland—

Relevant Locations." It was seven pages of handwritten names, addresses, and maps scrawled on a legal pad, listed in order of relative investigative value. Number one in Eddie's estimation was Mateo, "Mickey's most frequently used chauffeur." His note included the address of a private lumber business that Mateo owned, and it went on to describe Miguel's driver in detail: "His beeper number is 671771, code 067. Mateo is appx. 5'5" tall, 160 pounds with black hair, a black moustache. He is in his 30's and likes sunglasses. He almost always drives 4-door sedans with tinted windows, which are owned by Mickey. He is light-skinned and has straight hair. According to appx. six sources, Mateo crosses paths with Mickey three or four times a day."

Feistl and Mitchell immediately picked up Mateo's trail only to have their eager anticipation turn to weary disappointment. For several days, they followed the chauffeur back and forth to his business address but never anywhere near Miguel. What the DEA agents didn't know was that as part of their routine rotation, Mateo was off duty. This was Jorge "Fercho" Castillo's turn at Miguel's side.

The DEA agents were still chasing the off-duty chauffeur on a morning in July when Jorge Salcedo picked up his copy of *El Tiempo* and read a small story out of Miami. It reported that a number of American lawyers for the Cali cartel were facing racketeering and conspiracy charges. In a brief mention, the newspaper article said that Joel Rosenthal had escaped the most serious charges but had pleaded guilty to a felony. Jorge understood instantly that a felony conviction was an especially devastating development for an attorney with Rosenthal's long ties with the government.

But Jorge could barely contain his excitement. He read and reread the brief lines about Rosenthal, almost in disbelief over his astounding good fortune. His American lawyer friend was in such serious legal trouble that all Jorge could say was *Thank God.* It was the answer to his prayers.

WHO IS PALLOMARI?

J ORGE SALCEDO COULD DROP PLANS TO SHAVE HIS BEARD. HE WOULD not be waiting, after all, in a line outside the U.S. embassy, exposed to suspicious eyes and hiding behind a disguise. No more blind calls to the CIA, either. He would not have to endure being treated like some delusion-peddling nut. He didn't even need directory assistance from the overseas operator. Jorge already had Joel Rosenthal's number.

He tossed aside his copy of *El Tiempo* with the story about Rosenthal's legal troubles and headed directly to a neighborhood Telecom office near his southern Cali home. By 10:00 a.m., Jorge was in a public phone booth placing an overseas call to Miami.

No phone call he had ever made was so charged with life-and-death consequences. Jorge saw it as the first step in saving Guillermo Pallomari. But it was also one big step past the point of no return—leaving him with the possibility of two very different outcomes: a bullet in the ear, or escape from the cartel. If this were a poker hand, Jorge was "going all in."

The phone was ringing fifteen hundred miles to the north. Jorge expected at any second to hear the reliably cheerful voice of Rosenthal's secretary. Instead, his call was routed to a recording device. Rosenthal's law offices were closed. Jorge had to think fast. He had not composed a voice-mail message for the occasion. It would have to be ambiguous enough to be safe no matter who retrieved it, but direct enough to be clearly understood by Rosenthal. The electronic beep signaled Jorge to begin: "Hello, Joel," he said in English. "This is Jorge calling from Cali. I'm so sorry to hear what has happened. I just wanted you to know that I am on your side. And if there is anything I can do, like we have done in the past, please—you can count on me."

Jorge left a pager number and hung up, expecting that it might take a day or so for Rosenthal to check his messages. Barely an hour later his pager went off with an insistent ding . . . ding . . . ding . . . ding. It flashed an unfamiliar Miami phone number.

Back in the same phone booth near the Unicentro shopping mall, Jorge dialed the Miami number and heard Joel Rosenthal answer. They greeted each other warmly, each thanking the other for responding. Jorge said that he was hoping there was something he could do for Joel under Rule 35, the sentence-reduction provision Jorge learned about working with Rosenthal on the Noriega case.

"Thank you, Jorge," Rosenthal responded. "You can help me a lot. I'm here now with Agent Kacerosky, and he would like to speak with you."

THE TIMING OF THEIR TELEPHONE RENDEZVOUS was extraordinary, another one of those coincidences that supposedly never happen in Colombia.

Jorge Salcedo had recently come to the attention of U.S. law enforcement, thanks mostly to Joel Rosenthal. The indicted lawyer had told Kacerosky he thought that Jorge was a candidate to defect from the cartel if properly approached. And he offered to make that approach personally—in return for sentencing leniency.

Kacerosky, in his seven-page list of people to watch in Cali, had included as number three "Jorge Salcedo at Avenida Cascajal #28." The address wasn't current, but it was the same Jorge Salcedo. Kacerosky's note to the DEA agents cautioned: "After you get this list and kick it around down there, call me on Salcedo. I think there's a chance in concert with a buddy of his here we grabbed in the last round up, that we telephonically can convince Salcedo to help you locate Mickey. Call me on this before doing anything. Obviously, Salcedo's buddy will push this in the hopes of a Rule 35 reduction."

Kacerosky's reference to "Salcedo's buddy" was, of course, a reference to Rosenthal. It was as if Jorge and Joel had been together over breakfast at the InterContinental hotel instead of plotting separately on two different continents. Each saw the other as his salvation. But the deal still had to be sealed—and Eddie Kacerosky was the key. He greeted Jorge in Spanish and with a round of verbal slaps in the face: "It's a good thing you called, Mr. Salcedo . . . you're in a lot of trouble."

Jorge was briefly taken aback as Kacerosky continued on the offensive: "I was about to indict you . . . I've got your bank records . . . There may be a way that you can help yourself . . . I want Miguel Rodríguez."

But Kacerosky had carried his bluff a bit too far. Jorge waited for the American to pause for breath and gently interrupted. "I don't have a bank account," Jorge said in English. "And I can get Miguel for you any day."

"You know where he is right now?" Kacerosky asked, again in Spanish.

"Yes, I know where he is," Jorge said, insisting on using English. "And I know where he will be tonight and tomorrow and every night. But we don't have time for that. First, you've got to save Pallomari. They're going to kill him."

There was no immediate reaction over the telephone line. Finally, Kacerosky asked, "Who is Pallomari?"

JORGE NEEDED A SAFE TELEPHONE somewhere to take a call from American agents that Kacerosky vowed were trustworthy. Jorge had doubts. They were drug agents attached to the embassy, and Jorge had heard too many cartel boasts about spies among the embassy staff. Jorge had doubts about a lot of things, including the Americans' grasp of the situation's urgency. He was still bothered that he had to explain to Kacerosky the importance of Pallomari. It was unnerving enough to be entering into a life-jeopardizing alliance with strangers. He hoped the Bogotá-based DEA agents were better informed. At least the agents satisfied one of Jorge's demands—they were not Colombians.

Before agreeing to meet anyone, Jorge told Kacerosky that he didn't trust anyone in Colombia—not the police, the army, the president, or General Serrano. Even those who were not corrupt too often had aides or friends or cousins who worked for the cartel. That's why no one could know Jorge's identity, not even any other Americans at the embassy. And Jorge insisted on one more condition: he did not want to see anyone who even appeared to be Colombian. Kacerosky had to send agents who looked American. He assured Jorge that he had just the guys. They were already in Cali and could call Jorge at any number he considered safe in order to set up a meeting.

Jorge turned to Lena for help. Without telling his wife the purpose, he said he needed a private telephone to receive a very sensitive call. It could not be a phone belonging to anyone in the family. She suggested her hairdresser's salon a few minutes' drive from their residence. The owner was a friend. The couple fibbed that their residence phone was out of order. Lena asked Jorge no questions. The call for Jorge at the beauty parlor came shortly before noon.

"I'm the guy Eddie Kacerosky told to call you," said the youthful male voice. "When can we meet?"

"The sooner, the better," Jorge said. "I suggest we meet outside Cali."

Jorge offered directions to the International Center for Tropical Agriculture (CIAT). It was a United Nations–supported experimental farm out near the airport, a half-hour drive from central Cali. CIAT's staff of scientists and specialists came from all over the world, so two North Americans in that area would attract no special attention. Long, straight rural roads also made it easy to spot tails or surveillance. Neither Jorge nor the agents trusted each other yet. For Jorge, the worry was being exposed, even accidentally. For the Americans, the worry was cartel treachery.

When Jorge drove up to the rendezvous point, about a half mile from CIAT's main gate, the American agents in a white Sprint economy car were already parked off the road next to a field of sugarcane. They had come early, circled around the area, and plotted a plan for retreat and counterattack if this meeting turned out to be a cartel setup. Jorge parked several car lengths in front of the agents to give them a good look at him. He was alone. He was unarmed. He approached the agents' car with both hands clearly visible. In one hand he carried his identity papers.

In the white car, Chris Feistl was seated behind the wheel and David Mitchell was in the backseat, leaning forward to watch Jorge amble toward them.

"You know, that guy reminds me of somebody," Feistl said.

"Yeah, right. It's that actor. He could double for Sean Connery," Mitchell said.

Jorge opened the front door, ducked, and dropped into the vacant front passenger seat, taking stock of his new partners amid the introductions. His first impression was that the DEA agents seemed just a little jittery. They spent more time at first checking their mirrors and watching the road than taking notes. But Kacerosky was right about one thing: both were blond and blue eyed and not the least bit Colombian looking. Like Jorge, both of them were over six feet tall and broad shouldered. The three big men pretty much filled the compact car. Feistl kept the Sprint's air-conditioning running.

From the backseat, Mitchell asked the first question: "Is it true you can get us to Miguel Rodríguez right away?"

"Yes, of course," Jorge said.

"Well, how is that possible?" Mitchell demanded.

"Because I am in charge of his security," Jorge said evenly. "You can have Miguel any day you want, but we have to save Pallomari before they kill him."

"Who's Pallomari?" asked one of the agents.

ASIDE FROM THE FACT that Kacerosky and the DEA agents seemed to Jorge to be woefully unaware of Pallomari's importance in the cartel scheme of things, he was very impressed with the Americans. They were men of action. He liked that. And they were beyond the corrupting influence of the cartel. He especially liked that. But Feistl and Mitchell also came across as sincere, good-natured, and strong willed, characteristics that eased Jorge's fears. "I'm putting my life in your hands," he told them. "And not just mine, but my family's."

Their roadside conference continued for more than two hours. It ranged across many subjects. Jorge told the American agents about cartel security procedures, the hidden vaults, the lookouts that patrolled the neighborhoods, the radio alert system—all the reasons why capturing Miguel would be difficult. He told them to trust no one in the Bloque de Búsqueda. He told them what to look for on a raid to confirm whether Miguel lived there—the Panasonic telephone equipment and certain kinds of food in the refrigerator for his hypoglycemic condition and a Mazda 626 in the parking garage. And he told them about Pallomari, the accountant.

Repeatedly, the young drug agents interrupted Jorge to ask him the same question in a number of different ways. It came down to "Why are you doing this?" Jorge told them that he originally came to the cartel on a mission to stop Pablo Escobar, but that he was being asked to do things now that he could not stomach. He said he was also fed up with the violence and corruption that he saw all around him.

"I'm an engineer. I don't belong in this world," Jorge told them. "But I'm trapped."

FEISTL AND MITCHELL did their best to give Jorge a thorough grilling. They tried to maintain their investigative skepticism. But twenty minutes into their marathon interview they knew Jorge Salcedo was a rare find. After a year of scraping and scratching for every little tip on the whereabouts of the Cali cartel boss, they had just been handed the virtual key to Miguel's front door. Jorge was soft-spoken, forthright, and utterly convincing. Everything he told them rang true. Much of what he told them was intelligence gold.

The agents wanted to move fast—grab Miguel now and then work on the accountant later. Jorge agreed to go along with that order of battle. The first challenge was to find out exactly where Miguel was. Jorge knew he was in a residential building called Colinas de Santa Rita, an upscale address with about eight floors near the Cali River. He had his first assignment as a DEA informant: pinpoint Miguel's apartment.

They agreed to communicate through pagers, leaving coded telephone numbers whenever they needed to talk or arrange for another meeting. The code was simple, but effective: subtract one number from each digit relayed to the pager. If Jorge sent the agents the phone number 567-3456, for example, they would reach him by calling 456-2345. Jorge liked the agents' care and obvious concern for security. He gained confidence as their meeting went on. By the time they parted, he was starting to call them Chris and Dave.

Of course, the agents could not refer to Jorge by his real name or by Richard, his cartel nickname. To avoid even an accidental slip, they bestowed a new name on their newest confidential informant. His DEA code name: Sean . . . as in Connery.

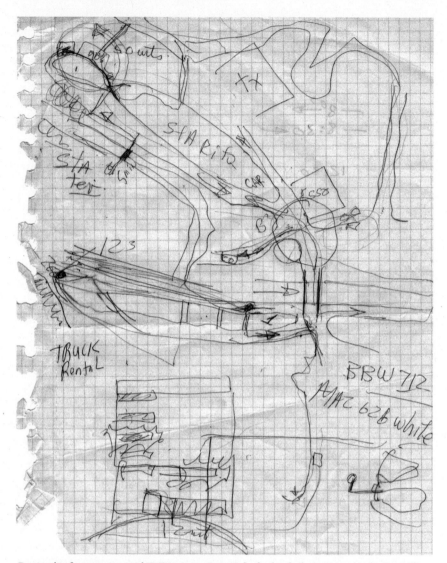

During his first meeting with DEA agents, Jorge Salcedo sketched out a map to the Santa Rita neighborhood where cartel godfather Miguel Rodríguez Orejuela was hiding. The residence was a building of six or eight floors circled in the upper left corner of the map. It is also depicted at the bottom of the page. At the time, Jorge didn't know whether Miguel was living on the fourth or second floor—both of which are highlighted in the drawing. Jorge also notes the license number of a white Mazda that, if found at the site, would confirm Miguel's presence. An intersection just across the Cali River is also circled where Jorge warned that cartel guards would be stationed. (Map from DEA files)

THEY'RE COMING

EVEN AT THREE IN THE MORNING, THE JULY NIGHT IN CALI WAS warm and sultry. Jorge Salcedo would have felt uncomfortable even under normal circumstances. But hiding in the shadows watching the world's biggest crime boss was anything but normal circumstances. Until the night before, he had been working for that crime boss. He still was . . . in a very complicated and dangerous sort of way. From a hillside vantage point, Jorge had watched through the night as one by one the lights went out in windows of the Colinas de Santa Rita apartment building. At least one of the windows in that building belonged to the secret residence of Miguel Rodríguez Orejuela.

Jorge knew well that Miguel's work habits kept him up and on the phones late into most nights, routinely until three or four in the morning. Before the boss was forced to move from the comfort and security of his favorite residence a month before, Jorge typically stayed at his side until some time past midnight. But the visitors Jorge ferried in and out—the politicians, the friends, the occasional journalist—were no longer welcome.

Miguel was a fugitive now, hunted so aggressively that he could not allow anyone to know precisely where he spent his nights. Even Jorge knew only the building. And Jorge's men, Miguel's early-warning system of street-level sentries, knew only the general neighborhood. They were restricted to a perimeter at least six blocks from the building. Such was the state of paranoia in the Cali cartel in mid-July 1995 that the godfather slept in hiding even from his own chief of security.

In Cali, everyone had secrets. The fact that Jorge had crossed the line to become a law-enforcement informant was only one of them— but it was a secret both from the cartel and from his wife and children. Ignorance was for the family's own good, Jorge reasoned, at least for now. It meant that he alone had the burden of acting normal while taking life-threatening chances.

It was nearly four in the morning when the last lit windows finally went out in a corner apartment. They were on the fourth floor and almost certainly the apartment of Miguel. Just to be absolutely sure, however, Jorge immediately pressed the call button on his phone. After two or three rings, a single light on the same floor came back on, and the weary voice of Castillo answered the phone.

"Fercho, the equipment is in place. Good night," Jorge said softly, a coded way of reporting that his sentries were at their stations and that he was going home. Jorge clicked off the connection and watched the last light go out again. It was confirmed. Miguel was in bed just down the hall from Castillo . . . on the fourth floor. Still to be determined: the precise apartment number.

JORGE AND HIS new DEA partners met the next day in the late afternoon. Jorge picked the place. Their original meeting site near the experimental farm was too far away, nearly a thirty-minute drive. Instead, Jorge summoned Feistl and Mitchell to a mall under construction on the north side of town. It was close enough to Miguel that Jorge could respond quickly and without excuses for delays if called by the boss. The future Chipichape shopping mall, then under construction, offered excellent privacy behind safety barriers, heavy equipment, and piles of debris. There was a lot of mud and no security at the site.

Both Jorge and the Americans arrived with fresh intelligence. The drug agents had investigated ownership of apartments in the Colinas de Santa Rita building. They found two apartments registered in the names of known cartel operatives. Feistl greeted Jorge with two closed fists extended, concealing something.

"Pick a hand," he told Jorge. "Left or right?"

Jorge tentatively tapped Chris on his left knuckles. The agent opened his left hand to reveal a piece of paper on which was written the number 402. He opened the other hand. The number was 801.

"It's the fourth floor," Jorge said, disclosing his overnight observations.

"Four-oh-two. We have a winner," Feistl said, grinning.

Talk turned to plotting the raid. Feistl and Mitchell intended to act immediately on their new information. Jorge realized for the first time just how fast things were going to change. The pace of developments was no longer in his exclusive control. They discussed strategies for how best to bring armed military personnel into the building. Jorge drew them a map, described the security watch, and shared some invasion advice. The Americans said they could be ready to launch a raid on the building by Saturday morning.

It was already Thursday evening. Jorge still hadn't told his wife or anyone else in his family that they very likely were going to have to leave their homes and flee for safety to another country. As quickly as things were happening, they could all be on a plane for the United States in a matter of days—maybe even hours. And that was if everything went right. He thought of all the ways that things could go wrong—and decided to page Feistl for a midnight meeting.

The American agents were parked on a lightly traveled street near the Unicentro mall when Jorge came out of the shadows dressed entirely in black. They thought he was "acting kind of strange." What they could not see behind his otherwise stoic demeanor was that Jorge was fighting his nerves. It helped ease his mind to plot strategies for the raid. He offered Feistl and Mitchell a chance to make a drive-by inspection of Colinas de Santa Rita. Jorge would pull his security teams out of the area for a very brief span—about thirty minutes—but enough time for the two agents to drive through and see the terrain firsthand.

Around midday on Friday, July 14, the DEA partners drove into the Santa Rita neighborhood just north of the Cali River. The street to Miguel's building was not a through street. It was lightly trafficked because only drivers with destinations along that street had any reason to approach the area. It was not a thoroughfare to anywhere else. It was the perfect setup for cartel security—one way in and one way out. As Feistl and Mitchell could see, a surprise assault would be difficult at any hour. Compounding their challenge was how to sneak in a raiding party of no fewer than thirty or forty armed policemen.

THE RAID WAS TOP SECRET. No one knew the target except Feistl and Mitchell, the agents had assured Jorge. Not even General Serrano, chief of the Colombian National Police, was in on the planning. A search warrant application filed with the attorney general's office said they intended to raid a lab suspected of making precursor chemicals for cocaine production. And to avoid involving the compromised Bloque de Búsqueda, the raiding party would come from Bogotá, traveling overland by night. Miguel's building would be invaded at five in the morning, when the drug lord would presumably be sound asleep.

Jorge checked in with his sentries stationed around the Santa Rita neighborhood. "Keep a sharp eye," he urged each one. Since the DEA agents knew all about the cartel security system, Jorge was counting on the Americans to beat his defenses. The more robust his security protection, the less likely he or his men would be blamed for Miguel's arrest. Such credibility could buy Jorge more time to save Pallomari and to get his family out of danger.

Finally, there was nothing more for Jorge to do but to wait—and to pray. On his drive home that night he sent up an endless stream of divine requests. His main prayer: *God, just get me out of this—it's time to stop.* Sometimes he added: *And please protect Pallomari a little longer.* He was preparing for bed when his pager sounded. It was Miguel trying to reach him immediately. Jorge went outside to return the call in privacy.

"Listen, Richard—it appears there will be a raid tomorrow morning," the godfather said in a low voice over Jorge's cell phone. Jorge asked if Miguel could tell him more, like where or when or anything else.

"A good source in Bogotá says that Serrano is flying into Cali tonight, but I'm sure they don't know where I am. And Buitrago would have called if the Bloque was coming for me," Miguel said. "But keep your eyes open. Alert your men to be especially careful tonight."

Jorge disconnected the call and tried not to panic. His first thought was to try stopping the raid. It was obviously compromised. The DEA had a leak, and Jorge feared disaster. But he also had to play an utterly convincing role as the cartel's chief of security no matter what happened. He immediately called in extra guards, assigning them to watch the gates of the Bloque garrison. He also called Enrique Sánchez, his most loyal aide who was already on duty, and directed him to the key vantage point—a traffic circle at the entrance to Miguel's lightly traveled street. "There may be a raid," he told Enrique. "Don't let anything get past you."

Then Jorge tried to reach Feistl and Mitchell. He hoped it wasn't too late to abort the mission. He dialed Feistl's SkyPager service and relayed a hastily conceived message to the operator.

"Stop dinner," Jorge dictated, his tone urgent even to the operator. "It won't be a surprise party."

Jorge returned home and prepared for bed, but he was having second thoughts about that last message. If the raid were called off now—right after Miguel's call to Jorge—it might look very suspicious. Now Jorge worried that he might have given himself away simply by reacting fearfully. Of course, a compromised raid could end badly, too. He was uncertain which outcome was worse. *God, I leave it in your hands.* Jorge prayed a final prayer and turned out the lights. He left his Motorola radiophone tuned in, its volume set low and its red indicator light glowing.

IN THE PREDAWN DARKNESS off of a deserted highway outside Cali, Feistl and Mitchell waited in the parking area of a closed pizza restaurant. They were meeting a contingent of antinarcotics police driving in from Bogotá. They had not seen Jorge's warning message. They were proceeding as planned. They had acquired two well-used delivery trucks—a pair of midsized box trucks used in Colombia to transport chickens. They were common sights on city streets in the wee hours of morning and therefore much less likely to draw attention than military trucks or troop carriers. Chris and Dave had paid 1 million pesos each (about $2,000 total) to hire these chicken trucks as makeshift troop carriers. Their hope was to get as close as possible to Miguel's building before being discovered.

The raiding party finally arrived, accompanied by a federal prosecutor to enforce the search warrant and assure that proper procedures were followed at all times. Feistl addressed the group and briefed them on the mission at hand. He said they were going to take down a lab making chemicals for cocaine production. He said everyone would ride in chicken trucks to protect the element of surprise. Mitchell took the wheel of one truck. Feistl climbed into the cab with the owner of the second, who had insisted on driving.

There were immediate murmurs of complaint as the uniformed, flak-jacketed, and heavily armed Colombian police climbed into the cargo compartments usually reserved for crates of chickens. The empty storage space reeked of unpleasant odors. Before the grumbling could turn to mutiny, the trucks hit the road for Cali.

It was still dark, a little after four in the morning. The two-truck caravan followed a circuitous route. Feistl called the turns in the lead truck and Mitchell followed. They meandered all over the city, making certain they were not followed and taking routes designed to confuse any cartel watchers along the way. When they finally approached the Cali River near the zoo, Feistl ordered the driver to slow down and to take the bridge at a slow and inconspicuous speed.

Enrique, a big man known around the cartel as El Gordo, was sitting astride his motorcycle when he watched the first chicken truck pass. He was immediately suspicious. But it was the second chicken truck only a few seconds behind it that alarmed him. He immediately activated his radiophone and, discarding any attempt to encode his message, shouted a warning: "Fercho! Fercho Castillo. Wake up. Wake up! Fercho, wake up!"

The cartel sentry kicked his bike into gear and raced down the street for a closer look at where the chicken trucks were stopped. Both trucks had pulled up at the Colinas de Santa Rita, and dozens of police were spilling out of them. Enrique called his boss: "Richard, Richard, Richard! They're coming! They're coming!"

In the Colinas de Santa Rita building, Enrique's voice had awakened Fercho Castillo, who, in turn, had time to alert Miguel. Across town, Jorge fumbled in the darkness for his Motorola.

"What is it?"

Enrique reported what looked to him like an invasion force suddenly surrounding an apartment building at the end of the street.

"Get away from the area," Jorge ordered. "Everybody move back. Put away your radios and get back. There's nothing anyone can do. We'll meet at the star."

The star was a Texaco gas station in the area. It would serve as a temporary command post, a place to exchange information without risking a radio intercept. Jorge complimented Enrique for his quick action, and then he ordered all of his people on duty at that hour to switch to a new radio channel. But he also ordered radio silence unless there was an emergency.

Jorge called Carlos Alfredo, his radio expert, and got him out of bed to disable the radiophones in Miguel's apartment. Their frequencies could be jammed remotely. His quick action would prevent police and DEA agents from making use of seized radiophones to compromise the cartel's secret communications network.

As a secret DEA informant, Jorge had precipitated this cartel emergency. As the cartel's chief of security, he was trying to minimize the damage. He was too scared to consider the irony.

PLEASE DON'T LEAVE

BY EARLY LIGHT ON SATURDAY MORNING, JULY 15, IT APPEARED THAT the sky was falling on the Cali cartel. Forty members of the National Police and a contingent of American drug agents had surrounded the Colinas de Santa Rita apartment building. A Bloque de Búsqueda unit arrived belatedly, along with the press and hordes of gawkers. Miguel Rodríguez Orejuela was believed trapped inside. The entire organization held its collective breath, hoping for a miracle escape—and darkly pondered: Who's the snitch?

Jorge Salcedo faced the day knowing that he would be one of the suspects—knowing, too, that his life depended on how convincingly he played his role as cartel chief of security under these circumstances.

Lena Salcedo did not ask about the flurry of morning calls. She said nothing about the urgent tones, the key words that revealed a crisis unfolding in her husband's world. He had refused breakfast. Jorge clearly was too nervous to eat. But she waited for him to say something.

"Apparently, they got Miguel," Jorge said as he prepared to leave.

She had guessed as much. She also knew it presented both opportunity and danger for her husband. Even though she had no inkling of his role as an informant, Lena worried for his safety. Like Jorge, however, she hid her feelings.

"Maybe now I'll get my husband back," she said gamely.

The morning was dragging on without news of any kind from the scene. He tried not to worry, but Jorge had expected to hear something within an hour or two. If Miguel had been caught immediately, he most likely would have been carted off for formal arrest procedures and a walk with General Serrano past every camera in Cali. The prolonged silence suggested that the drug boss might have escaped, most likely into a vault but possibly out of the building. For the first time Jorge considered the possibility that the raid could fail, a truly terrifying prospect. He imagined a cartel internal affairs inquiry that could get very nasty.

Jorge kept checking his DEA-provided pager to make sure that it was working and that he hadn't missed a message. It was set on vibrator mode and concealed in his pants pocket. Finally, he decided to check out the search scene for himself. Sometime around 9:00 a.m., Jorge parked across the Cali River from the Santa Rita neighborhood. Trees and buildings blocked his view of the Colinas de Santa Rita building, but Jorge spotted a group of his men gathered on a nearby pedestrian bridge. He was annoyed. He had ordered his men to leave the area and specifically not to congregate anywhere near the search scene. They could attract attention and, like Mario del Basto's ill-fated gathering, draw some sharp-eyed investigator to check them out.

One of those on the bridge was Rolando Mantilla, a former del Basto aide assigned to Jorge against both of their wishes. The former army corporal in his mid-thirties had a high opinion of himself, chafed at Jorge's egalitarian management style, and harbored deep-seated suspicions that Jorge might have been responsible for del Basto's shocking arrest. Mantilla seemed to be in a particularly surly mood that morning on the bridge, and Jorge chose not to make an issue of his orders being ignored.

"What's going on?" Jorge asked pleasantly.

"They're on the money," Mantilla growled with a nod toward the search site. "They're in his building, and he's in there, too."

"You're sure about that? Maybe he had time to get out," Jorge responded.

"No, he's in there. William told me."

Miguel's son had no experience whatsoever actually running the crime syndicate or marshaling forces in a crisis. There was no question, however, that cartel operatives would rally around William's leadership while his father was in jeopardy.

William's sudden authority mixed with fear and anger over his father's predicament combined to make him perhaps the most dangerous man in all of Cali. If he suspected Jorge was behind his father's capture, there would be no trial, no proof beyond a reasonable doubt. Natural instincts might suggest staying far away from the potentially volatile Rodríguez kid, but Jorge thought more strategically. If Jorge was worried about keeping William's trust, there was only one place to be: very, very close.

"Where is William now?" Jorge asked.

Mantilla clearly enjoyed telling Jorge something he didn't know. He said that Miguel's son was at Benito's bakery, a cartel favorite in the center of town. It was William's makeshift command center until further notice. Jorge worried that Mantilla might already be undermining William's confidence in him.

JORGE FOUND PARKING a half block from the bakery and was crossing the street when Amparo Rodríguez Orejuela stopped her car and called him over. Miguel's sister looked tired. She may have been crying.

"Richard, tell me—what do you know?" she pleaded.

Jorge tried to be reassuring, telling her that the raid caught everyone by surprise but that one of his men was able to send an alert before authorities reached the building. Maybe he got away. Maybe he found a place to hide, Jorge told her.

"I'm just praying to God that they catch him," she said. "That will finally stop the nightmare we've all been going through. I just hope they respect his life."

Jorge knew that the sister's concern was rooted in fear for the safety of her brother, not a family rift. Pablo Escobar's bloody end in the 1993 shoot-out still haunted the Rodríguez Orejuela family.

"I understand," Jorge said. "Hopefully, if he gets out of this, he can work out a surrender. We will do everything we can to protect him."

Amparo drove off, and Jorge continued to the bakery. He found William sitting alone at an outdoor table. Other cartel operatives were milling around, but none had sufficient rank to sit with the boss's son. Jorge joined him.

"How did it happen?" Jorge asked immediately, hoping that his feigned bewilderment was believable.

William looked grim as he shrugged and shook his head. He was trying to stay hopeful. He told Jorge not to jump to conclusions. "Just wait and see what happens," he said. He thought his father might have had time to escape into a *caleta.*

"Oh, so there is a vault there?" Jorge acted surprised and relieved.

As they talked at the table, their pagers and cell phones repeatedly interrupted conversation. Between those distractions, however, Jorge told William about Miguel's call the night before warning about a raid . . . about how extra security was arrayed . . . about how his early-warning system saved the day and sounded a last-minute alarm for Castillo. The young Rodríguez seemed intrigued and asked a lot of questions.

Jorge was just starting to feel relaxed when the DEA pager in his pocket suddenly vibrated and startled him. Its soft hum was masked by nearby traffic noises, but Jorge stood quickly and excused himself to visit the restroom. Behind a locked door he read the digital message on the luminous screen. "Call Patricia," it said, and included a local phone number.

Jorge Salcedo was a man of many names that morning. He was Richard to his cartel colleagues. He was Sean to the American DEA agents. But for this specific operation at the Colinas de Santa Rita building, he would be Patricia—as were Feistl and Mitchell. Patricia was their interchangeable code name. "Call Patricia" simply meant for Jorge to contact the DEA agents or vice versa.

Just outside the restroom was a telephone available for bakery customers. Jorge had used it on many occasions for cartel business. It was located in a private area where he could see if anyone approached. He was alone. He decided to dial the number, a pay phone at the Pizza Hut near Santa Rita. Moments later, it was ringing.

BUREAUCRATIC CONFUSION and jurisdictional politics had delayed the raiding party's access to Miguel's apartment. When the Colombians realized that the chemical lab mission was a ruse and that they were searching a building for the boss of the Cali cartel, they stopped everything. Colombian rules had to be followed, they informed the frustrated American agents.

First, the colonel in charge of the National Police insisted that the Bloque be contacted and allowed to send backup. It was the collegial thing to do. That delayed matters for about twenty minutes. When the backup team of at least fifty men arrived, it included Captain Efrén Buitrago, Miguel's secret informant.

Then the Bogotá prosecutor said she lacked the proper search warrant for this address, and she insisted that a local prosecutor be summoned with appropriate legal papers to oversee the police entry. That delayed matters another forty minutes or more. The cartel's friend in the Cali prosecutor's office sent over one of his trusted legal men. The element of surprise, or whatever remained of it, was lost in the red tape. Feistl and Mitchell were helpless to do anything about it.

It was more than ninety minutes before a search team was finally allowed to enter apartment 402. The investigators found a Panasonic phone system with multiple lines. They found a refrigerator filled with Miguel's favorite fruit and vegetable juices. They had already found a Mazda 626 in the garage, parked in space 402. Its license tag, BBW712, matched the car Jorge said Miguel was using.

They found three people in the apartment—two housekeepers and a man who said he lived there. He said his name was Fercho.

"Fercho?" said Chris Feistl. "Are you Jorge Castillo?"

"*Sí,*" he answered.

Feistl turned to his partner and grinned. "We've come to the right place, Dave—he's here."

Finding Miguel proved a more frustrating challenge, however. After a futile couple of hours searching the apartment and grilling Castillo, they were running out of ideas. Feistl and Mitchell had paced off some of the rooms and tried to spot false walls indicating a hidden vault or *caleta*. All they found was what Feistl called shoddy workmanship. In one powder room off the living room, the cabinetry was installed so close to the commode that the doors did not open without banging into the porcelain toilet bowl.

"Look at this lousy construction," he told Mitchell.

They decided it was time to call Patricia, not only for help locating the secret chamber, but also to confirm whether or not Miguel had managed to escape the apartment during their long-delayed access to the building.

The agents left the apartment and drove to a nearby Pizza Hut where they were familiar customers. It had pay phones. Both the DEA agents and Jorge felt less vulnerable to intercepted conversations by speaking to each other over random public phones. They waited for Jorge to ring back. Dave Mitchell grabbed the receiver after one ring.

"He's there," Jorge told him in a low voice. "Miguel is in the vault."

"You're sure?"

"Absolutely."

Jorge quickly explained that he was at the bakery with William and a number of his operatives, that they were worried about Miguel but confident he was in the vault. Dave asked if Jorge had some idea where the hidden chamber might be. Jorge recalled Tanga's boast.

"Is there a small bathroom near the living room?" Jorge asked. "Focus there."

The apartment had no fewer than five bathrooms, the DEA agent said, but he would concentrate on the powder room. Then someone was coming. Jorge signed off.

* * *

RETURNING TO WILLIAM'S TABLE, Jorge was greatly relieved to know that his DEA friends were inside the apartment and on the hunt for Miguel. It was only a matter of time, he was sure, until they found the vault and El Señor in it.

During his brief absence, Jorge found that the crowd had swelled around William. Dario was there, along with Marta Lucía's brother, Óscar, and another friend, the *sicario* Nicol Parra. This was William's "rat pack." Jorge called them "the brothers four." Jorge also found a sudden chill in the air. He wondered if Mantilla had called. William greeted his return with an exaggerated show of bonhomie that immediately put Jorge on guard.

"I have good news, Richard," he called out. "He was able to escape. When the police came, he got away."

How odd, Jorge thought, even as he feigned joy. "That's great," he said, and pulled up another chair to join William's table.

Privately, Jorge was troubled. Why was William telling him such a story? It seemed like a lie intended to persuade the raiding party that they were too late, that they should call off their search. If William really suspected Jorge was a conduit to the police and would relay that message, Jorge was in big trouble. He was still trying to understand the implications when a messenger from one of Miguel's wives arrived with keys to Miguel's next safe house in the Normandía section of town.

"It's ready," said the messenger. "And easy to find. It's the tallest white building in Normandía." He offered the apartment keys to William, but Miguel's son stopped him.

"Give them to Richard," he said.

Reflexively, Jorge waved off the keys. He said he didn't know the area. Secretly, he didn't want anyone to know that he had any inkling of Miguel's hiding place.

"You can't miss it," the messenger insisted. "It rises like a monster over—"

"Shut your mouth," Jorge interrupted. He seized the opportunity to play the role of security boss with gusto. He turned on the hapless messenger and berated him: "You talk too much. In such a public place you must be more careful. Don't make me tell you again."

Jorge ordered the man to give the keys to a friend of William's at another table and then told him to arrange for a car for Miguel's use to be parked in the garage of the new building. In fact, Jorge was full of orders. To William's friend who would check on the apartment's readiness, Jorge warned, "Nobody should know this address. You must be very discreet." No one challenged his orders.

William's initial suggestion that Jorge handle the keys seemed to Jorge to be a hollow show of trust, maybe even a setup. Or . . . maybe he was simply being paranoid. Jorge couldn't be sure. He was nervous and confused, that much was certain. He tried to hide it behind a vigorous demonstration of sound judgment and smart defensive moves. His performance as chief of security had to be nothing short of Academy Award quality.

The DEA pager in his pocket vibrated again. He ignored it. A few minutes later he consulted the cartel pager on his belt. It was approaching lunchtime, and Jorge often went home for a midday meal with his family. This time he invented a pager message.

"Lena is serving lunch. I'll be home for the next hour or so," Jorge told William as he stepped away from the table.

Jorge took the long way home, stopping first at the InterContinental hotel. A bank of public telephones in an isolated section of the lobby was unoccupied. He sent Feistl and Mitchell the number for one of those phones. A few minutes later, it rang.

"WHAT ARE WE LOOKING FOR?" Mitchell asked, after disclosing that they were still frustrated in their efforts to locate the hidden vault.

"I don't know. I've never been there. I haven't seen it," Jorge said.

He suggested that the agents call on the neighbors in apartments above and below 402. Take a look, he said, at apartments 502 and 302. The floor plans around the powder room area should be identical. Take along a measuring tape. Wherever there is a difference, "there you will find Miguel," Jorge assured them.

When he got home a short time later, Lena's kitchen smelled of fresh cilantro, garlic, and onions. Under normal circumstances Jorge would have taken one whiff and plunged into a bowl of his favorite oxtail soup. But his appetite had lost out to his edgy nerves. He sipped a fruit juice with Lena. He hadn't really noticed that the radio was on until the soft salsa music was interrupted by a news bulletin: "Miguel Rodríguez has been captured in Cali."

Jorge immediately turned up the volume, but the RCN radio commentator had little to add to his brief report. The couple hovered over the radio, hoping for more. Jorge tried not to show his delight. Not yet. Not even to Lena. They had neighbors who were in the cartel. Jorge could imagine one of them reporting: *You should have seen how happy he was when Miguel was arrested!*

But Jorge's relief was obvious to his wife. As the radio station resumed its regular salsa music programming, Jorge ladled a big helping of Lena's soup into a bowl and sat down to savor it. Moments later the music stopped again.

"We have a correction," said a radio voice. "Miguel Rodríguez has *not* been arrested. We repeat, Miguel Rodríguez has not been arrested." The commentator was apologetic and pledged to update the news as additional details were known. Jorge pushed aside his unfinished soup. He had to get back to work, he said.

William was no longer at the bakery. Jorge realized he was too uncomfortable to be around the young Rodríguez anyway. He decided to make the rounds of cartel businesses, like the radio shop of Carlos Alfredo to confirm that he had disabled the radiophones in apartment 402. Mostly, however, it was to play the role of a working security boss, to see and be seen by as many cartel operatives as possible. It was a tactic intended to avoid any impression that he might be holed up alone somewhere whispering in the ears of the police or U.S. drug agents.

The pager in his pocket buzzed again in the mid-afternoon. He returned to the InterContinental hotel.

DAVE MITCHELL'S MESSAGE was chilling. Still no success finding Miguel and pressure was building to call off the search. The problem was that after about seven hours of finding nothing to prove that Miguel was still there, police and legal advisers were getting antsy. Even General Serrano was impatient. He had paid a visit to the search site but didn't stay long. His arrival had no doubt set off the premature news reports of a capture. But he left when it became clear that searchers were nowhere near locating the missing drug boss.

Most of the Colombian police had withdrawn to one of the bedrooms where a soccer match was playing on a big-screen television. The commanders needed their idle men put to work—or sent home. The prosecutors were talking about how long they could occupy the flat and detain Castillo and the maids. It seemed that there might be some sort of legal limit.

"We know he's here," Mitchell said, assuring Jorge that he and Feistl had unambiguous confidence in his information. But, he said, there was growing skepticism among the search team. "I gotta tell you, Sean—we don't know how much longer we can keep this going," the American said.

Jorge absorbed the comment like a punch in the gut. He needed to prove his credibility to the Colombians who didn't even know who he was—give them something to help the DEA agents convince everyone that they had an excellent informant who knew what he was talking about. Jorge had hoped to reserve mention of the desk filled with cartel · records until after Miguel was found. He knew how sensational they would be, especially to the Colombians. He didn't want the cartel treasure to distract anyone from finding Miguel first and foremost. But now, fearing premature abandonment of the apartment, Jorge altered his timetable.

"Wait a minute," he said. Had the agents noticed in the apartment a reddish wood desk with an unusual top—a very thick top of maybe four inches? Yes, as a matter of fact, they had, Mitchell said. Then go back and break it open, Jorge urged him. It should contain briefcases full of cartel records in a secret compartment.

"It's Miguel's treasure," he said.

The agents were eager to get back and seize the prize, but Jorge would not hang up the phone just yet. "You are in the right place," Jorge repeated. "He is in that wall. You've got him. Whatever you do, please, please, don't leave. Don't stop now."

Once again, Jorge felt a surge of confidence. Disclosure of the desk and its sensational documents would certainly confirm the bona fides of "Patricia," he thought. It also figured to help Feistl and Mitchell keep the raiding party in place.

Jorge resumed his rounds of security checks, pressing his daylong campaign to see and be seen all over town. It was the perfect way to stay busy, cope with his nerves, and convey his sense of responsibility. He already felt as if everyone were watching him—so let them watch a security boss taking care of business. But he was eager, even impatient, for his next call from the Americans.

He imagined the stir caused by the document discovery. He imagined the news announcements reporting Miguel's actual arrest. He was mentally prepared to mask his delight and to act the part of a worried, angry cartel operative, throwing himself into the search for whoever betrayed the godfather.

Finally, his DEA pager buzzed again, its luminous screen lighting up on the car seat next to him. Jorge turned his silver Mazda back toward the InterContinental hotel and its bank of pay phones. This had to be the call he was waiting for.

I'M DEAD

FOUR AMERICAN DRUG ENFORCEMENT AGENTS SURROUNDED THE odd-looking desk in the living room of apartment 402. Jorge Salcedo—a.k.a. Sean, a.k.a. Patricia, a.k.a. the informant—had described it without ever having seen it himself as a custom-made piece of furniture with a reddish wood stain and an unusual top that was at least four inches thick. He had been right again. Of course, it was also the only desk in the room.

What the assembled DEA agents were pondering was how to get at what Jorge had called its treasure, records hidden away in some secret compartment. The Americans opened and shut drawers, ran their hands around the edges feeling for recessed buttons or levers, and crawled under it looking for clues to spring a lock or expose a chamber.

"I don't see it," said Chris Feistl in clear frustration.

At that moment, Agent Jerry Salameh grabbed one edge of the heavy desk, picked it up off the floor, and with great exertion toppled it over. The desk landed on its side with a heavy thud and the sounds of splintering wood. The commotion brought policemen away from their TV soccer to investigate. The toppled desk had broken open like a cracked wooden egg. Now Feistl could see behind a broken drawer what turned out to be one of three leather briefcases. They were full of documents.

Captain Buitrago was especially interested. "What are you doing?" he asked. "Who told you about this?"

But his questions went unanswered as the Colombian commander, Colonel Barragán, and the American agents collected the briefcases and stacks of loose documents from among the debris of the shattered desk. It was all moved to the dining room table, where they leafed through reams of what were obviously cartel records. Feistl found a photocopy of one canceled check for $40,000 made out to an official of President Ernesto Samper's election campaign. There were lots of other canceled checks, a telephone directory of cartel lieutenants, lists of payments to politicians and police and media figures, cartel correspondence, and more—piles of evidence and examples of corruption sure to shake the political foundations of Colombia.

"I've got to get this to General Serrano," said the colonel. He and an aide quickly gathered up everything from the desk and left the Santa Rita building. They would not return that afternoon.

The search for Miguel Rodríguez Orejuela resumed with new enthusiasm, at least among the Americans. Agents Salameh and Ruben Prieto were burning up drill bits boring through the concrete walls in and around the small bathroom. Most of the Colombian police stayed close to the big-screen TV. The colonel's abrupt departure with the documents also left the line of command a bit uncertain. Captain Buitrago of the Bloque de Búsqueda stayed close to the Americans.

The raid had effectively shifted hours earlier from a joint effort to the exclusive enterprise of the four American drug agents. Resistance to their tenacious and continuing search efforts mounted as the day wore on. At first, it was passive—lots of complaints and suggestions that time was being wasted. After the powder room became a focus of attention, the American agents discovered that someone using the toilet had urinated all over the floor. They suspected Buitrago. Whoever was responsible, it seemed to be a deliberate tactic to discourage anyone from getting down on the floor to inspect floorboards, moldings, or spaces under the sink.

When Chris Feistl defied the wet conditions to take a closer look, he let out a muffled shout with his head inside the floor cabinet: "What the hell is this?" It turned out to be a plastic oxygen tube that disappeared into the wall behind the sink, further proof that something was back there. Jerry Salameh's drill bits confirmed an air space between the walls. Dave Mitchell proposed getting a sledgehammer. First, they searched one more time for an access door.

There was no rush. The godfather of the Cali cartel was inches away with no place to run.

THE WRECK OF THE RED DESK remained in the living room, and some of the concrete walls were riddled with three-quarter-inch holes, when a small man carrying a small typewriter case opened the front door to apartment 402. He stood for a moment in the entryway surveying the damage. No one noticed until he cleared his throat and declared with a barrister's authority: "You are to cease and desist immediately."

In the puzzled silence that followed, the little man with jet-black hair directly addressed the Americans gathered around the doorway to the powder room. He wanted to know, he said, "who you are, what you're doing, and under what authority." Feistl and Mitchell looked at each other and shrugged. Mitchell muttered, "Who's Napoleon Bonaparte?"

"Napoleon" was head of the regional attorney general's office, a man whose legal authority trumped the other two prosecutors supervising the search. He was the Law in apartment 402, and there was no appeal. Before proceeding further, the regional prosecutor locked the front door, removed the key, and slipped it into his pocket. Technically speaking, "Napoleon" had just made the DEA agents his prisoners.

Feistl struggled to tamp down his anger. "We're here," he said evenly, "with the Colombian National Police," responding to information that Miguel Rodríguez Orejuela was hiding in the apartment. "We're looking for him."

The little man was unmoved. He set up his manual typewriter on the dining room table and declared that as foreign agents the Americans did not have authority to conduct raids in Colombia or to damage private property. He inserted a sheet of blank paper, then started typing a formal complaint charging the Americans with unlawful search.

"Wait a minute!" Mitchell almost shouted, barely able to contain his temper. They were so close—inches and minutes away from the most wanted man in the world. "Miguel Rodríguez is right there! He's right behind that wall."

It didn't matter. Friends of the Rodríguez Orejuela brothers had interceded. The regional prosecutor ignored Mitchell's protest. He turned to the other Americans and demanded their identification papers, then kept typing. Feistl checked the front door. It was, indeed, locked.

"Am I under arrest?" he asked.

"No," said the prosecutor.

"Then I'm leaving," Feistl said.

"No, you can't leave," said the prosecutor.

"Then I'm under arrest," Feistl said. "I demand the right to call my embassy."

The back-and-forth grew angrier. The prosecutor fired a legal warning shot, noting that the Americans were armed in violation of Colombian law. He could take them into custody on serious weapons charges.

The U.S. embassy was notified. Diplomatic channels were opened, and face-saving understandings were reached. The complaint was typed and presented to the Americans—who then refused to sign it. The agents were cited for violations, but they were never taken into custody. And they were not disarmed. When the front door was finally unlocked, however, they were ordered to leave. The search for Miguel was over.

Feistl and Mitchell didn't know what to do about Jorge. He could help them make another run at Miguel . . . but only if he wasn't murdered as the suspect in their failed raid. They would leave that decision up to Jorge. But first they had to break the news of their failure. It was the call they didn't want to make.

IT WAS EARLY EVENING IN CALI, the time of day when the western range of mountains blocks the setting sun and the city is dimmed by shadows that spread eastward across the Cauca valley. The sultry heat of the day also eases just a bit. But for the agents at the Pizza Hut and for Jorge at the InterContinental hotel the chill was as if the Ice Age were back.

"Leaving?" Jorge repeated Feistl's message as if he didn't believe it. "But—" He stopped himself before he could finish his thought . . . *but I'm dead!*

"Yeah, there's nothing we can do. We're already out of the building," Feistl said.

"But how? How can you leave when you're so close?" Jorge pressed again. Feistl said nothing. Jorge tried another tack: "And what about you? This could be the pinnacle of your careers."

"Sean, what can I say? I'm sorry, but they're making us leave. He's there. We know he's there, but we had to go," Feistl said, pleading for understanding. "We just got arrested, for God's sake."

Jorge had spent his last ounce of strength. He sounded especially weary as he asked if the Bloque was keeping a twenty-four-hour guard on the building. They must do that, he insisted. Miguel was going to come out of that vault eventually. Feistl said he had already asked for an overnight watch inside and outside the Santa Rita building. The DEA agent urged Jorge to be very careful. If he wanted out, if Jorge wanted protection immediately, Chris and Dave would do anything they could to help bring him and his family to safety.

"No, not yet," Jorge said.

There seemed nothing more to say. After a long pause, Jorge ended the pained conversation. "I know you did your best," he said.

FEISTL AND MITCHELL had not slept for nearly two days. They started July 15 rounding up the chicken trucks at three in the morning. Now they headed to the airport to fly back to Bogotá—exhausted, defeated, and in fear for the safety of their informant. They didn't need Jorge Salcedo to tell them how close they had come to the biggest prize in international law enforcement. And they didn't need Jorge to remind them how great was the peril he faced because of their failure to finish the job. Flying back to Bogotá through the black skies of midnight over Colombia, they shared their frustrations.

"Man, we let him down, didn't we?" Mitchell said. "He came to us—he put his life in our hands, now this. What do you think will happen?"

"I'm afraid they're gonna kill him," Feistl said. "God, I feel terrible. This is the worst day of my life."

VERY STRANGE

JORGE SALCEDO DID NOT DRIVE STRAIGHT HOME AFTER LEAVING THE InterContinental hotel lobby. His phone conversation with the American DEA agent left him shaken. He needed time to reflect, to re-examine the harrowing day he had just lived through. At least he had lived through it so far. He drove the long way, using the solitude of his silver Mazda to play out in his mind what he should do next to stay alive another day. It was a measure of his peril that Jorge suddenly viewed his future in hourly increments.

He expected to be a prime suspect inside the cartel. He already felt the suspicion from William. All of his natural instincts urged Jorge to lie low, to call in sick, to follow the example of Guillermo Pallomari and hide. But Jorge also knew that he had to do the opposite. He had to be confident, show no hint of guilt. In fact, by the time he parked outside his apartment building, Jorge realized he had to take the lead investigating who had betrayed the godfather. He had to investigate himself.

It was dark, around nine o'clock or a little later, and Jorge was dead tired. He hadn't eaten, and he was emotionally drained. As he dragged himself out of his car, a voice in the shadows called to him from across the street: "Don Richard, I need to speak with you."

Jorge was startled, but only for a moment. It was the familiar voice of Enrique Sánchez, his most loyal and trusted aide. The rotund man was resting against his motorcycle as if he had been waiting for some time. Jorge walked closer.

"Do you know about the meeting?" Enrique asked.

"What meeting?"

Enrique was half expecting that answer—but he was also disturbed by it. He told Jorge that William had. called an emergency security meeting. It was set for sometime between ten and eleven at Genaro Angel's disco. The fact that Jorge was not informed was alarming—the security chief not invited to an emergency security meeting. It could not be more clear that Miguel's son and his crowd did not trust Jorge.

Genaro Angel was a potential problem, too. He was close to Miguel and could easily share his doubts about Jorge with the boss. He was the cartel carpenter who had designed and built some of the secret vaults and, of course, the desk now in shambles in apartment 402. Angel was also a budding drug lord who retained his own team of *sicarios*. His disco was a favorite late-night dance spot for thugs and thug wannabes, but that night it was reserved for a private party.

"This is a bad thing. You have got to be there," said Enrique, stating the obvious.

Jorge knew he could not afford to let this meeting convene without him. Everything Jorge had said or done—or not said or failed to do— would be sliced, diced, and dissected by the small group of insiders without anyone there to defend him. Dario Delgado, his number two, was useless. He could be counted on to vote with the majority in any lynch mob. The only person Jorge could count on, in fact, was Enrique.

"Wait for me," Jorge told him, then headed to the elevators. Jorge had time for a quick meal and a change of clothes. He needed to freshen up. He had been in a cold sweat much of the day—and this day still was far from over. He thought he might also grab a ten-minute nap. He needed to be sharp and alert when he walked into Angel's disco.

*   *   *

JORGE'S CARTEL PAGER went off as he was finishing his leftover soup. It was Fercho Castillo. The return phone number was to one of the Panasonic lines in apartment 402. Jorge made a quick decision to forgo routine security precautions. He picked up his residence phone and dialed Castillo's number. A moment later Jorge heard the low, raspy voice of Miguel Rodríguez Orejuela. He had emerged from the vault, but he was trapped in the apartment.

"Señor! Thank God you're all right," Jorge said.

"Where are you?" Miguel growled.

"I'm home."

"Now listen, Richard—the goddamn police are everywhere. Here's what I want you to do to get me out of here . . ."

Miguel's plan for escape was a lame one. He wanted Jorge to fetch fancy dinners for fifty or sixty policemen patrolling the apartment building, its grounds, and the streets approaching it. Jorge was to pose as a good citizen who brought food to them out of the goodness of his heart. Then what? Jorge asked. Did Miguel really think that a little roasted chicken or grilled steak would buy fifty pairs of blind eyes? Well, apparently, that was exactly what Miguel thought. Jorge could dismiss it as the irrational idea of a man cooped up for too long inside a wall, but he dared not mock it as a crazy idea. In the end, Jorge simply said, "Yes, sir."

The godfather's phone call had made Jorge late for the security meeting. He hurried downstairs and drove for ten minutes to Angel's disco on Avenida Roosevelt. Enrique followed. The nightclub was upstairs in a two-story building. Discussions were already under way when the two latecomers entered. Maybe it was Jorge's imagination, but he got the feeling that they were talking about him. No one questioned why he was there, however.

The disco, usually a magical and seductive place with lights low and the music throbbing and strobes flashing, looked small and seedy in the harsh glare of overhead lights. The walls and ceiling were painted black. To Jorge it felt like a well-lit tomb. Eight or nine familiar cartel operatives, including the "rat pack" of William's close friends, were seated in chairs around Miguel's son in the middle of an empty dance floor.

"I've just had a call from El Señor," Jorge announced. He had everyone's immediate attention. And it was the perfect calling card. He needed no other excuses for crashing the party to which he was not invited. Jorge went on to explain Miguel's order for fifty meals, hoping that he could enlist William to help beat back the plan. Not only was it unlikely to work as the boss hoped, but Jorge could see it backfiring badly—getting him, or whoever made the delivery, caught on tape or photographed by a news outlet. The tactic worked. William labeled it a terrible idea and said he would talk to his father about a different plan.

Relieved of his responsibility to serve takeout to police, Jorge sat back in his chair and tried to act nonchalant. He realized that his hands were shaking. He hoped no one else noticed. He tried to cover the fact by folding both hands behind his head and leaning back. He imagined that he looked like the lazy teen at the back of the class. It bothered Jorge that his nerves were so obviously shot. He wondered what other signals he might be sending. His shirt showed signs he was sweating again.

Talk turned to setting up rescue teams in key areas that Miguel might be able to reach just outside the Santa Rita building. The apartments backed up to a steep hillside. If Miguel could get out of the building and climb that hill, he would emerge on the side of the winding highway to the Pacific coast and the port of Buenaventura, where he could be scooped up by friends and whisked away to safety. But those ifs were substantial. The obstacles were under discussion when William's cell phone rang.

Listening to only one side of the conversation, Jorge quickly realized that it was Captain Buitrago of the Bloque de Búsqueda telling William that he, too, had just received a call from Miguel. The drug boss wants the police captain to find a way to get him out of the apartment building, but Buitrago tells William that it is impossible. National Police guards surround the place.

"Don't give me that shit," protested William. "You tell me you can't do it, but you can always take the money. That's no problem. That's never impossible."

The men sitting around the disco had all fallen silent listening to

William. He was entirely unsympathetic to his caller's predicament—and growing more impatient. His face reddened as Buitrago still resisted. But there would be no compromise. William shouted into the phone: "This is why we pay you. It's for this moment, so it's up to you. Find a way. Just do it."

William cursed and disconnected the call. Someone asked what the captain was going to do. William shook his head angrily. They couldn't count on Buitrago for anything. "We'll do it," he said.

CLIMBING THE HILL immediately behind Colinas de Santa Rita would pose a challenge to the young, fit, and agile. From its base outside the building's ground-level entrance up to a point where the slope crests at the shoulder of the coast road was about a hundred yards—roughly the length of a football field. In this case, however, the field is tilted at a severe incline of about sixty degrees and covered with thick, thorny brush. It was not clear that Miguel could make such a hard climb even if he succeeded in reaching the hill undetected. But it was the only plan in the cartel playbook that night. William conferred by phone with his father, who agreed to make a try at it.

The disco security meeting adjourned well after midnight to the coast road. Jorge and Enrique parked along the shoulder of the two-lane highway and raised the hood, feigning car trouble. Periodically, others came by to feign assistance. Once Miguel started up the hillside, someone would climb down from above to help him complete his ascent. It would not be the overweight Enrique under any circumstance. He had bull-like strength, but at five feet four and 240 pounds he was more likely to start an avalanche than perform a rescue. Jorge considered the irony that he might be the one to risk breaking his own neck trying to save Miguel.

Periodically, the cartel men switched roles, moved in a different "disabled" car, or pulled back to avoid drawing attention. But the roadway had little traffic in the wee hours of a Sunday morning, and the would-be rescue team's security never seemed in jeopardy. The eastern sky beyond the Cauca valley plains was showing signs of first light when William's cell phone rang again. It was Buitrago.

While Jorge and William were waiting for Miguel to scale the steep hillside, Captain Buitrago had found another way to extricate the godfather. Already, Miguel was resting at a new safe house. According to William's account, Buitrago had somehow managed to clear a path to the parking garage, where he hid Miguel in the trunk of his car—and then drove him away right under the noses of at least fifty armed guards.

At sunrise over Cali, Jorge joined in the celebration of Miguel's safe return to leadership of the cartel with hugs and backslaps all around.

NEWS REPORTS BEGAN trickling out later Sunday confirming that the Cali cartel boss had narrowly escaped arrest by hiding in a vault in the wall. Police inspecting apartment 402 earlier that morning had found the *caleta,* its secret door left open when Miguel fled. Inside the hidden chamber was an oxygen tank and a bloody shirt, the latter prompting speculation that one of Jerry Salameh's drill bits took a bite out of the godfather.

The clash between American drug agents and an unidentified Colombian prosecutor was also disclosed. A television news account named the four Americans cited for exceeding their authority. Chris Feistl was barely awake when he got the call to be at the ambassador's residence later that afternoon. The U.S. ambassador Myles Frechette was on the warpath. He was having enough trouble already navigating the rocky relations between Washington and Bogotá in the aftermath of President Samper's controversial election. Now his drug agents were getting arrested. Frechette was famously intolerant of political sideshows in his tightly run embassy. Feistl feared the worst.

The DEA attaché Tony Senneca and the agents who helped raid apartment 402 were escorted to the ambassador's personal library. The comfortable chairs and sofas turned into hot seats when the scowling career diplomat marched into the room and demanded that someone explain to him what the hell happened.

Feistl took the lead recounting how the raid was planned and executed, what valuable leads their highly placed informant provided, and how close they were to Miguel Rodríguez Orejuela when the regional prosecutor intervened.

"Why were you people even in there?" Frechette wanted to know. He was under the impression that the Americans stayed outside and let the Colombians do their own searches and arrests. When Feistl started to explain, the ambassador cut him off. "And why were you drilling holes and looking for the vault instead of the Colombian police?"

Most of the Colombian police had lost interest an hour into the twelve-hour raid and were watching television, Feistl said. "We were just helping."

The ambassador seemed no less annoyed after the agents' explanations than before. Nonetheless, he eased Feistl's mind when he growled that it was a very good thing police did find Miguel's *caleta* in the apartment earlier that day. Otherwise, he told the agents with unmistakable menace, they all would be "on the next plane to Miami."

How could it be, Feistl pondered, that the biggest break in his law-enforcement career was turning out so badly? Instead of being showered with accolades, he was teetering on the edge of professional ruin and worried that his informant of a lifetime was about to be murdered. If it wasn't already too late, there could be no more mistakes.

IN CALI, THE SEARCH for guilty parties began in earnest first thing Monday morning. Jorge was to drive down to Santander and interview Fercho Castillo, debrief him thoroughly about what he heard and saw during the twelve-hour occupation of apartment 402. Find out, too, if he said anything damaging, even inadvertently.

"Don't go alone," Miguel said. "Take Valencia with you."

Miguel's demonstration of continuing trust was a welcome relief. Jorge was not the prime target of the investigation—he was running the investigation. On the downside, however, he regarded Valencia as a potential problem. The former sergeant's long experience with military intelligence made him especially dangerous. Jorge could not afford to make even the smallest mistake. Any inconsistency in his words or actions could expose him to Valencia's trained and critical eye.

Jorge picked up Valencia at the man's home shortly before dawn. Amid polite greetings, the intelligence veteran mentioned something about the suspected informant being a woman. It caught Jorge off guard. Maybe Jorge was on the wrong end of this investigation after all. Meetings over key evidence were going on without him. He was more out of the loop than he thought. After a moment, he realized that Valencia was still talking to him. He hadn't heard a word since mention of the woman informant.

Valencia had insisted on bringing along Dario Delgado, William's friend and Jorge's second-in-command. The last passenger climbed into the silver Mazda as Jorge tried not to show discomfort. He felt vulnerable with Dario seated behind him, and he watched his rearview mirror more than usual as he drove south out of the city.

It was for just such occasions that Jorge had rigged a tape recorder in his car. It was stashed inside the driver's door pocket, under a window rag. As he steered through light morning traffic with one hand, Jorge reached into the side pocket with the other and fumbled for the record button. It made no sound as its cassette spools turned out of sight and undetected. Along the road, Jorge made excuses for three different stops, allowing Dario and Valencia time to talk unwittingly for the hidden recorder.

About an hour's drive outside Cali they found Fercho Castillo still in an anxious state from the ordeal of the raid. He had gone twenty-four hours without food or sleep, he said, and worried constantly about the safety of El Señor. He had also endured frequent questioning by police and American drug agents. What did he tell police about Don Miguel? "Nothing. I said no one was there when I went to bed; no one was there when police woke me at my door." Castillo was most eager to talk about the informant. The Americans, he said, had someone who knew all about the apartment.

"And it was a woman," he said.

"How do you know?" Jorge asked.

"I overheard—they called her Patricia."

Valencia scoffed. He said she was probably using a code name and was just as likely to be María, Ingrid, or Monica. Jorge agreed.

"Whoever it was, she knew about the desk, the papers, the vault—everything," Castillo said.

"What women can you name who visited that apartment?" Jorge

asked, settling in to conduct what would have every appearance of a thorough interrogation.

"On my shift? No one," Castillo said. He had of late been alternating with Mateo and Memo Lara, he said, so he could not vouch for which female visitors might have been to the apartment during days when he was off duty. For several minutes, Jorge challenged him to recall every name—operatives, family members, maids, everyone who called on Miguel or made any kind of delivery at apartment 402. It was entirely for show. Jorge knew his own name was on no such list.

During the next half hour, Jorge solved one mystery in his own mind. Castillo said that it was General Serrano's personal pilot who had tipped Miguel the night before about the raid. Jorge did not feel he could safely ask questions about the pilot, but Castillo went on to say that the aviator was a longtime friend of the Rodríguez Orejuela family and that Miguel's brother Gilberto had funded the man's flight training years earlier.

Castillo could offer little more, and the debriefing session ended after about forty-five minutes. Valencia warned the aide that police were likely to be looking for him now that they knew Miguel had been hiding in the apartment. Castillo could be charged with the crime of harboring a fugitive. The boss wanted him to lie low for a while, to stay with friends or move into a hotel, not to go home. Valencia reached into a pocket and pulled out some cash—about 1 million pesos, or $1,000. "Use this," he said.

Back in the silver Mazda, Jorge wondered what Valencia thought of Castillo's story. More than that, he wondered what Valencia and Dario thought about him. On the drive back to Cali, he made another stop—this one outside the Colmena Bank, where a friend of his was working. It was purely a play for time and a chance to let the tape run while his passengers thought they were alone.

AT EACH OF JORGE'S STOPS during the morning, his departure from the car had the expected effect—setting off conversations about Jorge between Dario and Valencia behind his back.

"What do you think of him?" Dario asked at an early stop.

"I don't know," Valencia responded, but he said that Jorge was act-ing very nervous and distracted.

Dario agreed. "The man is very jumpy, isn't he?"

Such critical observations resumed each time Jorge left the car, stopping when he returned. Valencia called Jorge a son of a bitch for warning him about a military roadblock that Valencia doubted was real. Behind Jorge's back, his colleagues on that drive spent most of their private moments sniping at his trustworthiness.

"I find him very strange," Valencia concluded.

At the last stop outside the Colmena Bank, Valencia had just begun to complain about Jorge when the two men in the car heard a noise. Were they being bugged? The recorder had picked up a faint but dis-tinct sound: buzz . . . buzz . . . buzz . . . (pause) buzz . . . buzz . . . buzz (pause).

"What is that?" said Valencia.

"It's a microphone," blurted out Dario, meaning that he thought it was a bugging device of some kind. Microphones make no sounds, but the mistake was irrelevant. Valencia knew what he meant and immedi-ately reached for the radio knob to turn up the volume. He also turned on the noisy air conditioner fan. And all conversation stopped.

ONCE JORGE HAD DROPPED off both passengers at their homes, he drove to a quiet street and retrieved his tape recorder from the side pocket. He also recovered his DEA pager from the trunk of his Mazda. The pager listed a coded DEA phone number.

Before returning the DEA call, however, Jorge rewound his tape recorder and listened to the voices over and over.

"The man is very jumpy, isn't he?"

"I find him very strange."

It confirmed Jorge's fears. Valencia and Dario were suspicious of him. He considered Dario little more than a nuisance, easily manipu-lated and possibly even useful as a conduit for misinformation. Valen-cia, on the other hand, was dangerous. And he wanted Jorge's job at the right hand of Miguel. Valencia's incentive for mischief was great. He could easily exploit the current atmosphere of distrust and possibly purge Jorge from the cartel inner circle—a potentially deadly demotion. Even if he managed to do everything right to conceal his cooperation with the DEA, Jorge was in danger from a jealous rival. Obviously, the Cali cartel was not big enough for Jorge and Valencia.

Finally, Jorge replayed the tape a couple of times, trying to hear the sound that prompted his passengers to stop talking and amp up the music. The faint buzz . . . buzz . . . buzz, he realized, was his DEA pager vibrating in the trunk.

The message to call Feistl and Mitchell had come in while Jorge was in the bank. He returned their page.

"Hey, Sean. How's it going? Do we need to get you out of there?" Feistl asked.

"No, I think I can handle it," Jorge said.

THE GAY CABALLEROS

THE AMERICAN DRUG AGENTS WERE ENCOURAGED BY JORGE SAL-
cedo's confidence. Unfortunately, they didn't share it. They remained anxious about his safety and the possibility that if he were
killed, they wouldn't even know it. They would simply spend their days
waiting by the SkyPager for a call that would never come.

Already, Jorge had turned off and stashed away his DEA pager.
After it had vibrated inconveniently in his trunk, he realized it was too
dangerous to carry. He no longer wished to risk having to explain it to
some cartel associate. For the time being, at least, Feistl and Mitchell
were cut off from direct access to their informant. They had no choice
but to wait and let Jorge call them when it was safe to do so.

When Jorge did not check in the next day, Mitchell's diary entry for
Tuesday, July 18, carried only the brief notation: "no contact." Wednesday ended with the same entry: "no contact." And before going to bed
Thursday night, Mitchell wrote it once again: "no contact." He did not
record how many times Feistl checked his SkyPager to be sure he hadn't

missed a message. By Friday morning, it had already turned into a long week for two agents who were counting every hour and imagining every possible disaster. A U.S. Treasury agent friend invited Chris and Dave for lunch. The antsy DEA agents needed some good company— and maybe a beer.

JORGE WAS STILL HOME with Lena one morning during that week when Miguel called from his new hideout. There was no introductory small talk. This was a business call.

"I'm concerned about you, Richard," said Miguel. "I've been told that you acted very nervous all during the day of the raid."

The godfather's tone was blunt and cold. Jorge knew immediately that the skeptics—chief among them William, Genaro Angel, and Valencia—had been busy undermining him. They probably noticed his shaking hands, his cold sweat, his distracted nature. Confronted by Miguel's stern tone, Jorge had seconds to refute that dangerous impression.

"Of course I was nervous," Jorge blurted out, as if relieved to admit it. "How could I *not* be nervous? I care very much for you. I had all the responsibility for your safety. I did everything you told me, and still I failed."

Jorge recited the additional security precautions that he had arranged in response to Miguel's call the night before the raid. He said that the one bright spot was his man Enrique Sánchez sounding an alarm in plenty of time for Miguel to escape. After a long pause, Miguel snapped, "Okay, you're right."

Miguel had reason to believe Jorge and dismiss the suspicions. He knew that Jorge had never visited the Santa Rita building. He knew that Jorge had never seen its secret vault—or the desk or its contents. Despite the suspicions of others, Miguel could not see how Jorge could possibly be the snitch since he knew nothing about these things.

There were, however, some concessions Miguel made to William and his group of doubters. Responsibility for close-in security in and around the new hideout was shifted to Genaro Angel and his men. Jorge was left in charge of outlying or perimeter security, his men monitoring local police movements and taking up sentry positions near key bridges across the Cali River. The bridges provided the only direct access to a small neighborhood between the river and the mountains where Miguel was hiding in a "tall white building." There were as many as four different possibilities, but Jorge was not cleared even to patrol— or roam around or snoop about—on streets just north of the river. "Don't even come into the area," Miguel told him.

JORGE COULD NOT AFFORD to wait any longer while Valencia's keen eye and suspicious nature gained influence within the cartel's dwindling circle of advisers. Miguel's trust could easily be eroded under such circumstances. From the moment Jorge had listened to the tape he secretly recorded in his car, he knew: Valencia had to go.

Legal authorities already wanted Valencia. Charges were pending against him for leaking secrets to the Cali cartel and for taking bribes. He had been paid $1,000 per month, plus periodic bonuses every few months of another $20,000, throughout his years as a cartel double agent inside the Bloque de Búsqueda. Jorge had just been to Valencia's home to pick him up for the drive to Santander. He leaked that home address to a family friend in the army officers' corps.

Valencia left his home one morning a couple of days later and found himself suddenly surrounded by plain-clothed army intelligence officers with machine guns. He surrendered without resistance. Miguel immediately called Jorge to report the troubling news and directed him to find the best attorney in town—someone new and previously unused by the organization. Miguel was hoping to disguise the fact that Valencia was a cartel operative, and he didn't want any of the four or five regular mafia lawyers showing up to take over his case.

"I believe I know someone," Jorge assured his boss. He had a personal acquaintance who could handle the case. A few hours later the man who had arranged for Valencia's capture and arrest had also arranged for his legal representation.

Jorge was busy doing more than looking over his shoulder in the days immediately following the failed raid. One morning, he received an unexpected telephone call from the police captain Efrén Buitrago.

Miguel's main man on the joint task force needed the security chief's intervention. The cartel owed him money, and he felt impolite hitting up Miguel or William at this sensitive time. He no doubt was anxious, too, that Miguel might be arrested before settling his accounts.

"I was promised fifty boxes, and they haven't been delivered," the police official told Jorge in their brief telephone exchange.

"I'll look into it personally," Jorge agreed.

The reference to fifty boxes was code for 50 million pesos. Jorge checked with Mateo, and a day later the aide brought him a pair of checks signed by Miguel Rodríguez Orejuela. One was written to Buitrago's mother, the other to the man's sister. Jorge was instructed to deposit the two checks—together totaling 50 million pesos, or about $50,000—into accounts of the two women at a bank in Palmira near the Cali airport. Jorge turned over the deposit slips to Buitrago a few days later.

MEANWHILE, JORGE WENT TO WORK immediately trying to verify Miguel's new hideout—hoping that another raid could be quickly organized. The swirl of suspicions around him only added to the urgency. The sooner he could get Feistl and Mitchell back to knock down Miguel's door, the sooner Jorge could get his family—and the accountant Pallomari—out of Cali and out of harm's way. He approached the challenge like a military field intelligence assignment, making terrain and approach observations and checking out potential infiltration routes. Barred from entering Miguel's neighborhood, Jorge enlisted a friend, no questions asked, to drive through and note down the street addresses of two buildings Jorge considered most likely.

He always was wary of being followed. When confident he was alone, Jorge made the rounds of scenic overlooks and other vantage points to photograph the suspected buildings. One evening when Jorge climbed steep hills behind Miguel's enclave looking for a good photo angle, he discovered a flood control channel. Its obvious purpose was to carry away the runoff from the mountain rains before the floods swept down into residential streets. But Jorge saw a tactical value, too. The channel was about seven feet deep with sloped concrete sides and a flat bottom. A raiding party using that channel could approach the apartment buildings unseen, especially at night, and emerge only a few dozen yards from the target.

It was time to beep Feistl's SkyPager. The incoming message interrupted lunch at the Treasury agent's house on Friday afternoon, July 21, but the callback was quick and celebratory. Jorge told Feistl and Mitchell that Miguel had moved and that only three or four people knew precisely where he was. Jorge said he had a pretty good idea which of two buildings Miguel was using but no idea which apartment or which floor level. He told them to watch for a package. He was sending photos of the suspect buildings by Avianca air courier same-day service. What about you? The DEA agents wanted to know that Jorge was no longer in danger. He acknowledged that he was one of the suspects but that so far he was doing fine because "Miguel doesn't believe I'm the one."

Now that the silence was broken, Jorge and the American agents renewed their intense schedule of meetings and intelligence gathering. Their focus narrowed to a white nineteen-story high-rise called the Hacienda Buenos Aires. Jorge said he was 80 percent sure it was Miguel's place. The American agents thought the odds were even better. Ownership of the building was in the name of a known cartel associate. But that still was not enough. No one was jumping into another raid without confidence approximating 100 percent.

They arranged for another secret meeting out of town, back in the cane fields near the CIAT experimental farms.

JORGE AND THE DEA AGENTS arrived separately and met at dusk along an isolated stretch of unpaved road. The spot was about a half mile from their original rendezvous about three weeks earlier—back when "Sean Connery" was introduced to a couple of wary Americans. The men had been through a lot together in that short time. They were Sean, Chris, and Dave to each other now.

They had picked the meeting area because they expected to see few if any cars at that time of day. The agricultural center was closed by then. However, they found traffic surprisingly heavy—and mostly yellow Renaults and Fiats, taxicabs from nearby Palmira. Some slowed as they passed. None stopped.

"What's with all the taxis?" Mitchell complained, and Feistl pulled the DEA car farther off the road, hoping for a bit more privacy.

Jorge had brought along a set of maps and photo enlargements depicting the Buenos Aires building from various angles. He came prepared to show them a layout of the hillside flood control channel, too. They had barely started when a white van with a distinctive green stripe pulled to a stop about twenty-five yards behind them.

"Oh, God!" Jorge gasped. "It's the police."

Feistl instinctively stuffed the photos and maps under the front seat. He worried that they might appear to be an espionage ring. Their car was parked close enough to the sugarcane that both agents were able to toss their handguns unseen out into the thick foliage. They did not want to be questioned about them. The agents carried no official gun permits, so explaining those weapons would almost certainly require a trip to police headquarters and a call to the embassy in Bogotá to sort it all out.

"If they arrest us, I'll be killed," Jorge whispered before leaving the car. Then he tried his best to affect an easy smile as he met the men climbing out of the police van.

Jorge and the DEA agents could not risk identifying themselves or telling police anything about the true nature of their meeting. A thorough search would turn up pictures and maps, not to mention the weapons. There were more than enough reasons to justify continued questioning at police headquarters. Jorge figured that the Vulture or some other cartel informant would be among the first to know. Getting hauled in for questioning was enough to get Jorge killed.

Five uniformed policemen from the Palmira station emerged from the van and were walking toward Jorge, each cradling an Israeli-made Uzi machine gun. Jorge could barely breathe. *There's no way out,* he thought. He offered a desperate last-second prayer: *God, help me. What can I do?*

He greeted the police in Spanish: "Hey, how are you doing? Can I help you?"

The young lieutenant in charge gave the overly friendly Colombian a careful look. Jorge was well dressed and apparently unarmed. The officer studied the two Americans still some fifty feet away and standing outside their compact car.

"We're investigating a murder—a cabdriver was killed not too far from this place," the lieutenant said. "I'd like to know what you're doing here."

That was too bad, Jorge responded, but they had seen nothing suspicious along this road. He said the two blond men were Americans who worked at CIAT. "We are friends, just here talking," Jorge said. "We don't want any trouble."

The lieutenant and his sergeant were determined to examine the parked cars and to question the Americans. When they stopped at his silver Mazda, Jorge did not wait to be asked. He quickly opened the trunk, eager to show that they had nothing to hide.

"You can see for yourself—no drugs, no contraband—and obviously we are not murderers," Jorge said. "There is no need to bother the Americans."

Just as quickly as Jorge opened the Mazda trunk, he closed it. He remembered that he had stashed five cartel radios in one of the wheel wells, not one of them properly licensed. In Colombia, having radios without permits was treated about as harshly as possession of unlicensed weapons. The officers didn't notice. They had moved on to question the DEA agents.

Feistl and Mitchell repeated the cover story: that they worked at CIAT, they were just meeting a friend after work, and they weren't doing anything wrong. The police asked to see ID. Jorge offered his Colombian documents. He had no choice. The Americans said they did not have their work IDs. During a feigned search for work badges in the car, Mitchell slipped Jorge a wad of pesos, the U.S. contribution to a bribery fund. When the lieutenant pressed the Americans to come up with some kind of documentation, Jorge asked the officer to step aside for a confidential conversation.

"You're embarrassing these Americans. It isn't necessary. Why don't you take this and forget about them?" Jorge said, as discreetly as possible offering him a fistful of pesos that amounted to a combined total of about $650. The lieutenant glanced at the wad of bills, and then ignored it. He wanted to search the DEA car. This time, Feistl objected: "Hey, man—this is crazy. We've done nothing wrong."

The Colombian officer calmly responded, "If you've done nothing wrong, why are you trying to bribe me?" Chris Feistl, an honest cop himself, was momentarily stumped by the question. He shrugged, then complained, "Don't you have better things to do? How about catching a thief?" Privately, however, Feistl cursed his fate: *How did I get the only honest cop in Colombia?*

Jorge intervened with the lieutenant again. In a low, conspiratorial tone Jorge said, "Listen, I told you this was very embarrassing for the Americans. I have to be honest with you. We are homosexuals. This rendezvous was a private matter. But if you continue, there could be scandal. It will be harmful and embarrassing for everyone. Please, just take this—and let us have our privacy."

The lieutenant stood rigid and silent, this time considering the proposition. Jorge extended the cash. The officer still hesitated. "Just a moment," he said and stepped away to confer with his sergeant. It was the sergeant who returned to Jorge and accepted the wad of bills. The deal was done.

The gay caballeros breathed a collective sigh of relief as the police van pulled away. They were still in business. Their plot to seize the Cali cartel boss remained a secret. It was going to be dark soon. Feistl and Mitchell hurried to recover their weapons from deepening shadows in the sugarcane field. Mitchell counted his cash and realized he had contributed nearly $300 to the bribe fund. He cringed at the paperwork ahead, but it would make for an interesting expense report.

Jorge drove home celebrating what he regarded as an answered prayer. The proof? He wasn't dead yet.

GO FOR IT

THE MARBLE-FLOORED LOBBY OF THE INTERCONTINENTAL HOTEL had become de facto headquarters for Jorge Salcedo's security operatives. Its central location, public phones, food service, air-conditioning, restrooms, and staff of cartel-paid clerks and bellmen all made it a natural hub. It was also just across the Cali River from the neighborhood where Miguel was in seclusion. Operating out of the hotel, Jorge dispatched his motorcycle patrol teams to watch for police or military movements, especially toward the bridges that accessed their fugitive boss's hillside enclave.

On Friday night, August 4, 1995, his deputy, Dario Delgado, accompanied Jorge across the lobby toward a set of glass doors where two motorcycle watchmen waited to go on duty. It was getting late, about ten o'clock, and the men preparing for the overnight shift needed their final instructions before Jorge called it a night and went home. The DEA pager in his pants pocket suddenly began to vibrate and hum softly. Jorge considered ignoring it. Dario was right there and might ask questions. On the other hand, Dario noticed almost nothing suspicious unless someone pointed it out to him. Besides, such a late page from Chris Feistl and Dave Mitchell could be important. Jorge reached into his pocket and checked the message screen. It was a familiar coded number—a pay phone at one of the DEA-favored pizza joints.

"Hey, I'm sorry," Jorge told Dario. "I need to call my wife. I'll join you with those guys in a moment."

Dario nodded without a blink of hesitation and pushed through the glass doors leading out toward the street. Jorge turned the other way to the bank of hotel pay phones against a far wall. Through the glass, Jorge could see Dario and the men exchange greetings and trade inaudible banter. He dialed the coded number but watched his men as he waited for the phone on the other end to ring.

Feistl answered. "Sean—hey, something's come up," he said. "You've got a decision to make."

EVENTS IN CALI AND BOGOTÁ had been moving quickly since the first of August, the night of their close encounter with a police van in the sugarcane field.

A series of late-night stakeouts by the American agents had pretty much confirmed that Miguel Rodríguez Orejuela was holed up in the Hacienda Buenos Aires. Feistl and Mitchell watched the nineteen-story luxury residence with high-powered binoculars from a hillside park nearby that they shared with lovers and sightseers. The agents saw Miguel's housekeepers in the building's tenth-floor windows, two black women in white uniform dresses. Jorge wasn't sure whether the building's first floor was its ground level or the next floor above it. The raiding party could not afford to exit onto the wrong floor.

Jorge said he would try to pin down conclusively which elevator exit was appropriate. He assumed he had at least another day to do so. Meanwhile, he had been busy trying to undermine Miguel's safety net. Jorge's primary target was the cartel's white-shoed man in the Cali office of the national telephone company, Carlos Espinosa. Jorge had slipped incriminating information to an army officer friend, disclosing that the man known to the cartel as Pinchadito had been highly paid for the secret installation of Miguel's phones, for creating electronic traps and decoys to block official traces on Miguel's phone lines, and for helping the cartel bug police hotlines.

While Jorge was getting his ducks in order, so were Feistl and Mitchell. They wanted to avoid the confusion of the first raid, when, at the outset, entry to the apartment was delayed over jurisdictional quandaries. This time, they met early with Colombia's attorney general and wrangled one-time-only concessions: they could handpick their prosecutor, and they could have a search warrant authorizing them to break down the door to Miguel's apartment. No delays, no questions, and no quibbles about damage to private property. They also asked General Serrano to stay home so as not to tip off his cartel-friendly pilot. And they arranged for primary raid support from the one branch of the government that had escaped cartel corruption: a Colombian navy special forces unit out of Buenaventura.

Things had moved so fast, in fact, that the Americans found themselves ready to launch before Jorge had given his green light. In deference to his life-risking role, Feistl and Mitchell had assured Jorge that he would make the crucial go/no-go call. He was anxious, still not convinced that Miguel was on the tenth floor, still wanting to know more about the security setup inside the Buenos Aires building. But there were also events and circumstances beyond the control of either the DEA agents or Jorge Salcedo conspiring to force a decision at the pay phones of the InterContinental hotel that night.

Press accounts and criminal proceedings had rocked the administration of President Ernesto Samper in recent days. His former campaign treasurer had been arrested and was talking. Santiago Medina confirmed what records found in the desk at apartment 402 showed: that the Cali cartel provided millions of dollars in campaign money to Samper. The president's former campaign manager—Defense Minister Fernando Botero—had just been arrested. He was being forced to resign the country's top defense post that very night.

In Botero's place, General Zúñiga—Colombia's top military commander—would assume the acting Defense Ministry post. He had already issued orders to National Police and all branches of the military that he wanted a complete description of all joint antinarcotics operations under way everywhere in the country—and he wanted it at 8:00 a.m. on the first day of business next week. That news alarmed Jorge.

The general was a friend of Miguel's. Jorge knew that from Miguel's own lips. The drug boss considered the general his most important contact in the Colombian military. Only in Colombia, thought Jorge, could the friend of a drug lord be left in charge of capturing him. But Feistl had called with a solution.

"We're ready to go tonight," he said.

"Tonight?" Jorge almost gasped.

Anticipating an assault on the Buenos Aires building as early as Sunday or Monday, Feistl and Mitchell had moved the navy commandos into position along with one of the specially vetted counternarcotics police units from Bogotá. A predawn Saturday morning strike simply meant no sleep that night. The DEA team was eager to launch immediately. They had called hoping to persuade Jorge.

For Jorge, there was no margin for error. It was a matter of life and death. He was not as certain as the Americans were that Miguel was in the tenth-floor apartment. Yes, it was likely. But it wasn't absolutely confirmed. Jorge would have liked a little more time to raise doubt about other potential fall guys. And now there was the Zúñiga dilemma. Jorge felt like Butch Cassidy or the Sundance Kid with the choice of facing the posse or jumping off a cliff. It was the Zúñiga news that pushed him over the edge.

"Let's go for it," Jorge said.

He hung up and hurried to join Dario and his men. Jorge had done his best over the previous three weeks to increase Dario's visibility as his security deputy. The young man was still lazy, slow, and unreliable, but he was also a very close friend to William. And if Miguel were captured that night, they were all going to wake up in the morning with William as the new king of the cartel. Jorge wanted Dario so deeply immersed in the security processes that he would have to share any blame for the catastrophic security failure that was about to happen. At least Jorge had managed to set up two potential fall guys—Dario and Pinchadito, the phone man—but with the time for schemes expired, he faced the hardest part of his plan . . . waiting.

Jorge tried not to show anxiety as he prepared for bed. He considered asking Lena to say an extra prayer. Instead, he told her nothing and offered up a silent prayer: *God, help Chris and Dave.* Then he turned out the lights. He had expected to toss and turn. But it was a sign of both his physical and his mental exhaustion that in a matter of minutes Jorge Salcedo was asleep.

WHILE JORGE SLEPT, a convoy of three canvas-covered civilian delivery trucks followed a four-door sedan through some of the most affluent neighborhoods of northern Cali. At one point they passed within two blocks of the private quarters of William Rodríguez. Concealed inside the canvas compartments were about a dozen navy commandos in combat gear, another twenty antinarcotics officers from the National Police—some of them in battle fatigues, others in plain clothes—and finally the handpicked federal prosecutor from Bogotá. The lone female on the mission was dressed for a court appearance, if necessary— wearing a turquoise blouse, white slacks, and high heels. She was not, however, dressed for what happened next.

The assault on Hacienda Buenos Aires began in darkness shortly before four in the morning. The trucks pulled up to an unlit and unde-veloped hillside. The approach was treacherous. The first phase was a steep ascent in night shadows, about a three-hundred-foot climb over rough terrain to a flood control channel. Mitchell and the navy com-mandos reached the concrete-lined drainage ditch first, startling a pair of teenagers necking on the slope above the city lights. The dark hillside lost its romantic appeal in a hurry as the commandos pounced on them and brusquely checked them for weapons or radios before letting them flee into the night. The raiding party continued without resistance.

Feistl and Mitchell took the lead guiding the group along the twist-ing quarter-mile route of the storm channel. They were virtually unde-tectable, concealed by eight-foot concrete walls and a pitch-black night. However, the movement of thirty-five mostly combat-booted invaders— and the one in high heels—set off a chorus of barking dogs from the squatters' shacks scattered across the ridge. Mitchell urged the group on and hoped that Miguel was not a light sleeper.

The channel finally came around the ridge and turned along a hillside literally a stone's throw from the towering white Buenos Aires building. Miguel's suspected tenth-floor apartment was a few hundred feet away—almost at eye level with the edge of the flood canal. Dave Mitchell dropped down on his belly and trained a pair of binoculars on the windows. He had a clear view into the residence, but there was no sign of activity. He and Chris Feistl waited for the rest of their contingent to catch up. Last to arrive was the prosecutor in high heels and white slacks, assisted by the DEA agent Ruben Prieto.

"You should have told me we were climbing mountains," she hissed.

Feistl shrugged apologetically, then he motioned for everyone to gather silently around him in the middle of the channel bed. For the first time he informed them that their target was the tenth-floor apartment in the tall white building looming over the channel walls.

"We are here to seize and arrest Miguel Rodríguez Orejuela, boss of the Cali cartel," Feistl concluded. The news was received with general excitement by everyone except the prosecutor, clearly annoyed that she had been kept in the dark about both the target and the physical difficulties of the mission. Worse yet, she had a fear of heights, and the most difficult portion of their night trek still lay ahead—a rough and extremely steep descent of about sixty yards.

Feistl left the team and backtracked to where he had parked the sedan. He drove to a prearranged position just outside the inner security ring being watched by Genaro Angel's men. With the car, Feistl could respond quickly—"just in case" something unexpected occurred.

The assault plan called for Mitchell to stay on the hillside near the channel with his binoculars and a radio watching the apartment as the raid developed. The rest of the raiders would follow the agents Salameh and Prieto down the rock-strewn mountainside in the dark. Almost immediately, their descent turned dangerous when the group encountered an unexpected ravine. Its near-vertical sides dropped away like a double black diamond on a ski slope.

Prieto peered over the edge. "Someone's gonna break their neck," he said in a worried tone.

"We can't wait," Salameh insisted. He was toting a twenty-pound sledgehammer intended to smash Miguel's door. "You stay with her." He nodded to the overdressed prosecutor. And then he jumped.

It was Salameh's first experience at skiing. He slid and skidded the first twenty feet on the soles of his boots, fell back and skidded several more on the seat of his pants, and finally went airborne the last eight or ten feet in an avalanche of dirt and gravel—still gripping the long-handled sledgehammer.

FEISTL'S FIRST HINT that the descent might not be going as planned came as he sat in his car waiting to hear that the commando team was ready to enter the building. Salameh radioed for assistance.

"We're here—at the building. We need help!" he said. The message wasn't desperate, but it was urgent.

"I'll be right there," Feistl responded. He figured that a car with a lone driver could enter the security zone without tempting an alarm. He drove slowly, fighting an urge to rush to the scene.

When he pulled up between the hillside and the main entrance to the Buenos Aires building, Feistl expected to see most of the thirty-five raiders he'd left on the ridge. He saw only Jerry Salameh, who walked up as a puzzled Feistl rolled down his window.

"Jerry? Hey, man—where is everybody?"

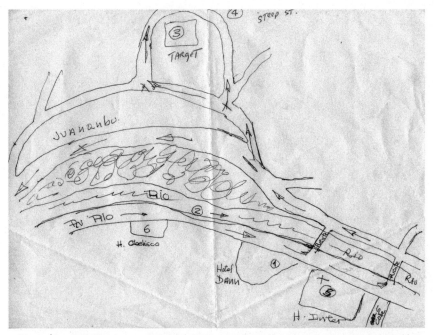

After the first raid failed, Jorge Salcedo provided DEA agents with this hand-drawn sketch of Miguel's new hiding place in a residential area just north of the Cali River. At first, Jorge considered the likely target to be either number 3 or number 4, but the location of Miguel's apartment was quickly narrowed down to the Buenos Aires building—here marked with a 3. Because normal approaches to the building were limited and easily monitored, the raiding party would instead descend from a steep hillside above and beyond areas covered by this drawing. (Map from DEA files)

The Buenos Aires building (3) and a second possible residence (4) that was briefly suspected as Miguel's hideout. The flood control channel is barely visible cut into the hillside behind the number 4 building and at the far right of the photograph. Jorge Salcedo took this photo and turned it over to the DEA. (Courtesy of the DEA)

The Buenos Aires building as seen from the hillside flood control channel that would be used to help conceal the approach of a joint Colombian-U.S. raiding party. Jorge Salcedo took this photo and turned it over to the DEA. (Courtesy of the DEA)

THE RISING SON

Chris Feistl looked up the steep hillside again and saw no signs of the thirty-odd cops and commandos still picking their way slowly down the dark slope. No reinforcements appeared anywhere near. The raiding party already at the entrance to Hacienda Buenos Aires amounted to only six men, two of them Feistl and his DEA partner Jerry Salameh. Ambassador Frechette's orders were for the Americans to stay back and let the Colombians take the lead on these raids. But there weren't enough Colombians on the ground to lead a respectable conga line. Of course, Ambassador Frechette wasn't faced with the dilemma of waiting outside the godfather's secret lair with time ticking away and the element of surprise about to blow up at any second.

"We gotta go!" Salameh insisted. "It's been ten minutes already."

The final assault team would be only five men. One of the Colombian policemen had detained two night watchmen, and he would have to stay behind to keep them silent and secure. That left one navy commando and two Colombian police officers to accompany Jerry and

Chris to the tenth floor. Not much of a force, especially if they encountered armed resistance. But Feistl doubted the likelihood of a shoot-out. Jorge had assured him that Miguel Rodríguez Orejuela relied on early-warning systems, not weapons, for his protection. What worried the DEA agent more was the possibility that Miguel would get a tip in time to escape again into a secret vault. And that risk was mounting with every tick of the clock. Feistl eyed his small team. The sledgehammer was the only piece of equipment they really needed. Everyone looked to Feistl for the signal.

"All right, let's go," he said. "We'll take the stairs."

Five armed men with a sledgehammer entered the building's stairwell on the run and took the ten flights of stairs at a brisk pace. Entry to the tenth-floor apartment unit was through a handsome, heavy wood door. The DEA agents took positions on either side of the door and, in deference to the rules of engagement, gave a Colombian policeman first shot with the sledgehammer.

Ka-thud!

The heavy steel head landed square in the middle of the wood panel and bounced off, leaving a dent but having little effect on the door's structural integrity. Salameh immediately grabbed the sledgehammer. Everyone stepped back to give him extra clearance for a big windup.

Feistl's radio crackled with static and then the voice of Dave Mitchell reporting urgently from his vantage point high on the hillside: "We've got lights!" Salameh landed his first hammer strike just above the lock and door handle. The latch still held, but it was damaged. The molding cracked along the doorjamb. A second blow left the door slightly ajar—and a third blew it wide open. It took seconds, but seemed like five minutes.

Feistl was the first one through the debris and into the dark entryway. He had never seen a floor plan and had no idea which way to turn. The single apartment took up the entire floor, sprawling across about four thousand square feet of white marble flooring. Feistl moved quickly to the right, groping along the wall for a light switch. Others scattered in all directions. Feistl found himself in the kitchen. There on a tiled counter was the multiline Panasonic telephone equipment, a reassuring sign. Ahead, down a dark hall, lights were coming on. He rushed toward them and encountered an unarmed man who had obviously been sound asleep until moments before. It was Mateo, the driver he and Dave had followed for nearly a week. Now Feistl was certain this was the right place. But he also feared that the godfather might have already slipped away.

From somewhere on the far side of the apartment, Feistl heard excited, muffled shouts. It was the navy commando's voice calling: "I've got him! I've got him!" Feistl ran toward the sound, down another hall, through the master bedroom, into a huge walk-in closet. There he found the brawny special forces officer with a big fist locked around the arm of a much smaller, unshaven man in boxer shorts and a T-shirt. They were standing beside a floor-level door that opened into a hidden wall chamber. Feistl reached for his radio and called Mitchell.

"We've got him," he said.

"You're sure?" Mitchell could see no one from his angle.

"Hey, man—I'm standing right in front of him," Feistl assured his partner.

MIGUEL WAS DRESSED, cuffed, and seated in the living room by the time the rest of the raiding party straggled in. Over the next thirty minutes, a parade of navy commandos wandered through the apartment for a peek at their quarry, the rather harmless-looking man in a blue jacket and black slacks.

One of the last to arrive was the prosecutor—her high heels ruined, her hair and clothes askew, and her white slacks smeared with dirt stains. Her humiliation getting down the mountain was only compounded by the apparent lack of trust the Americans demonstrated by keeping secret the real target of the morning's mission. It seemed to the DEA agents that she remained somewhat aloof from their celebration. The four DEA agents posed for pictures with their trophy fugitive. Miguel sat watching the flurry of activities around him and occasionally shaking his head. He said nothing.

Feistl wandered back down the hall to the master bedroom for another look at the *caleta*. It was the most sophisticated example of its kind he had seen. The chamber itself was a claustrophobic three and a half feet square and more than six feet high, large enough for Miguel to stand but barely wide enough for him to turn around. It was equipped with an oxygen tank, a folding stool, full water bottles, and a large bag of peanuts. Investigators also found another stash of cartel records inside. An air-conditioning vent provided a constant flow of fresh, cool air. The access door was eight inches thick, made of cement, and disguised to appear as part of the closet's built-in cabinetry. The door was mounted on heavy-gauge steel hinges to glide open and shut easily. It had a set of four sliding steel rods to secure it from the inside.

This time, it was Feistl shaking his head. Not in a million years would they have found this vault had the door not been open when they arrived. The commando who nabbed him said that Miguel was already halfway through the vault doorway when he arrived, and that he had grabbed him just in time to pull the drug boss back out.

It had been that close.

THE TELEPHONE NEXT TO Jorge Salcedo's bed woke him with a start at about six that morning. He fumbled to answer it before the ringing bothered Lena.

"Do you know what happened?" the caller said.

Jorge was pretty sure it was Dario, but his voice was so low that it could barely be heard even in the quiet bedroom. "What happened, Dario?" Jorge answered and held his breath. The man sounded so miserable.

"They captured Don Miguel," Dario said.

"What!?" Jorge almost shouted. He hoped his relief came across as shock and surprise. Dario remained glum.

"Yes, it happened last night," he went on. Dario said that Miguel had been arrested sometime around four in the morning and that just a few minutes earlier, around a quarter to six, he was transferred to the air force base.

"How could this happen?" Jorge said.

Dario had no idea. "No one saw them come in," he said. "We don't know where or how they came in. What can I say?"

"Well, is there anything we can do? Will there be any chance for a rescue?"

"No, there's nothing—nothing we can do." Dario said the size of the police and military force surrounding Miguel was massive. Jorge knew that, of course, and realized he had pushed his response far enough. Instead of pressing for explanations, he offered comfort and re-assurance.

"You did your job, Dario. We all did," Jorge told him.

It was Sunday morning, August 6, 1995, and Jorge Salcedo had suc-cessfully served up the world's biggest crime boss to law-enforcement au-thorities. If he was not in immediate danger of retribution, it was only because there were but two people in all of Colombia who knew about his role. One of them paged Jorge later that morning.

"Hey, Sean. We got him. Thanks to you," Feistl said in a brief tele-phone exchange.

"Thank God; thank God," Jorge responded.

The agents said it was time for him and his family to come in for government protection. The DEA would arrange for a plane to fly them all out of Cali the next day. Not so fast, Jorge protested. What about Pallomari? If he left now, someone else would be put in charge of killing the accountant, and Jorge's invaluable insider vantage point would be lost. No, the Americans had to act quickly now and rescue Pallomari, he insisted. Jorge also felt reasonably confident that he could dodge blame for a few more days. He was ready to play out his charade a little longer.

In the vernacular of the spy world, Jorge was not yet ready to come in from the cold. Besides, he needed time to prepare his family for the upheaval that was about to strike their lives. He still hadn't told his wife that she was married to a double agent.

WILLIAM RODRÍGUEZ SUMMONED Jorge to an urgent meeting shortly after lunch on Monday afternoon. Miguel's son had just returned from Bogotá, where he conferred with his father and the drug boss's legal team. He had brought back a message for Jorge.

Jorge drove immediately to William's law offices downtown. He was ushered in past a coterie of heavily armed toughs lounging in an outer office and brought directly to the new acting boss of the Cali cartel. Dario was already there, head down, shoulders drooping. William's friend was clearly absorbing some of the guilt for the security breakdown.

"Do we know what happened?" Jorge asked.

"They arrested Pinchadito—and, of course, he talked," William said, so matter-of-factly that Jorge felt instantly in the clear. He still had to hide his relief.

"Ah, of course. But tell me, how is your father?"

"He will be fine," William said. "He tells me you are in charge of the Pallomari project. He wants that taken care of now, immediately. It's the absolute priority."

Jorge nodded and said it could be done but that Pallomari had moved since he last had an address for him. No problem, said William. He would call in Pallomari's lawyer and get the accountant's latest address from him. A good idea, Jorge acknowledged, but he also reminded the new boss that César Yusti was the *sicario* assigned to the killing. Jorge was simply the coordinator.

"Yes, but I don't know this man, Yusti," William said. "I want you to find him and bring him here. I need to speak with him."

"Now?" asked Jorge.

"Now. Today. Immediately."

Jorge called Yusti and arranged a meeting downtown. He waited until they were together in person to report that William wanted to see him.

An hour later, back in the downtown law offices of Miguel's son, Jorge introduced Yusti to William for the first time. It was a moment rich in opportunism. William was the new king of the cartel; Yusti was the loyal servant eager to impress.

"I've been ready to do this for some time," Yusti said. "But we've all been so busy. I just need to know the target's location."

All eyes turned to Jaime Gil, Pallomari's personal attorney and a longtime legal adviser to the cartel. While Jorge had been rounding up Yusti, William had called in Gil for just this moment. He wanted Gil to tell them where to find Pallomari. His hired assassin needed to know.

Gil resisted. "I really don't remember," he said.

"You better remember, Jaime, or you will pay the consequences." William could not have been more menacing. Jorge was struck by how quickly and enthusiastically he had assumed the role of mob boss.

"Well, maybe I can find the place again by driving to the area," said the shaken lawyer, still insisting that he could not recall the actual address.

William dispatched Jorge, Yusti, and Dario to ride along so everyone could see where Pallomari was in hiding. But before they filed out of William's office, the young Rodríguez emphasized one more time: *"Mi papá,"* he said. "My father wants Pallomari dead by the end of this week."

RACE THE ASSASSIN

O N Monday, August 7, Colombia celebrated once again the 1819 rout of Spanish forces at the Battle of Boyacá that brought independence to Panama, Venezuela, Ecuador, and Colombia. The streets of Cali were empty, allowing Jaime Gil's little orange Renault to sprint from the north side to the south side of the city in little more than fifteen minutes. Not that the lawyer behind the wheel was in any hurry. He was not at all eager to show the cartel assassin in the backseat where his client Guillermo Pallomari was hiding. In the end, however, he drove directly to the neighborhood and made no further pretense of forgetting how to find the accountant who knew too much.

"That one," said Jaime Gil, pointing to an eight-story brick building. "He lives there."

"Which apartment?" César Yusti, the compact balding man behind him, was leaning forward to study the terrain around the building, the street approach, and the main entrance. But the lawyer didn't respond immediately.

"I don't know the apartment. And I don't know the floor," said Gil, though he hastened to add, "But whatever floor he's on, he's in the apartment across the hall from the elevator."

Jorge Salcedo said he would check the building's numbering system and find out who lived in the elevator-facing apartments on every floor. He said it might take a day or two. Privately, he imagined that he could eke out an extra day of delay, if necessary. Yusti said he would start surveillance on the site that very night. Clearly, he was determined to make a good impression on young William.

Jorge had to move fast. Feistl and Mitchell returned from Bogotá the next day and met with Jorge at a construction site where they felt secure. They were just as alarmed as Jorge was about the heightened danger to Pallomari, but they were unsure how to approach him. Jorge was of little help because the accountant deeply distrusted him, just as he did everyone else in the cartel hierarchy. They finally agreed to approach Pallomari through his wife—Gladys Patricia Cardona Pallomari. Everyone knew her as Patricia.

PATRICIA WAS A VIVACIOUS BEAUTY with long hair and big dark eyes. Along with a family friend named Fredy, she ran a Pallomari-owned computer company called Universal Link out of a building just down the street from William Rodríguez's law offices. Even as her fearful husband slipped deeper and deeper into seclusion, Patricia continued to work openly—coming to the office daily, going home to the couple's empty home every night. The cartel kept her under constant surveillance but never picked up any leads to the missing spouse.

At six thirty Tuesday afternoon, the two American drug agents walked into Universal Link and asked for Patricia. When she emerged from an office, they asked to speak to her in private. They were aware that a pair of six-foot-three gringos asking about Pallomari's wife could set off repercussions, but they had no more time. There were at least a dozen employees watching as they moved to a private office in the back. Patricia sat behind a desk and waited.

"We're agents with the U.S. Drug Enforcement Administration

and we're here on a very sensitive matter," Feistl began in Spanish. "We advise that you keep what we are about to tell you confidential."

He waited for some sort of acknowledgment. She nodded for him to go on.

"There is a very advanced plan put in motion by Miguel Rodríguez to kill your husband," he said.

The information clearly did not surprise her. She said the couple had suspected as much and for that reason Guillermo had gone into hiding. She said she hadn't seen him for nearly a year and had no idea where he was at that moment. Mitchell interrupted. "We are obligated to tell you that your life, too, is in great danger," he said.

She shrugged and appeared unruffled. She agreed to try passing along a message to her husband—but it could take a day or more. Before leaving, the agents warned her that she was under surveillance by the cartel and that she was being followed in hopes of leading hired killers to Guillermo.

Outside the Universal Link offices, Feistl and Mitchell weren't sure what to make of their encounter with Patricia. They thought she was taking their warnings far too lightly, maybe even flippantly. It seemed to them that Jorge Salcedo was more concerned about her husband's peril than she was.

That evening César Yusti paged Jorge. The *sicario* had obtained an apartment number for Pallomari and was considering mounting his attack that night. Slow down, Jorge cautioned. Without having a phone number for the apartment, it was not possible to verify he was in that night. A premature hit would scare Pallomari even deeper underground. Jorge advocated another day or two of delay to work cartel telephone company sources for a valid phone number. Don't move in for the kill, Jorge advised, until confirming that Pallomari was home.

The next morning, on Wednesday, August 9, Jorge met early with Feistl and Mitchell at the shopping mall construction site. He warned them that he couldn't hold off Yusti much longer. The agents left to renew their negotiations with Patricia Pallomari. She still had not heard from her husband, she said, but now she wanted to meet with the ambassador. She was concerned about her husband's potential legal liabilities in the United States. The request meant at least another day's delay.

The agents arranged for her to meet the next day at the Bogotá embassy with the DEA attaché Tony Senneca.

At a second rendezvous on Wednesday back at the shopping mall site, Jorge was sitting with Feistl and Mitchell in their car when his cell phone rang. It was William, and he was angry about the pace of the Pallomari project. William's voice was so strong that Jorge could hear it even while holding the receiver two or three inches from his ear. Feistl and Mitchell could hear it, too. All three listened in silence as William raged to Jorge: "Listen, I want Pallomari killed by the end of this week, or I'll have you killed."

Jorge would have to dispatch Yusti that night to make an attempt on Pallomari's life. He had no choice. He needed an external source of delay this time. He asked Feistl and Mitchell for help to orchestrate another ploy. They, in turn, enlisted the services of the major crimes division of the Colombian National Police—its F-2 unit.

That night, when César Yusti drove into Pallomari's neighborhood, he stopped well short of the apartment building. There were roadblocks at key intersections manned by officers wearing the distinctive black and yellow F-2 armbands. They were inspecting cars and checking identities of everyone moving through the area. After waiting a few hours without any sign that the barricades would come down during the night, Yusti apparently retreated.

ON WEDNESDAY, after a midday meeting with the American agents, Jorge came home and asked Lena to go for a ride with him. "I need to talk with you," he said. Their three-year-old and five-year-old were in the care of a housekeeper. They drove only a short distance to a favorite scenic spot, a field of wild grasses with a view of the mountains. It was late afternoon, and the shadows were creeping down the eastern slopes. The couple sat together in the warm grass near the road.

"I have to tell you that Miguel's capture and all these exposures and scandals with President Samper—these were not by chance," he began. "I am behind them. They are all the result of my involvement." Lena seemed confused. "What are you saying?" she asked.

"Our lives are in great danger," Jorge said. "We have to leave—in two or three days, we will be going to the States. All of us—the children, your sister, my parents."

"What?" It was all too much to absorb so quickly.

"I will be cooperating with U.S. authorities. It is important for me; it is important for our country," he said. "But it may be some time before we can come home."

She began to weep. Jorge took her hand and began to tell her the story of his last two months—of the Pallomari murder orders, of the failed raid and the secret documents, of the need to wait a few more days to rescue Guillermo and Patricia. As the initial shock ebbed, Lena's practical nature recovered.

"You have to know too much," she said. "I know it can't be safe. But why haven't you told me sooner?"

Jorge tried to explain that it was for her own safety and the children's, saying that their ignorance might have protected their lives if he had been discovered. She didn't buy it. "You really think they would not come for all of us when they came for you?" she said. There were so many things he admired about Lena. She was strong, direct, nononsense, and practical. But most important, sitting in the grass on that August afternoon, she held his hand and said she was with him—wherever that might take them.

"When you think it's time for us to go, we will go," she said.

After talking for about forty minutes, many practical questions arose, including financial ones. What would they do for income in the United States? Jorge had not discussed such things with the Americans except to say that he was not seeking any cash rewards as a condition of cooperating. He assured his wife, however, that he expected some sort of government support to assist them in getting settled.

On their brief drive home, Lena was already planning the move. She had to get some things to the laundry, she had to buy extra luggage, she would get started that night packing. "No, no, no—" Jorge stopped her. "Not yet." The simple act of packing suitcases could be incriminating. The entire family could be massacred at the first hint of flight.

Lena wept again.

* * *

For the U.S. embassy, the Pallomari affair threatened to be a significant diplomatic headache, or worse. The betting among U.S. agents was that if the Colombians arrested Guillermo, he wouldn't live to testify in any court proceedings. The nation's highest officials and its most ruthless mobsters shared the same powerful interest in seeing Pallomari silenced. For the United States to intervene, however, was a tricky proposition. Pallomari faced criminal charges in Colombia that took legal priority over any foreign allegations—and those pending Colombian charges were hardly routine. Pallomari was a central figure in the national scandal that threatened to topple Colombia's presidency. The United States could not take such a prominent fugitive into custody and simply whisk him from the country—not legally, not without violating Colombian sovereignty. In fact, Pallomari was going to have to escape from Colombia without official U.S. assistance under whatever scenario was devised. Otherwise, Feistl and Mitchell might be headed back to the ambassador's woodshed once again.

On Thursday morning, Patricia Pallomari was at the embassy in Bogotá to talk about Guillermo and how he could take advantage of the DEA's offer of protection—specifically, what it would take to get him out of Colombia, what sort of legal exposure her husband faced in U.S. courts, and what quality of life the family could expect if relocated to the United States. She raised a number of personal issues, many of them financial. The couple had investments, furniture, property, and businesses. What would happen to those? How much time could they take to liquidate assets? Feistl, Mitchell, and the DEA attaché Senneca could only underscore the risks of doing nothing. At one point, Feistl's pager went off and he excused himself from the embassy office to respond.

It was Jorge. The cartel had successfully wiretapped a telephone in the apartment where Pallomari was hiding. César Yusti had confirmed that Guillermo was there. He was going to make another attempt to kill Pallomari tonight. Feistl returned to Senneca's office.

"Guess what?" he said, standing in the middle of the room. "That was our guy. They're listening to Guillermo's phone now. He's got to get the hell out of there. Now."

*   *   *

IN CALI THAT THURSDAY AFTERNOON, Lena Salcedo went shopping for suitcases. Even if she couldn't start packing just yet, she would soon need the luggage. She anticipated having to pack for Jorge and herself, for her teenage son by her previous marriage, and for the couple's two preschoolers—not to mention helping her sister and fiancé, who would be evacuated with them. The one-way nature of the trip posed considerably more of a challenge than preparing for a long vacation abroad. They could take only what they could carry, not knowing whether they would ever return.

Her emotions faltered at times, thinking about family and friends she might never see again—and about the Lot. The ten-acre plot was still undeveloped with little more than a caretaker's shack. But it represented the couple's fondest dreams. Jorge had designed various versions of a family home. Lena had spent many hours planting the grounds with flowers and fruit trees. A row of elegant coconut palms marked the future entrance to Casa Salcedo. It was just one of so many dreams they would have to leave behind.

At a discount market in the city, Lena found the large matching set of suitcases she needed for family preparations. The complete set was not in stock but would be available for pickup on Friday morning. She left her home phone number for the proprietor to call when her shipment was delivered.

"You left our home number with the luggage store?" Jorge was incredulous. He had to assume that his home phone was one of those routinely monitored by the cartel—especially now. He worried what William might make of a call to the Salcedo residence from a store advising them that their luggage was ready. Jorge did not want Lena to feel bad, but they drove immediately to the market to say that their phone was out of order. No problem, said the proprietor with a shrug. Just come back Friday morning and pick up the cases.

Pallomari's slow and uncertain response to the DEA's rescue offer was becoming a serious burden for all sides. From the sidelines, Jorge could do nothing to speed it along. He sensed that his own double-agent role had about run its course. False suspicions about Pinchadito, the telephone man, were going to be discovered eventually. That the misperception had lasted nearly a week was remarkable. And with the safety of his wife and children eroding, Jorge's stubborn commitment to saving Pallomari was finally giving way to other priorities. He had his own family to save.

On Friday, August 11, Jorge got the call he was dreading. It was William. His voice was neither friendly nor angry—simply ice-cold. "Can you be here at three?" he said. It was a demand, not a question.

A WEEKEND FUNERAL

Something was wrong. Jorge Salcedo was picking up signals everywhere he turned. The phone call from William Rodríguez was ominous. There was unmistakable contempt in his voice. Jorge had never been fired from a job, and he imagined that a cartel firing might not resemble standard business models. He hoped that nagging uncertainty about whether he was or was not the informant would prevent, or at least delay, harsh measures. Jorge had a few surprises in reserve, if he needed them.

His long wait in William's outer office was another troubling sign. Goons with big guns lolled about in chairs or leaned against the walls, lending an aura of menace to the surroundings. Jorge had never been asked to wait outside for more than a moment or two—never even time to take a seat—but this delay felt like punishment. This was the wait imposed on those who were disrespected. It had already extended beyond twenty minutes.

Jorge was sharing a small couch with one of William's *sicarios,* a slovenly man pushing three hundred pounds in a loud orange shirt and white pants. A shiny .357 Magnum was stuffed into the front waistband—and stuffed was the only appropriate description. Since the orange shirt failed to cover the man's substantial girth, Jorge could not help but notice the butt of the gun keeping a roll of belly fat from tumbling out over the top snap of his pants.

Across the room another revolver-armed bodyguard was sprawled on a chair thumbing through porno magazines and keeping up a running commentary for all to hear on the modeling talent he discovered on the pages. This was the new generation of Cali cartel security men, Jorge mused—crude, undisciplined slobs and thugs. Not the cool and efficient professional security force assembled and maintained by Jorge and Mario del Basto since 1989. Jorge couldn't help himself. He had been proud of his men and of his protective services for the families. But things had changed.

He reached down to pat a bulky paging device on his belt. It looked like an old-fashioned model, but it was not what it appeared to be. Jorge had replaced its electronic guts with a powerful charge of C-4 plastic explosives. A delay switch rigged to the little red reset button would give him five seconds to escape or seek cover before it blew and spewed BB-sized shrapnel. It could cause serious harm to anyone too close, but mostly Jorge counted on his handcrafted mini–claymore mine to cause a diversion, to buy time for his escape.

Jorge had only briefly considered making a mad dash for the U.S. embassy instead of meeting with William. But that might have left some of his family stranded and unprotected. Jorge had not yet told his elderly parents what he was doing, though he hoped they would join him relocating to the United States. Also, sudden flight to the embassy risked setting off a diplomatic storm that could jeopardize both Jorge and Pallomari. The Colombian government might assert the right to prosecute them, denying the United States custody of either man. Of course, that most likely would mean both would die in Colombian jail cells. Jorge preferred his chances with William.

It was a cold, pragmatic calculation, but Jorge acknowledged the risk. Besides his explosive pager, he brought along a wingman—someone to make certain that he didn't suddenly disappear without a trace. His watcher was a family friend who waited in a car around the corner from William's office armed only with a cell phone. If Jorge failed to check in every fifteen minutes, the watcher was to call the army, where Jorge had friends. Jorge had already called down to the car once, letting the man know he was still waiting.

A heavy wooden door at the far end of the waiting area finally opened, and Jorge was summoned to the inner chamber. He entered facing William, who was tilted back in a big leather swivel chair behind his desk. Two men seated across the desk with their backs to Jorge stood and turned toward him as Jorge approached. It was Captain Efrén Buitrago of the Bloque de Búsqueda and the Shadow. Jorge greeted them with a cordiality that seemed markedly out of place.

"Captain, how are you?" Jorge said, smiling and extending his hand. "Tell me, did you catch any shit over taking out Miguel?"

"No, no problem," Buitrago said quickly, and just as quickly dropped it. He was not going to engage in conversation.

Dario Delgado entered through the big wooden door without a knock. Jorge couldn't help noticing that his assistant had a higher security clearance now than he did.

"Richard," said William in a low, deliberate tone, "do you have anything going, any projects besides Pallomari?" He was still tilted back in his chair, legs crossed, the fingertips of his left hand touching the fingertips of his right hand, assuming a contemplative pose—and staring at Jorge.

"No, nothing," Jorge responded. "Let me know whatever you need and I'll—"

"Delgado will take over supervision of Pallomari," William interrupted. "What else are you doing?"

"Well, we need to reorganize my people. They are waiting for new assignments, perhaps taking care of the families, you, and—"

"Delgado will take care of this," William said.

Jorge was being fired—apparently, one duty at a time. He imagined his epaulettes being ripped from his shoulders. It seemed almost ceremonial. Neither policeman said a word. Delgado said nothing. But at that moment, Jorge's cartel beeper chirped and vibrated. He excused himself and slipped it from his belt.

"Do you mind if I take this call?" Jorge said, nodding toward a telephone across the room. "It's from Yusti."

William shrugged, and Jorge, grateful for the interruption, moved to the phone and dialed Yusti's number.

"We're going to do it tonight," Yusti said when they connected. The *sicario* was using his cell phone, so he was cautious about how explicitly he discussed the Pallomari hit. He said that he had enlisted help from friends in the local prosecutor's office, the *fiscalía,* and that he was going to have all the proper documentation to get through the police roadblocks if they returned that night.

"No, please, be very careful," Jorge cautioned, instinctively playing his role as security counselor to the very end. "You don't want to take chances getting caught with false documents under these circumstances."

"No, no, no," Yusti insisted. "These are the real *fiscalía.* They have a warrant. We'll hit him after one in the morning. It's all arranged. Tonight's the night."

Jorge hung up and repeated Yusti's report for Dario. William seemed annoyed that Jorge knew so much about Yusti's plan. Clearly, the assassin had not yet been informed of Jorge's new status as an outcast. And there was nothing left to discuss with William.

"Well, then—I'll be going home now," said Jorge.

He gave a polite nod to Buitrago and his corporal, to Dario, and to William, and then walked out the door. No one stopped him. It seemed obvious to Jorge that William had just learned from the Bloque snitches that Pinchadito, the telephone man, had not talked to police after all. That meant the most likely informant was the one William had suspected all along—his father's security boss. It was fresh information. Their response was reactive. A more calculated response would come later. For now Jorge was allowed to exit without so much as a question.

And so, on Friday afternoon, August 11, 1995, Jorge Salcedo was finally, if not officially, an ex-member of the Cali cartel—and no doubt the newest name on the list of *sicario* targets.

* * *

WITH THE EXCEPTION OF a seven-shot Walther pistol, Jorge did not keep weapons around his home. He maintained a locked and secure storage space in town, however, that contained a virtual arsenal—rifles, machine guns, explosives, ammunition—everything necessary for the well-stocked family bunker.

That afternoon Jorge took home an MP5K rifle, a German-made submachine gun, several magazines of ammunition, and five live hand grenades. They were stashed under his bed, out of sight from his small children. But they were loaded and in easy reach.

The Salcedo residence was in a secure apartment building. They lived near a supreme court justice who required armed guards twenty-four hours a day supplied by the Administrative Department of Security (DAS). The armed guards were near enough to be a potential deterrent. Of course, they were no guarantee against some rogue prosecutor or crooked cops cloaked in official authority trying to arrest him, but the DAS guards did minimize the prospects of Yusti or Memo or Freckles making a solo run at his door—a door that was now heavily guarded by Jorge's in-house armory. If anyone attempted to enter his home, even with a warrant for his arrest, Jorge intended to resist with all the firepower under his bed.

Jorge called Feistl and Mitchell with details of Yusti's new plan to use prosecutors with an arrest warrant to seize Pallomari some time after one in the morning. The status of the fugitive accountant's rescue or surrender or whatever it had become remained uncertain. The DEA agents couldn't talk about it. But Jorge had done all that he could to make it happen. As far as he was concerned, Pallomari was now in the hands of God and the DEA. And so was he.

As midnight approached, Jorge turned out the lights, made sure that in the dark he could still find his German-made MP5K submachine gun, and then said his bedtime prayers. He was content with incremental progress: *God, get us through this weekend.*

GUILLERMO PALLOMARI'S STATUS as a highly sensitive political figure, already wanted on criminal charges by Colombian authorities, complicated every stage of efforts by Feistl and Mitchell and their DEA colleagues to move him to safety. As the agents flew to Cali that Friday night in hopes of bringing him back to Bogotá and the protection of a safe house, they were also flying well beyond their limits under international laws and treaties. It had to be viewed as a humanitarian mission, not law enforcement.

The six-man DEA contingent arrived in an eight-passenger aircraft. They told Colombian airport authorities that they would be returning later with an additional passenger, a sick colleague. If anyone should press further, Feistl and Mitchell also brought along a spare DEA identification badge. Its mug shot of a colleague named Tommy was of sufficiently poor quality that it might pass for Pallomari in the dark.

The rendezvous arranged through Pallomari's wife and their family friend Fredy was set for around eleven o'clock that night outside a southern Cali hospital, the Clínica Valle del Lili. It was a place where groups of people gathering at late hours were a common sight, where tall blond men and swarthy Colombians could be seen mingling without drawing attention.

Feistl and Mitchell, both familiar to Patricia Pallomari and Fredy, made themselves as visible as possible. And at 10:45 p.m., an entire family emerged from the shadows. It was Patricia, Fredy, two boys aged fifteen and eleven . . . and Guillermo Pallomari. They had arrived with suitcases and a bad case of nerves.

"Don't worry. We're here to help you," Feistl said.

But there was no way they could accommodate the entire family. It was going to be dicey enough sneaking Pallomari aboard a government plane on an official trip while posing as Tommy, the sick DEA agent.

It was finally agreed that Patricia and the kids would fly to Bogotá on a commercial flight the following morning. Pallomari climbed into a car with Feistl and Mitchell for a midnight dash to the airport. A second DEA car ran ahead, clearing the route and checking for roadblocks. It was just as important that night to avoid Colombian authorities as it was to dodge cartel assassins. Under the circumstances, both posed equally grave dangers to the man in the backseat.

*　*　*

JORGE SALCEDO WAS FAST ASLEEP with his MP5K comfortably near when a ringing telephone jarred him awake. It was Dario.

"Richard, have you heard from Yusti?" he asked.

Jorge checked the clock. It was nearly two thirty in the morning. Dario hadn't been in charge yet for twelve hours and already he was calling Jorge for advice. Didn't he notice that William fired him that afternoon?

"No, Dario. No, he hasn't called. Why?" Jorge was patient with him, as usual.

"I can't find him. I thought maybe you knew about a change of plans," Dario said. "We were supposed to meet at two. But he didn't show up. I don't know what to do."

Jorge said he was going back to bed and could only advise Dario to stand by and wait for Yusti to call. The Salcedo household was back to sleep at six o'clock, when the phone rang again. It was Dario again, this time in considerable agitation.

"Richard, guess what?"

"No, what?" Jorge was a bit short with his former assistant. He was in no mood to be awakened for riddles.

"It's Yusti—he's been shot. The sons of bitches killed him."

Jorge's mind raced. Was there a shoot-out with the DEA? Dario talked on excitedly about what he knew and didn't know. Yusti had been shot in the head while sitting in his car somewhere between Pallomari's apartment hideout and the Clínica Valle del Lili. Who did it was a big mystery, but one loudmouthed cartel operative known as El Guajiro, "the Peasant," was blaming Dario, of all people, for the execution-style hit. Dario was undone by the suspicion and openly fearful that he might be killed in unwarranted retaliation.

"Of course, that's nonsense. No one will believe it," Jorge tried to reassure him.

Dario said a funeral would likely be organized for Sunday at a neighborhood parish. He asked if Jorge would attend.

"I'll see you there," Jorge said. It was an easy lie.

He hung up, his mind racing. Was it possible Yusti wasn't dead, that this was a ruse to lure him out from behind his barricade? But Dario was incapable of acting. Did the CIA do it? Was it part of the Pallomari rescue? That made the most sense at six in the morning in a barricaded apartment with an arsenal under his mattress.

It was nine o'clock when Feistl and Mitchell, checking in from Bogotá, paged him. Pallomari was safe, and the DEA agents were on their way to the airport to pick up his family on an Avianca flight from Cali.

"That's wonderful," Jorge said. "Hey, did you hear Yusti's dead?"

What? The Americans expressed shock. It seemed to be news to them. Of course, Jorge figured they were capable of acting, unlike Dario. Yet it sounded like genuine surprise. He reconsidered. Maybe it wasn't the CIA.

"Whoever did it is an angel," Mitchell said.

Jorge laughed and took mock credit for eliminating the hit man who might also have harmed the agents in his attempt to gun down Pallomari. "Yeah, well, I couldn't let anything happen to you and Chris," he joked. Jorge worried later that his DEA friends might have taken him seriously. It was something about Mitchell's silence.

But Jorge had more immediate concerns. He asked the agents what time he should have his family ready to leave. They were standing by, ready in an hour or two if necessary. Mitchell said a DEA plane would be at the air force base to pick them up on Monday.

"Monday!" Jorge was stunned. He felt that he and his family were already in the line of fire. And it was only Saturday morning. He tried to ask calmly, "It can't be sooner?" But Feistl and Mitchell were fully engaged. They could not do everything at once. Jorge hung up and told Lena that she would have two more days to get ready.

As it turned out, Jorge would still be in town for Yusti's weekend funeral. He was curious, but not that curious. For the next two days he dared not venture anywhere beyond his barricaded front door. It promised to be a very long weekend.

WE KNOW WHAT YOU'RE DOING

IN THEIR BARRICADED FOURTH-FLOOR APARTMENT, JORGE SALCEDO and his family spent two days packing the new suitcases, watching television, and staying out of sight. Jorge manned a window vantage point that provided a commanding view of the apartment building entrance. He worried most that he might spot Freckles, the *sicario* whose mother lived in the same residential complex. Freckles, who tipped generously throughout the year, was on excellent terms with the building's security guards.

After two days of waiting, watching, and worrying, Monday finally dawned and along with it a flurry of last-minute activities. If any cartel *sicarios* were going to get him today, they were going to have to hit a moving target.

Jorge had arranged for a friend to drive his Ford E-350 van, filled with the luggage, to Bogotá. That was launched early in the morning. Next, there was the disposal of weapons and munitions. Jorge was uncomfortable simply abandoning so much firepower where it could fall into anyone's hands. He returned to his storage space and loaded up everything he didn't already have in hand and then drove to a rural area just outside town. In an empty field overgrown with grass, Jorge tossed out twenty rifles and several boxes of ammunition and explosives. He marked the location on a map he would pass along to the American drug agents. The discarded arsenal included every weapon he owned, except for his Walther pistol and the MP5K submachine gun. He would keep those with him for a few more hours. There was no sign of anyone tailing him, but Jorge remained watchful and took routes designed to expose anyone trying to follow.

THE DEA PLANE to Bogotá was at the Marco Fidel Suárez Air Base, and departure was scheduled for around two in the afternoon. The family was asked to arrive by one, leaving time enough for one last family meal at home. During lunch, the residence telephone rang. It was Freckles. The *sicario* who once killed a brother for crossing the cartel was solicitous. He sounded concerned, like a friend—like a brother.

"We need to talk," he said. "Where can we meet?"

"All right," Jorge agreed, hoping to buy some time. "But I'm having lunch with my family now. Let's meet at two o'clock. I'll come to your place."

It was possible that having confirmed Jorge was home, Freckles would not wait. He might be watching the building already. He might have called from his mother's apartment next door. Jorge had to move his family to a safer place. It was time to go.

The family climbed into the silver Mazda, Jorge's cartel company car. He would drive one-handed in order to keep the MP5K in his left hand, tucked out of sight next to the driver's door. Its short, pistol-like muzzle made it very nimble and especially suitable for close-quarters combat situations. Once again taking a circuitous route to foil pursuers, Jorge tried not to speed or draw attention to his driving. He relaxed only when he spotted Feistl and Mitchell at the base.

At two o'clock, when Jorge was supposed to be meeting Freckles across town, he was introducing his family to Chris and Dave. Shortly before two thirty they were cleared to board the plane to Bogotá. Jorge and Lena shepherded their family toward the twin-engine Beechcraft across the tarmac. Jorge's cartel beeper had started chirping earlier, but it seemed to beep nonstop as they approached the plane's open door. Jorge stopped and slipped it from his belt holder. Holding it up for Lena to see, he pressed the off button and silenced the pager.

"It's over," he told Lena.

"Finally," she said, smiling.

And they boarded the U.S. government plane. By the time they reached Bogotá, Jorge's disengaged pager had received 158 new messages.

THEY ARRIVED IN a Bogotá swept by intrigues—a president fighting for his political life over ties to the Cali cartel, members of his cabinet facing criminal charges over those links, and rising turmoil in the defense establishment and justice systems over allegations of corruption. Both Jorge and Pallomari could corroborate damaging evidence against powerful figures throughout the government, as well as the cartel leadership. Jorge considered the city a nest of powerful enemies.

He and his family moved into the five-bedroom penthouse apartment of an embassy official who was out of the country. The makeshift safe house had several unusual features. The front door had four separate locks. And the powder room had a deadbolt lock . . . on the outside. Jorge feared it was not safe enough, but there were no better options short of sleeping on the floor at the embassy.

Eventually, Jorge's parents moved out of their private residence and joined them in the penthouse. The old general was seventy-eight and reluctant to leave his home in Bogotá. But it was too dangerous to stay. If the cartel could not get to him, the son argued, it would go after his family. Please, he said to his father, don't risk becoming a pawn of cartel vengeance. The general and his wife agreed to come along to the United States, but with the understanding that they intended to return as soon as possible.

They were a family of nine, gathered on short notice for international transit. Some needed travel documents. Embassy officials set about solving that problem, while Jorge settled in for a longer wait than originally anticipated. He could not leave the apartment, so visitors came to him instead. On Wednesday, August 16, his visitors were Feistl and Mitchell. They came bearing an alarming question.

What did Jorge think would happen, they asked, if Pallomari's wife returned to Cali?

"Whatever you do, don't let that happen," Jorge said. "She'll be dead."

Jorge read their silence instantly. It was too late, wasn't it? She had already gone, right? The agents nodded.

FOUR DAYS EARLIER, back on Saturday morning, August 12, about an hour after Jorge and the DEA agents had talked about the mysterious overnight death of the cartel killer César Yusti, Feistl and Mitchell drove out to the Bogotá airport to meet Patricia Pallomari. She and her two boys were flying in by commercial carrier, and the agents intended to meet them at the gate and escort them to a reunion with Guillermo at his embassy safe house.

Instead, Patricia turned her sons over to the agents, said good-bye, and said she was catching a return flight to Cali. She was nonchalant, as if the trip were routine and her safety not in question. She had business, she said, that would keep her until midweek. She said she also had some financial instruments to cash out and property to sell, including furniture.

"Is your furniture worth your life?" Feistl sputtered in disbelief.

Mitchell called her plan crazy and foolish, even suicidal. They argued for nearly an hour, but without success. She was going back to Cali. They had no authority to detain or arrest her, even for her own safety, and eventually had to throw up their hands in defeat. Before she left, the agents insisted that Patricia take the direct phone number of the DEA chief Tony Senneca, just in case she needed to reach someone urgently who might be able to marshal a quick rescue team.

Feistl and Mitchell arrived at Pallomari's Bogotá safe house with his two boys, but they had to explain to the accountant why his wife was missing. He cried out in despair and literally beat his head and fists against the wall. His fear for her safety had immediate implications for the United States.

"I won't leave the country without her," he vowed.

BY THAT WEDNESDAY NIGHT, when Feistl and Mitchell came to visit Jorge in his Bogotá hideaway, Patricia was supposed to have rejoined her family. An impatient Guillermo Pallomari called the couple's housekeeper in Cali and was reassured that his wife was fine when she saw her that morning. However, the maid also reported a haunting message left by a male voice.

"We know what you people are doing," said the anonymous man.

Patricia Pallomari did not return home that Wednesday night. The housekeeper said she left suitcases packed by the door, but never re-trieved them. Patricia and Fredy Vivas had left their offices at Universal Link around seven thirty in Fredy's red Fiat, and no one knew where they went.

"I think she's already dead," Jorge told the DEA agents that night.

Over the next couple of days Pallomari risked his security in Bogotá by launching a number of desperate telephone calls searching for news of his missing wife. He ended up on the phone with Bruno Murillo, a top *sicario* for Gilberto and a longtime aide to both Rodríguez Orejuela brothers.

"Your wife has been kidnapped because you have not obeyed Miguel's orders," he told the accountant. When Pallomari pleaded for her life and asked what he could do for her safe return, Murillo told him to return to Cali and have nothing to do with the DEA. "Don't co-operate with the authorities," the *sicario* said.

The hopelessness of Pallomari's situation was overwhelming. It was obvious that to go back to Cali was to be killed, and Patricia was doomed as well—if not dead already. A grieving and distraught Guillermo Pallomari flew off to Florida on Saturday, the nineteenth, and into the federal witness protection program. To avoid diplomatic complications, the fugitive accountant chartered a private plane and departed without the official assistance of American agents.

During the next week, eight members of the Salcedo family followed Pallomari's route north, boarding two separate commercial flights to Miami. Only Jorge stayed behind. The Americans feared that Colombian authorities might detain and hold Jorge if he risked a routine passport check at the airport. Some of his most dangerous enemies wore uniforms of the state. A team of federal police broke into the Bogotá home that his parents had left, apparently looking for clues to Jorge's whereabouts. With his security in mounting jeopardy, Jorge waited for high-level Washington approval to be spirited out of his own country without Colombian government notice or authorization.

He had been alone for more than twenty-four hours, rattling around his empty apartment fighting off waves of impatience and anxiety, when the telephone rang. Jorge rarely used that phone and knew that the cartel had bugged a number of phone lines into the United States embassy. He didn't trust this one, either. But maybe it was a call from his family in the States. He had to know.

"Hello, I'm taking a survey," said a female voice when Jorge answered.

The woman on the phone said she had a few questions about Jorge's television viewing habits. "But I don't live here. I work here. I'm—a house painter. The owners are away," Jorge sputtered. He prepared to hang up, but the voice was persistent. The survey would take only a few minutes, she said. Surely he watched television, and his opinion was very important. She chatted away brightly, keeping the line open. Suddenly an alarm went off in Jorge's head. Abruptly, and uncharacteristically rudely, he slammed down the receiver. He wondered if she might have been working for the cartel—or the government. *Maybe they were tracing the call; maybe they know where I am.*

Maybe it was simply paranoia, but Jorge was badly spooked. He called the embassy, described the phone encounter, and requested immediate relocation. By that time, however, Jorge's regular contacts were out of the country. Chris Feistl was in the States with Pallomari, engaged in around-the-clock debriefings. David Mitchell was in Florida with Jorge's family. The substitute minders at the embassy tried to minimize Jorge's risk and assured him that he was safe where he was. Don't worry, they said.

Jorge pondered the long list of powerful people he considered his enemies—from ruthless cartel *sicarios* to the highest officials of the Colombian government. There were the top police officers he had bribed, the politicians he had chauffeured to meetings with the godfathers, the powerful military leaders he knew to be friends of the cartel—from street cops to the president and his cabinet. Jorge knew enough to ruin the lives and careers of so many. The four locks on his door seemed increasingly insufficient.

"I'm not going to stay here tonight," Jorge declared in his last attempt at a new safe house. "I'll find my own place. I promise to stay in touch, but I'm moving."

It was no bluff. And it worked. An embassy official agreed to arrange a late transfer. The new place had not been cleaned or serviced since its last occupant. The embassy man apologized, but since Jorge was in such a hurry, there wasn't much to be done. No problem, Jorge said. He was grateful for the fresh address.

After settling in, he went through the apartment tidying up. It was quite a mess. It appeared that a family of three or more had stayed there. Empty pizza boxes and fried chicken containers, stale French fries, used paper cups and plates, and more, all of it left scattered about the kitchen and living room. Jorge was trying to stash it in bulging trash receptacles when he found something that made him crumple into a chair.

It was a child's drawing, a loving rendition of a mother, almost certainly. It had the look of something done by a ten- or eleven-year-old, a juvenile portrait of a distinctive-looking woman with long hair and big dark eyes. Jorge knew that woman.

He studied the image and began to weep. It was Patricia Pallomari.

THE MAN WHO USED TO BE

THE HEARTBREAK THAT JORGE SALCEDO FELT FOR THE PALLOMARI children gave way shortly to anger and disbelief. His embassy minders had moved him from one dangerous location to an even more dangerous place. He was sure that Guillermo's last desperate efforts to find his wife had jeopardized security of this safe house. Rogue police or cartel *sicarios* no doubt knew the address—or soon would—and might be watching already.

Compromised security had to be one of the reasons that Pallomari finally gave in to U.S. prodding and left the country without confirming Patricia's death. Not that her death was in any doubt. Jorge guessed that she died like the lovely Emilia had that night a year before. He had to stop himself as he imagined Patricia's big eyes staring out at him from a plastic bag.

Between the numbers of cartel killers looking to win favor with their bosses, the corrupt police already on the cartel payroll and eager for bonus money, and the politically powerful hoping to silence a witness, Jorge figured that the number of people looking for him in Bogotá could be a thousand or more. Even radically discounted for excess paranoia, he had a right to feel menaced. His primary American handlers considered Jorge and Pallomari the two most targeted men under U.S. protection. There were concerns that the Colombian government might attempt to block Jorge's departure, asserting its right to question or even prosecute him before turning him over to the Americans. It was one of the reasons why his exit was hung up, still pending more than ten days after leaving Cali.

Jorge insisted that his wait, whether brief or extended, would have to be in a safer safe house. And just when he was starting to get seriously impatient again, he was advised to be ready to move on Saturday. He was expecting another local transfer when two bulletproof black Suburbans arrived. A team of armed American agents ordered Jorge politely onto the floor of one SUV. It roared off, lurching through a series of sharp turns and bone-crunching bumps. It felt as if the big vehicle were taking shortcuts over curbs and median dividers. Jorge couldn't tell for sure. He could see nothing.

The two-car caravan came to a stop, and Jorge was assisted off the floor and out of the Suburban. He found himself standing inside the walled compound of the U.S. embassy, inside the very gates he almost tried to enter in disguise two months earlier. Tony Senneca, the DEA attaché, stepped up to shake hands. He called Jorge a man of extraordinary courage and joked that among cartel assassins and crooked cops Jorge was "probably the most wanted man in Colombia" at that moment. He officially added: "I just wanted to tell you in person that the people of the United States are especially grateful for what you've done."

That's when Jorge learned he was leaving the country. Immediately. Back on the road and back on the floor of the SUV, Jorge was not allowed to raise his head until the Suburbans had driven inside a U.S. government-leased hangar at the Bogotá airport. The hangar doors closed behind them. A white twin-engine Beechcraft turboprop sat waiting for him. His American escorts hurried him aboard.

Jorge found himself with a choice of seats. He was the only passenger. He sat forward, nearest the cockpit. The hangar doors were still closed, but the pilot and the co-pilot invited him to buckle up. They immediately started their engines. The captain radioed for tower permission to take off. Only after they received that clearance did they signal for the big hangar doors to slide open. The plane sprinted from its confines and taxied quickly to the end of its assigned runway. It came around into the wind and, without a pause, powered into its takeoff roll. From hangar to liftoff seemed like no more than three or four minutes.

The sleek aircraft rose up over Bogotá, banked around to the north, and climbed toward thirty thousand feet. Out the cabin window Jorge watched the towering Andes give way to the lush green landscape of the Magdalena River valley and then to the jungle lowlands of the north coast. Colombia was fast slipping away under the Beechcraft's wings.

Jorge was leaving Colombia with a mixture of pride and melancholy. He was proud of his role bringing down the Cali cartel, proud of helping save the cartel accountant's life, proud of leading authorities to records that exposed official corruption on a massive scale. Investigations, indictments, high-level resignations, wholesale dismissals, and early signs of reform were already visible, spurred by a fresh wave of public outrage. It couldn't happen overnight, but Colombia's imperfect democracy was showing signs of recovery.

Six and a half years earlier Jorge Salcedo had been enticed by the Cali cartel to hunt down the notorious Pablo Escobar, a mission of public service with potential to make him a national hero. But it was by bringing down the crime boss who hired him that Jorge finally became an acknowledged champion of Colombian democracy.

On August 26, 1995, aboard a DEA plane rushing for the edge of Colombian airspace, Jorge was already a hero without a country. He knew he might never return, that the cost of his actions almost certainly meant permanent exile from his homeland. It was a wrenching moment for the whole family. His elderly parents were forced to flee a country that the proud general had devoted his life to defending. There was no way to measure the cost of lost friends, lost contact with extended family, and a lifetime of community ties severed forever.

They were heading into hiding in a foreign land where, for security reasons, their names would have to be changed and their pasts erased.

But they were alive. Jorge and Lena and their children still had a future together, somewhere in the United States. For that, Jorge whispered a prayer of thanks.

It was a beautiful clear day, not a cloud in the sky, when the sleek white plane cruised over the northern coastal city of Barranquilla and banked out across the turquoise waters of the Caribbean.

The man who used to be Jorge Salcedo looked back once more at the receding shores of his lost homeland and tried to tell himself that he had no regrets.

BACKGROUND
Stories Behind the Story

JORGE AND ME

I DON'T KNOW WHERE JORGE SALCEDO LIVES—NOT HIS STREET, NOT his city, not his state. I've never met his family. I don't know their names. Salcedo is the family name they left behind in Colombia. Federal marshals gave them new identities about fifteen years ago when they entered the U.S. witness protection program. And after nearly a thousand hours of highly revealing interviews—all but a tiny fraction of them on the telephone—there remain substantial secrets between us.

Those secrets are intended to protect Jorge's life and the lives of his family. I cannot, for example, arrange to meet him. Over more than a decade working on this story, we have met outside a federal courthouse three times—each time at his request and under strict security rules dictated by Jorge.

Also, Jorge calls me. Before he agreed to participate in this book project, those calls were irregular and unpredictable, but they produced hundreds of hours of interviews spanning nearly eight years. During

that period, months and sometimes even years went by between interviews. More recently, during the height of this book project, his calls
were frequent and lasted hours at a time. He answered every question I
asked. We are friends now—an odd thing to say, perhaps, for someone
I can't visit and whose name I don't know.

I met Jorge in a courtroom at the Miami U.S. District Courthouse
in October 1998. He was making an unannounced appearance before
the federal judge William Hoeveler to enter a negotiated plea—guilty
to one felony count of racketeering—and to receive his formal slap-on-
the-wrist probation sentence. The sources in Los Angeles who had
alerted me to the legal proceedings across the country remain confidential to this day.

That morning in Miami, Jorge was standing in the well of the court
between two large bodyguards, a pair of U.S. marshals. Jorge was easy
to spot. Stepping to the low railing separating court personnel from the
gallery, I offered my *Los Angeles Times* business card to one of the marshals.

"I'd like to introduce myself to Mr. Salcedo," I said. The guards
stepped aside.

It was the beginning of a challenging saga—a tantalizing story,
years of frustrating interruptions and denied access until finally, more
than a dozen years later, this book.

Jorge's story has been corroborated where possible by historical
records, investigative documents, and law-enforcement sources. The
U.S. Drug Enforcement Administration provided extensive assistance,
including access to records and case agents.

From our earliest conversations, Jorge has been eager to tell this
story. He says he wants history and his family to know the truth. His
children were very young when the family fled to the United States.
Jorge says that for security reasons—and to avoid scaring them—he
shared little of his Colombian story, even as they grew older. He said
they will learn about it now, when they read this book. His wife, too,
will find details Jorge had not told her. For the record, Lena Duque was
not her name. It is the only fictional name in this story, and it was
changed to protect the family's continued anonymity.

Finally, Jorge also hopes that his experience with the Cali cartel will deter others from making similar pacts with the Devil. "People should know what I know now," he told me. "My story should start by saying, if you are invited into such an organization, stop—stop and run away. Don't think you can ever fully escape."

WRAPPING UP

R ELATIONS BETWEEN THE GOVERNMENTS OF WASHINGTON AND
Bogotá remained rocky beyond the summer of 1995. A year
later, the Clinton administration revoked President Samper's visa, taking the highly unusual step of barring a friendly head of state over corruption issues. The visa of General Zúñiga, Samper's military chief, was
not renewed, and he was forced to resign as the United States refused to
certify Colombia as an antidrug ally. That action denied the Bogotá
government billions of dollars in loans and credits. Samper survived efforts to remove him from office thanks to support in the Colombian
congress from members of his majority Liberal Party.

Following are highlights of what happened to others involved in
the Cali cartel story after Miguel was captured.

JORGE SALCEDO
Upon arrival in the United States, Jorge was reunited with his wife and
family in the lobby of an Embassy Suites hotel. Together with Jorge's

parents, the family disappeared into the federal witness protection program. Transition into their new life was eased by a total of $1.5 million in reward money provided by the U.S. and Colombian governments. However, a promise that he and his family would be granted U.S. citizenship remained unfulfilled more than fifteen years later.

GUILLERMO PALLOMARI

Pallomari left Colombia distraught over the loss of his wife. Her body was never found. The cartel accountant arrived in Florida with his two sons and immediately submitted to marathon debriefings by the DEA agent Chris Feistl, naming names, explaining documents, and providing invaluable insider information about the crime syndicate's personnel and operations. He said that during his last six months in Cali he feared that he and his family would be slaughtered. He especially feared the cartel security boss Jorge Salcedo.

"The one we called Richard—he was trying to kill me," Pallomari told Feistl.

"Really? Why do you think that?" responded the agent.

"He was Señor's man. He was the obvious choice. Besides, I once saw him outside my window. I'm sure he was trying to find a way to kill me."

Feistl jotted down some notes. "We'll get back to that later," he said.

The debriefings went more than a week. On the last day, Feistl closed his notebook and asked one final question: "Guillermo, do you know why you're here today?"

The accountant shrugged. "Of course, because you and Dave rescued me."

"No," Feistl replied. "It was Salcedo."

"What do you mean?"

"Salcedo saved your life."

"Impossible!"

"He refused to leave until you were safe. Remember the roadblocks in your neighborhood?" Feistl asked. "Salcedo warned us a *sicario* was coming for you. He told us where to set up barricades to protect you. And he told us how to find your wife and pushed us to make contact. I just wanted you to know—the main reason you're here and not dead is Jorge Salcedo."

The debriefing had concluded.

The accountant became the key witness in prosecutions of American defense lawyers who had worked for the cartel. He also provided sworn statements and testimony supporting other investigations into the cartel in the United States, Colombia, Mexico, and Europe. In Colombia, evidence gathered from Pallomari led to widespread indictments of political figures and dismissals of hundreds of police and military officials. His assistance helped a joint task force of federal agents trace, expose, and dismantle major elements of the cartel organization throughout the United States. As part of a plea deal, Pallomari served a brief sentence in a U.S. prison and is now in the federal witness protection program.

Like Salcedo's, Pallomari's new identity and whereabouts are unknown.

THE GODFATHERS

Miguel and Gilberto Rodríguez Orejuela

Cooperative efforts between law-enforcement agents in the United States and Colombia to dismantle the Cali cartel accelerated after the brothers' arrests, assisted in large measure by investigative advances made possible by Guillermo Pallomari and Jorge Salcedo. Also, Colombia finally restored its extradition treaty with Washington in 1997. By law, extradition of Colombian nationals applied only to trafficking violations occurring *after* December 17, 1997.

That left the Cali godfathers with the same option they had once sought from Colombian officials—a chance to retire from drug trafficking without fear of being prosecuted in the States. But the brothers did not retire. They turned their Colombian prison cells into luxury apartments and cartel headquarters. A police raid found cell phones, cable television, stereo equipment, carpets, and French wines. They were living "more like guests than criminals in La Picota prison," wrote Ron Chepesiuk in his book *The Bullet or the Bribe*. Some days, they had dozens of visitors. *The Miami Herald* reported that in a one-week period Gilberto was visited 123 times by people signing in as his lawyers.

Unfortunately for the brothers' future legal defenses, they did not take into account how badly compromised the organization had become. Salcedo and Pallomari had provided so much information about the cartel—even about its second-tier messengers, couriers, and operatives—that both U.S. and Colombian law enforcement knew whom to watch. Investigators confirmed that the brothers continued to engage in trafficking operations well past 1997.

First Gilberto, and later Miguel, were extradited to Florida, finally ending the long and lucrative reign of the Cali cartel. And in 2006— with the brothers in their mid-sixties—they agreed to forfeit more than $2 billion in accumulated assets. They were sentenced to thirty years in federal prison. Family members told the Colombian media in 2010 that Gilberto had a colon ailment and Miguel suffered hearing damage working in the prison laundry.

With credit for good behavior, they can expect release around February 9, 2030.

JOSÉ "CHEPE" SANTACRUZ LONDOÑO

After his arrest at the Carbón de Palo restaurant in Bogotá, the number three godfather spent six months in maximum security at La Picota prison—then bribed his way out in January 1996. He was driven away from the prison in broad daylight, apparently pretending to be part of a team of prosecutors who had come to interrogate him. Colombia offered a $2 million reward for his capture. He was rumored to be trying to form an alliance with FARC guerrillas when he was betrayed. According to the official account, Chepe was gunned down in a police ambush near Medellín two months after his escape. However, American drug enforcement agents found significant discrepancies between police statements and evidence gathered at the shooting, including signs that the Cali godfather was tortured and likely killed before police found his bullet-riddled body. U.S. investigators suspected Medellín-area traffickers who were angry over Chepe's FARC alliance—or north Cauca valley rivals. Whoever did it also likely stole $2 million in cash that the drug lord reportedly carried around in the trunk of his car for bribery emergencies.

Hélmer "Pacho" Herrera

The fourth godfather was the last taken into custody. He surrendered to General Serrano on September 1, 1996. Pacho was sent to prison near Palmira, his hometown. He was in his soccer shorts and cleats on November 5, 1998, after playing soccer on the prison field, when a man posing as a lawyer approached, pulled out a gun, and shot Pacho five times in the face. Trafficking rivals in the north Cauca valley had hired the killer. A series of vendetta killings followed during which one of Pacho's brothers was killed in his prison cell. Two other Herrera brothers were gunned down in trafficking feuds during 2001—one in Venezuela and the other in Ecuador.

KEY CALI CARTEL FIGURES

William Rodríguez Abadía

With his father and uncle in a Colombian prison, day-to-day operations of the Cali cartel fell to the young lawyer whom Jorge once warned: "Whatever you do, don't inherit the throne." While Miguel and Gilberto still directed the sprawling criminal enterprise from prison, William ran much of the family's financial empire—notably handling money laundering and bribery that continued unabated under new management. He also tried to hunt down Jorge. William offered one friend of the Salcedo family $2 million if she could provide cartel *sicarios* with his U.S. residence.

About nine months after Miguel's arrest, the Rodríguez family's hold on cartel power was briefly challenged. It was a Friday in late May 1996. William went to lunch at an upscale Brazilian restaurant with his regular coterie of friends and bodyguards, among them Marta Lucía's brother, Óscar Echeverri, Jorge's former assistant Dario Delgado, and William's favorite *sicario,* Nicol Parra.

At precisely one thirty that afternoon, hit men with silenced handguns instantly killed two of William's sentries outside the restaurant. Inside, at least a dozen armed men suddenly stood at tables overlooking William's luncheon party and emptied their automatic weapons into the group. A moment later, it was over.

It appeared at first that all were dead—until William struggled to his feet. Nicol Parra had shielded him with his body. Still, Miguel's son suffered dangerous abdominal wounds and had to be saved in emergency surgery. He alone survived the massacre.

About six weeks later, the DEA agents Chris Feistl and David Mitchell were seated at a small pizza restaurant in southern Cali when an entourage of bodyguards swept in escorting a young man with a limp.

"Hey, that's William," Feistl told his partner. "Let's go say hello." Even as Mitchell objected, Feistl started toward the table of traffickers.

Feistl introduced himself and pointed out his partner across the room. "We're glad to see you're feeling better," he said to smiles and friendly gestures from William and his bodyguards. William even waved to Mitchell, who could not wave back. The DEA agent's hands were under the table, one of them gripping a handgun stuffed inside a fanny pack he was holding on his lap.

"I just wanted you to know that we'd be glad to help you," Feistl continued to William. "If you need medical treatment in the States, let me know and we can arrange a medical visa."

It was a ploy, of course. Feistl knew that a pending indictment would lead to the gangster's immediate arrest if he entered U.S. jurisdiction for any reason. But the young gangsters probably knew that, too. "Thank you, but I'm doing very well," William said.

In 2006, William faced extradition to Miami on money-laundering and bribery charges when he surrendered to U.S. authorities and agreed to testify against his father and Gilberto. He was sentenced to twenty-one years in prison, but after he helped authorities identify more than a billion dollars in cartel assets, his jail term was slashed to eight years— then further reduced for good behavior. He was released from prison during the summer of 2010. There were reports that he feared returning to Colombia and had petitioned U.S. officials to take him and his family into witness protection.

MAJOR MARIO DEL BASTO
After serving time for espionage violations related to his arrest at the soccer field with secret government documents, Jorge's friend and fel-

low security chief received additional jail time for illicit enrichment. He spent seven years in Colombian prisons.

Guillermo "Memo Lara" Restrepo Gaviria

The Cali cartel's senior *sicario* was wanted in the States in connection with at least two murders. In Colombia, he was convicted of financial crimes related to drug trafficking and sentenced to La Picota prison. There were intelligence reports in the past decade that he had become blind. U.S. officials now believe he is dead.

Andrés "Freckles" Vélez

The loyal *sicario* who told Jorge he had killed one of his own brothers for betraying cartel godfathers was reportedly gunned down and killed in Cali within a year after the Rodríguez Orejuela brothers were captured.

Henry "the Delinquent" Gaviria

The *sicario* who led a raiding party that riddled Claudio Endo's body with more than one hundred bullets was killed in Cali late in 1995, reportedly in a vendetta by friends of the Endo family. An Endo family secretary who had helped Gaviria secretly obtain Endo's mobile phone was also killed.

OTHERS WHO SERVED THE CARTEL

Captain Efrén "the Vulture" Buitrago

The Bloque de Búsqueda officer and cartel snitch was fired from the Colombian National Police force after Miguel's arrest and after evidence of cartel payoffs was provided by Salcedo and Pallomari. The captain's sidekick, the police corporal Jorge called "the Shadow," was also fired.

José Estrada

The former Cali cartel security man who handled drug shipments and warehouse storage went into hiding as the godfathers were rounded up.

He was captured about six weeks after Miguel was arrested, holed up at a ranch in his hometown of Sabaneta. He was convicted of illicit enrichment and sentenced to eight years in prison. The Colombian government seized his warehouses and other assets, and he was fined $2 million. He served three years in the Palmira prison before being released on parole.

Carlos "Pinchadito" Espinosa

The telephone company official was one of several Telecom employees convicted of aiding the Cali cartel. He served two years in prison. He had installed Panasonic phones in Miguel's offices and made certain that any government taps of those lines would be misdirected to false addresses. He was gunned down and killed in 1999 after his release and amid reports that he had agreed to cooperate with investigators.

Enrique "El Gordo" Sánchez

A short time after Jorge Salcedo went into U.S. witness protection, DEA agents informed him that his most trusted aide on the motorcycle bodyguard crew had been named in a cartel murder contract. Jorge immediately contacted Enrique to warn him. He also provided a DEA name and phone number and advised his friend to turn himself in as soon as possible. Two days later, cartel gunmen killed the former assistant.

Ricardo Bilonick

The former Panamanian ambassador became the key government witness in General Noriega's drug-trafficking trial, then served a brief prison term. He has since returned to Panama, where he practices law. He maintained in sworn statements to the court that he had not been bribed by the Cali cartel, calling such claims "idiotic," according to a *New York Times* account. After an e-mail exchange with the author, he declined to comment further.

David Tomkins

The British arms dealer returned to the United States in 2003 looking for private contractor opportunities in the Iraq war. Instead, he was arrested at Bush Intercontinental Airport in Houston and charged with violating the U.S. Export Act, a felony springing from his attempt to purchase the A-37 Dragonfly bomber for the Cali cartel. Tomkins refused to cooperate with prosecutors and spent nearly thirty months in federal custody—some of it in the same prison where Manuel Noriega was being held. Tomkins remains a soldier of fortune. In an exchange of e-mails with the author during 2010, the Brit adventurer responded from Somalia and Uganda. His 2008 memoir, *Dirty Combat,* includes accounts of his missions to Colombia. In it, he also declares, "I'm a gangster and I always have been. I've had the yacht, the Rolls-Royce, the racehorses and the country club lifestyle . . . I'm morally ambiguous. I'm not going to apologize for anything and I don't give a damn what people think about me."

Peter McAleese

The former British special forces sergeant settled down in Birmingham to run a chain of English pubs, including the Victorian redbrick Gunmakers Arms in Small Heath. But he continued to dabble in mercenary assignments. For a time, the old communist foe worked in post-Soviet Russia teaching security techniques to bodyguards. More recently, he provided security services under private contracts in Algiers and Iraq. In his 1993 memoir, *No Mean Soldier,* McAleese described his role in the ill-fated raid on Pablo Escobar, and he quoted Theodore Roosevelt's tribute to a man who strives valiantly: "at the worst, if he fails, at least fails while daring greatly."

ANTICARTEL FIGURES

Colonel Carlos Alfonso Velásquez

The by-the-book former head of Cali's Bloque de Búsqueda survived the sex scandal engineered by the cartel bosses and became chief of staff to the general of the Seventeenth Brigade, assigned to counterguerrilla duties in the northeast. His dream of promotion to general was finally and fatally ended when he reported his commanding officer for improper alliances with paramilitary forces in the area. Velásquez, in turn, was accused of being too chummy with human rights groups. He was forced to resign from the army on January 1, 1997. He later became a professor of communications and public policy at the Universidad de la Sabana in Bogotá.

Chris Feistl

The DEA special agent Feistl remained in Colombia until 1997, when he was promoted to agency headquarters in Washington, D.C. He returned to Bogotá for a second tour of duty in 1999 and again in 2004. His last Colombian assignment lasted six years. In the spring of 2010 he moved to Arizona, where he became assistant special agent in charge of the DEA's Phoenix office.

David Mitchell

The DEA special agent Mitchell, whose South American drug enforcement experience included a stint in Bolivia, was also promoted in 1997 to a series of management assignments in Tampa and Miami. He remains with the agency today, working drug investigations in southern Florida.

Jerry Salameh

Like Mitchell and Feistl, special agent Salameh earned a management promotion and left Colombia in 1997. He was assigned to Washington headquarters, where he supervised the agency's Colombia program. He remains with the agency today, coordinating the DEA's Organized Crime Drug Enforcement Task Force for Florida and the Caribbean.

Edward "Eddie" Kacerosky

The U.S. Customs Service special agent who passed up promotions to spend nearly ten years investigating the Cali cartel—and who arranged for Jorge Salcedo's cooperation with American drug enforcement agents—retired from the government in 2006 after thirty years. Among his duties in those last years were interrogations of the Rodríguez Orejuela brothers. Eddie escorted the extradited Gilberto from Colombia to Florida in December 2004. During the flight north, the godfather called Kacerosky a *sabueso,* a term the agent mistook as a derogatory remark. "No, no! I'm not calling you a dog. It's a compliment," Gilberto insisted. He was calling the investigator a supersleuth, in Spanish "a bloodhound." Later, while questioning Miguel in 2005, Eddie used the occasion to set the record straight about the four people murdered at Pacho's ranch a decade earlier, apparently over cartel suspicions that Rhadamés Trujillo was cooperating with drug agents. "Rhadamés was not the informant. Your men killed the wrong people," Kacerosky said. The retired federal agent now works as a private investigator in the southeastern United States but continues to advocate cooperation between federal investigative agencies. He cites the Cali case as a prime example of interagency cooperation. "We showed how well it works," he said.

OTHER PROMINENT FIGURES

Ingrid Betancourt

The Colombian politician, who would go on to international fame as a longtime captive of FARC guerrillas, has acknowledged her meeting early in 1995 with the Cali cartel bosses. While some details in her previously published accounts of that meeting differ from the version Jorge Salcedo provided to U.S. authorities, they agree on who attended and what prompted the private session. The Rodríguez Orejuela brothers and José Santacruz wanted amnesty legislation. And financial rewards were explicitly tendered. "Most of your fellow representatives are in our pay," Gilberto told her, a clear invitation.

When asked in a telephone interview about Chepe's fifty-million-peso check, Betancourt said: "I didn't see it. I never saw anything like that."

In the weeks after their meeting, she said she noticed congressional colleague Alonso Lucio's warming relations with the cartel bosses and with President Samper. "It broke our friendship," she said. Press accounts disclosed that Lucio was a regular jailhouse visitor to the imprisoned Rodríguez Orejuela brothers. And when the Colombian congress tried to impeach Samper over his millions in cartel campaign funds, Lucio strongly supported the president. Betancourt, however, voted to impeach and publicly condemned Samper's ties to the Cali cartel, declaring that her country was "governed by criminals." Nonetheless, Samper and his allies prevailed in a congressional floor fight by a margin of 111 to 43.

The daughter of wealthy Colombian oligarchs—a diplomat father and a beauty-queen mother who was elected to congress—Betancourt first won national office in 1994 as a reform candidate. She won a senate seat four years later with the highest vote total in Colombian history, and ran for the presidency in 2002. In that campaign, a band of FARC guerrillas seized her during an ill-advised visit to disputed territory. She was held in jungle hideouts for more than six years before her rescue in July 2008. Betancourt wrote about her hostage ordeal in a 2010 memoir, *Even Silence Has an End.*

GENERAL MANUEL NORIEGA

The Cali cartel's role in delivering the key prosecution witness against Noriega was disclosed during government debriefings of Jorge Salcedo. The revelation set off a flurry of legal challenges that nonetheless failed to reverse the former Panamanian dictator's conviction. He remained in federal custody in the United States for more than twenty years and in 2010 was extradited to France, where he began serving a seven-year sentence for money laundering. He will next face extradition to Panama, where a sixty-year prison term awaits him from earlier convictions in absentia for murder and corruption.

JOEL ROSENTHAL

The Florida defense lawyer who represented various Cali cartel clients, most notably Lucho Santacruz, pled guilty to money-laundering charges in 1996. His cooperation with federal prosecutors and his key role introducing Jorge Salcedo to American drug agents earned him a reduced sentence. The former assistant U.S. attorney's private law license was reinstated in 2005 and he has resumed his legal practice in Miami.

ONE LAST MYSTERY

The shooting death of César Yusti, the cartel killer who was hunting down the accountant Pallomari, remains a mystery. He was found sitting in his car, shot in the head, on the very night that his assassination target was being whisked to safety in Bogotá by American DEA agents. From Jorge's point of view, the timing was miraculous. He confided to the author that he suspected a CIA hit team did it. DEA agents Feistl and Mitchell rejected such a scenario, but declined to discuss the matter further. "Whoever did it is an angel," Mitchell had told Salcedo in a phone conversation the next morning. Jorge got the distinct impression that the DEA agents were thanking him. "But I had nothing to do with it," he insists to this day. All that night and all that weekend, Jorge says, he was holed up in his apartment with an arsenal of weapons, fearful of *sicarios* targeting him and his family.

No physical evidence has ever linked anyone to the Yusti killing. However, high-level Colombian authorities speculate that his shooting may have been the first shot fired in a power struggle with north Cauca valley traffickers. The rivalry may have been behind Chepe Santacruz's death, and it was directly blamed for the Cali restaurant massacre that left Miguel's son William badly wounded.

| *Acknowledgments* |

My ability to tell this story started with support at the *Los Angeles Times,* my professional home for thirty-six years. Reporting for the original newspaper version spanned most of a decade, requiring an investment of resources and patience by editorial management that defied traditional cost-benefit analysis. It's an old story in newsrooms around the country. Challenging stories have always cost more—and investigative projects cost the most. They are still being delivered, though at a diminished rate in the face of nationwide staff reductions, economic hold-downs, and fearful corporate ownership. The *Los Angeles Times* suffers, too, but it was—and remains—an ambitious and extraordinary news organization. And it deserves credit for making this story possible.

I owe special thanks as well to individual editors and colleagues at the newspaper who played key roles. The deputy managing editor, Marc Duvoisin, guided my original *Times* story into print, and more recently he provided strong advice that transformed key portions of this manuscript. The national editor, Roger Smith, a partner on many of my journalistic adventures, contributed both story suggestions and moral support from the outset. Scott Kraft, the former national editor, saw the potential and backed my efforts before it was clear that any story would develop. And the former *Times* researcher Nona Yates—

who over the years often made me look good with her information-gathering skills—filled my files with important background material, key documents, and reliable data of all kinds.

This manuscript also benefited from the assistance, suggestions, criticisms, and encouragement of friends and family. Thanks to William Blaylock, Lee Chemel, Doug Frantz and Cathy Collins, Paul Goldsmith, Jim and Lynn Kouf, Teresa Reyes, Brian Sun and Stacey Cohen, and Jason, Lara, and Emma. I am especially grateful to Barbara Pierce, who did the first edit of every page of every draft—and so much more.

I will always be thankful to the U.S. Drug Enforcement Administration special agents Chris Feistl, David Mitchell, and Jerry Salameh for generous contributions of time and details. And thanks, too, to Garrison Courtney and Michael Sanders in the DEA public information office, who opened so many doors.

At the Robbins Office in New York, my literary agent, David Halpern, has been a skilled advocate and story consultant. His advice and consistently wise counsel made him an invaluable partner in this project and a great friend.

Special thanks also to Will Murphy, my editor at Random House. His keen sense of story and demanding critiques set a high standard. And his unwavering enthusiasm helped fuel many long rewrite sessions.

Finally and foremost, thanks to Jorge.

SOURCES AND NOTES

As disclosed earlier, this narrative account is based predominantly on details provided to the author by the former Cali cartel security chief Jorge Salcedo. Prosecutors and agents of the DEA and Customs Service offered extensive corroborating information, including access to investigative reports, documents, and interviews with field agents and supervisors involved in the case. The author relied further on transcripts of sworn testimony by the former cartel accountant Guillermo Pallomari and on various other court records. Documents made public by the National Security Archive in Washington provided additional historical insights.

Among the Colombian news archives frequently consulted by the author were *Semana, El Tiempo,* and *El País.* In the United States, *Time* magazine, the *Los Angeles Times,* and *The New York Times* provided useful contemporaneous coverage of the period. But the best by far—and the most valuable in preparing this manuscript—was the work of *The Washington Post* Latin America correspondent Douglas Farah.

One of the few books with extensive historical information about the Cali cartel is Ron Chepesiuk's *The Bullet or the Bribe* and its updated paperback version, *Drug Lords.* The most comprehensive coverage of Pablo Escobar and the rival Medellín cartel is in Mark Bowden's *Killing Pablo* and Simon Strong's *Whitewash.*

Interviews and Correspondence

Among sources other than Jorge Salcedo contacted in person, by phone, or by e-mail in the preparation of this book were: Ingrid Betancourt, Ricardo Bilonick, the Miami defense attorney Robert F. Dunlap, Chris Feistl, Robert S. Gelbard, Edward Kacerosky, David Mitchell, Joel Rosenthal, Edward Ryan, Jerry Salameh, Tony Senneca, Dean Shelley, Susan Snyder, and David Tomkins.

Bibliography

Betancourt, Ingrid. *Until Death Do Us Part: My Struggle to Reclaim Colombia.* London: HarperCollins, 2002.

Bowden, Mark. *Killing Pablo: The Hunt for the World's Greatest Outlaw.* New York: Atlantic Monthly Press, 2001.

Chaparro, Camilo. *Historia del Cartel de Cali.* Bogotá: Intermedio, 2005.

Chepesiuk, Ron. *The Bullet or the Bribe: Taking Down Colombia's Cali Drug Cartel.* Westport, Conn.: Praeger, 2003.

———. *Drug Lords: The Rise and Fall of the Cali Cartel.* Lytham, U.K.: Milo Books, 2007.

Clawson, Patrick L., and Rensselaer W. Lee III. *The Andean Cocaine Industry.* New York: St. Martin's Press, 1996.

DiCanio, Margaret. *Encyclopedia of Violence.* New York: Facts on File, 1993.

Duzán, María Jimena. *Death Beat: A Colombian Journalist's Life Inside the Cocaine Wars.* Translated by Peter Eisner. New York: HarperCollins, 1994.

Eddy, Paul. *The Cocaine Wars.* With Hugo Sabogal and Sara Walden. New York: W. W. Norton, 1988.

Escobar, Roberto. *The Accountant's Story: Inside the Violent World of the Medellín Cartel.* With David Fisher. New York: Grand Central, 2009.

García Márquez, Gabriel. *News of a Kidnapping.* Translated by Edith Grossman. New York: Penguin Books, 1998.

Gugliotta, Guy, and Jeff Leen. *Kings of Cocaine: Inside the Medellín Cartel—an As-

tonishing True Story of Murder, Money, and International Corruption. New York: Simon & Schuster, 1989.

Hylton, Forrest. *Evil Hour in Colombia.* New York: Verso, 2006.

Kenney, Michael. *From Pablo to Osama.* University Park: Pennsylvania State University Press, 2007.

Kirk, Robin. *More Terrible Than Death: Massacres, Drugs, and America's War in Colombia.* New York: PublicAffairs, 2003.

Kohn, Michael, Robert Landon, and Thomas Kohnstamm. *Colombia.* London: Lonely Planet, 2006.

McAleese, Peter. *No Mean Soldier: The Story of the Ultimate Professional Soldier in the SAS and Other Forces.* London: Cassell Military Paperbacks, 2003.

McGee, Jim, and Brian Duffy. *Main Justice: The Men and Women Who Enforce the Nation's Criminal Laws and Guard Its Liberties.* New York: Simon & Schuster, 1996.

Noriega, Manuel, and Peter Eisner. *America's Prisoner: The Memoirs of Manuel Noriega.* New York: Random House, 1997.

Pollard, Peter. *Colombia Handbook.* Bath, U.K.: Footprint Handbooks, 1998.

Strong, Simon. *Whitewash: Pablo Escobar and the Cocaine Wars.* London: Pan Books, 1996.

Tomkins, David. *Dirty Combat: Secret Wars and Serious Misadventures.* Edinburgh: Mainstream, 2008.

Vásquez Perdomo, María Eugenia. *My Life as a Colombian Revolutionary: Reflections of a Former Guerrillera.* Translated by Lorena Terando. Philadelphia: Temple University Press, 2005.

| *About the Author* |

WILLIAM C. REMPEL spent thirty-six years as an investigative reporter and editor at the *Los Angeles Times*. Rempel has been recognized with numerous journalism honors, including an Overseas Press Club Award and a Gerald Loeb Award, and he was a finalist for the Goldsmith Prize for Investigative Reporting.

| *About the Type* |

This book was set in Garamond, a typeface originally designed by the Parisian typecutter Claude Garamond (1480–1561). This version of Garamond was modeled on a 1592 specimen sheet from the Egenolff-Berner foundry, which was produced from types assumed to have been brought to Frankfurt by the punchcutter Jacques Sabon.

Claude Garamond's distinguished romans and italics first appeared in *Opera Ciceronis* in 1543–44. The Garamond types are clear, open, and elegant.